$22.45

POLITICS IN SINDH, 1907–1940

MUSLIM IDENTITY AND THE DEMAND FOR PAKISTAN

Political Map of Sindh – 1935

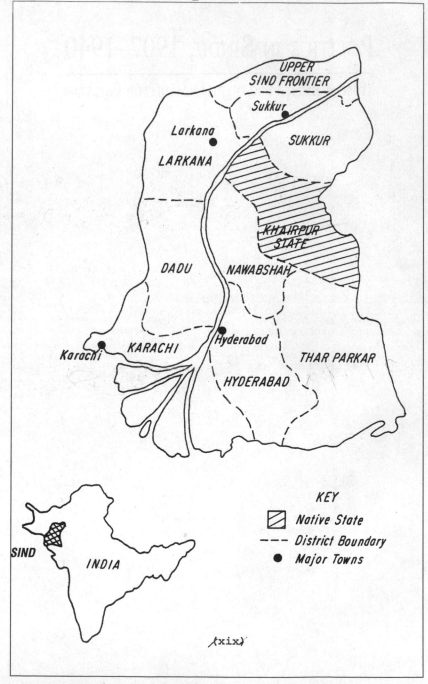

UPPER SIND FRONTIER

Sukkur

SUKKUR

Larkana

LARKANA

KHAIRPUR STATE

DADU

NAWABSHAH

KARACHI

Hyderabad

THAR PARKAR

Karachi

HYDERABAD

KEY

Native State

District Boundary

Major Towns

SIND

INDIA

POLITICS IN SINDH, 1907–1940

MUSLIM IDENTITY AND THE DEMAND FOR PAKISTAN

ALLEN KEITH JONES

OXFORD
UNIVERSITY PRESS

OXFORD
UNIVERSITY PRESS

Great Clarendon Street, Oxford ox2 6DP

Oxford University Press is a department of the University of Oxford.
It furthers the University's objective of excellence in research, scholarship,
and education by publishing worldwide in

Oxford New York

Auckland Bangkok Buenos Aires Cape Town Chennai
Dar es Salaam Delhi Hong Kong Istanbul Karachi Kolkata
Kuala Lumpur Madrid Melbourne Mexico City Mumbai Nairobi
São Paulo Shanghai Taipei Tokyo Toronto

Oxford is a registered trade mark of Oxford University Press
in the UK and in certain other countries

ISBN 0 19 579593 8

Photographs courtesy Dr Hamida Khuhro

Second Impression 2003

Typeset in Times
Printed in Pakistan by
Kagzi Printers, Karachi.
Published by
Ameena Saiyid, Oxford University Press
Plot No. 38, Sector 15, Korangi Industrial Area,
Karachi-74900, Pakistan.

To my parents, Keith and Ruth Jones,

to my wife, Beverly, and son, Andrew.

CONTENTS

LIST OF TABLES

LIST OF ABBREVIATIONS

AIML	All-India Muslim League
AIMLCC	All-India Muslim League Central Committee
BPML	Bombay Presidency Muslim League
CID	Criminal Investigation Department
D.G.	*Daily Gazette*
F	File (Archives)
I.C.S.	Indian Civil Service
INC	Indian National Congress
IOR	India Office Records
K.B.	Khan Bahadur
MLA	Member of the Legislative Assembly
MSLA	Member of the Sindh Legislative Assembly
NWFP	Northwest Frontier Province
PDH	Papers of Daulat Hidayatullah
PGMS	Papers of Ghulam Murtaza Sayed
PIS	Papers of Inayatullah Suleman
PMA	Papers of Matlubul Hasan
PSA	Papers of M.H. Saiyid and Rizwan Ahmed
PSAMS	Papers of Sheikh Abdul Majid Sindhi
PSLA	Proceedings of the Sindh Legislative Assembly
psm	per square mile
PWD	Public Works Department
QAPC	Quaid-i-Azam Papers Cell
SAC	Sind Azad Conference
SAP	Sindh *Azad* Party
SGG	*Sind Government Gazette*
SMA	Sind Muhammadan Association
SMP	Sind Muslim Political Party
S.O.	*Sind Observer*
SPML	Sind Provincial Muslim League
SUP	Sind United Party
UP	United Provinces

FOREWORD

The publication of Allen Jones' book is a welcome addition to the twentieth century history of politics in the subcontinent. It is also a significant addition to the political history of Sindh. Although Jones' thesis was completed in 1977, it has not been replaced or superseded by any other important research on the 1938 session of the Sind Muslim League that sponsored Resolution V, the precursor of the Lahore ('Pakistan') Resolution of 1940.[1]

Sindh was amalgamated with the vast Presidency of Bombay, one of the oldest colonial possessions onwords in India, a few years after the British conquest of Sindh. From 1847 on Sindh became a remote appendage of the Presidency where the writ of the colonial bureaucracy reigned supreme. The demand for the separation and autonomy of Sindh grew with the introduction of the local government in the 1880s and the growth of social and political organizations in the province. By the late nineteenth century there was a reasonably mature body of politicians in Sindh able to articulate their grievances and put forward their demand for a government more responsive to local needs. Three generations of Sindh's political leadership would have to struggle for over two decades to achieve the separation. They succeeded largely by their own efforts though with some help from all India political organizations, notably the All India Muslim League (AIML).

This book traces the history of the Muslim League in Sindh from its earliest stages, when in 1906 Agha Khan III wrote to Chagla, a Sindhi businessman to set up the organization in the province. It discusses the attempts of the provincial party to gain affiliation with the Central organization, and to get adequate representation there. These demands were mostly refused even after Jinnah assumed the leadership of the party. The All India

Muslim League did support Sindh's struggle for separation and passed a resolution to that effect in 1925 but, 'as the resolution's substance makes it clear the AIML partly wants to demonstrate its solidarity with Sindhi Muslim's case for separation. But of greater interest to the League was its intention to make the separation issue one of the several all-India Muslim demands as the basis of a platform to secure adequate representation of the Muslim minority in India's present and future constitutional order.'

The issue of the separation of Sindh was taken up on all the main Indian political platforms such as Muslim League, All India Congress and the Hindu Mahasabha in the years 1925 to 1927. In Sindh itself the issue became a popular cause with the emergence of new, young leaders determined to secure the separation. Foremost among these were Mohammed Ayub Khuhro and G.M.Syed. Allen Jones points out that, 'they represented a new breed of leadership: rural-based, progressive minded, less obsequious to the British and militantly pro-Muslim.' This was the third and last phase of the struggle to gain an autonomous status for Sindh—a phase of the struggle that was crowned with success when the Government of India Act of 1935 proclaimed the constitution of the autonomous province of Sindh. Unfortunately, the twenty years also saw a rift occurring between the Hindus and Muslims in Sindh.

This book answers at least partly, the question as to why Sindh, an overwhelming Muslim majority province, felt it had to join the Muslim League, an exclusively Muslim party, and why it supported the extreme position of a separate state for the Muslims of the subcontinent. This particular question is the key to the understanding of the creation of Pakistan because were it not for Sindh's support the creation of Pakistan would have been impossible. Jinnah understood this well and attached immense importance to the politics of Sindh and to the status of the Muslim League in the province.

In researching this subject Allen Jones has brought into focus a major milestone on the path of the struggle for Pakistan. The 1938 conference of the Sindh chapter of the All India Muslim

League has a unique position in the evolution of the idea of a separate Muslim state in the subcontinent of India. For the first time a bold and imaginative initiative was taken at the provincial level and that too by one of the newest and smallest of the branches of AIML. It was also remarkable that a mere two years later the Sindh initiative was translated into the landmark Lahore Resolution of 1940 which was to launch the struggle for a separate Muslim State in India. The present book discusses the background of twentieth century politics in Sindh and brings out the factors that led to the demand for a Muslim state in India at the 1938 conference.

Allen Jones points out that Sindh's leadership learnt several valuable lessons from the movement for the separation of Sindh from the Bombay Presidency. Foremost among these were organizational skills, the ability to sustain a political cause, and the expertise that is developed out of grappling with a formidable opponent. It was expected that a background such as this should give Sindh the required political tools to run an autonomous province without undue problems. Why then did the political process flounder? Why was there not a strong political party to represent the interests of the majority that had suffered so badly in the last hundred years? Why were the governments of Sindh unable to rectify the injustices and ease the hardships of the agriculturists of Sindh and to give the badly needed opportunities to the incipient middle class?

To some extent Allen Jones is right in blaming the selfishness and the narrow self-interest of the majority of the Sindhi politicians. We see this in the wrecking of the proposal to make the highly successful Sind Azad Conference into a political party; we see it in the infighting of Sind Azad Party and the Sind United Party most of which was about party posts; and in the lack of commitment of some politicians who were able to change their loyalties for personal gain. But at the same time there was the unity of objectives that the Muslim politicians shared. They had a real grasp of the economic situation in Sindh where the agricultural class was suffering because of the unbridled play of capitalist forces. The moneylender had the *hari* and the *zamindar* in his grasp. The manifestos of all the newly formed parties included legislation to safeguard the interest of the agriculturist and prevent 'land alienation'. The parties were also keen that their agendas should be secular and that the communities should work together in the larger interests of the province. In fact, they gave absolute priority to a Sindh programme and chose to ignore any overtures from All India parties.

So why had the situation changed so much within a year that the Sindh Muslim leaders staged a very high profile Muslim League Session in Karachi and joined the Party?

The answer lies with the behaviour of the Hindu leadership in Sindh. It failed to respond to the overtures of the Muslim leadership, and did not join any of the new parties that had been formed. This dashed the hopes of organizing any Sindh parties working across communal lines like the Punjab Unionist Party. Instead the Hindu leadership chose to activate the Congress Party in Sindh thus forcing the Muslims to go to an All India party that in their case was inevitably the All India Muslim League. An experiment in inter-communal co-operation in the post Manzilgah period when a Coalition Ministry was formed in 1940 between Muslims and Independent Hindus was wrecked when Congress chose to interfere.

This failure to bridge the political gap between the Hindu and Muslim communities made the Muslims throw their lot in finally with the All India Muslim League, and from 1942 onwards Sindh was to be an unwavering supporter of the All India Muslim League. This stand of Sindhi Muslims was the decisive factor in the achievement of Pakistan.

Hamida Khuhro
Karachi, 2001.

NOTES

1. The other major research work on twentieth century history of Sindh is my book, *Mohammed Ayub Khuhro: A Life of Courage in Politics* which covers the period 1901-1980.

PREFACE

The aim of this book is to analyze the origins and development of political support for the All-India Muslim League in the western Indian province of Sindh during the later years of the nationalist period in India. Traditionally, historical accounts of the growth of political consciousness among Indian Muslims, and the rise of the movement to create the separate nation-state of Pakistan, have tended to focus on those Muslims from northern and central India who, quite indisputably, were the first to become politically aware, and who were prominent in providing the Muslim League's leadership of the Pakistan movement.[1] These Indian Muslims have also attracted a large measure of historical attention perhaps because they were a dominant presence in the League's movement to create a separate homeland for Indian Muslims, not out of the provinces of their birth, but from among the provinces of India's northwestern and eastern extremities.[2] As a consequence of the concentration of historical interest on the Muslims from the United Provinces, however, the Muslims of the Punjab, Bengal, Sindh, Northwest Frontier province and Balochistan, provinces with majority Muslim populations which, in 1947, constituted the new state of Pakistan, have largely escaped the light of historical scrutiny, and relatively little is known of their contribution and the role they played in the Pakistan movement.[3] It was largely for this reason that I felt compelled to select Sindh as a case-study of one of the Muslim majority provinces with a view to providing a deeper, and more complete understanding of the Indian Muslim's struggle for national identity during India's nationalist period.

There were other reasons for choosing Sindh. Next to the Punjab, Sindh was the most important province in the bloc of Muslim majority provinces in northwestern India in terms of both population and economic strength. In 1932, the Sukkur Barrage irrigation scheme, the largest of its kind in the world, brought seven million additional acres in Sindh under cultivation. Partly as a result of increased arable land, and partly as a result of inflated war-time grain prices, Sindh's treasury contained a surplus of 500 million rupees when the province joined Pakistan in 1947.[4]

In addition to Sindh's intrinsic importance as a province, a further reason for its selection stemmed from its close symbolic relationship with the very idea of Pakistan. In 1936, Sindh was separated from the Bombay Presidency and became an independent, autonomous province which, in a sense, foreshadowed the larger partition of British India a decade later, into the two separate sovereign states of India and Pakistan.[5] Finally, Sindh was chosen because of the importance of the Sindh League's leadership in promoting the cause of Pakistan. On three different occasions at the 1938 Sindh League conference, and twice in the Sindh Assembly in 1943 and 1946, the Sindh League leadership, secured passage of three resolutions favouring or calling for the creation of Pakistan, and in each case it represented it was the first time such a resolution had been passed, either at a League meeting or in any Indian provincial legislature.

The notable leadership of the Sindh Leaguers on the issue of Pakistan might lead one to conclude that the League had always been strong in Sindh, but this was only true during the latter part of the final decade before 1947. During the first half of that decade, the League experienced considerable difficulty in establishing itself in Sindh and, in effect, failed to become the dominant political force in the province's politics. There were primarily two forces that served to forestall the League's early establishment in Sindh and inhibited the League's establishment of a strong, organized party base. Once these forces were overcome, or at least accommodated, the League succeeded in becoming the province's most powerful political force for the remaining years of the decade.

Disunity, in its various guises of division, infighting and factionalism, was one of the principal forces which weakened the League's impact during the early years of Sindh's provincial autonomy. In terms of the Muslim political elite in Sindh, disunity manifested itself among the League's leaders as well as within the broader spectrum of Sindhi Muslim leadership. The factors that created disharmony and conflict were not the same in each case. The division between the League-minded Sindhi Muslims and the anti-League Sindhi Muslims, most of whom were known as Muslim Nationalists, stemmed from a difference of outlook based largely on ideological considerations. The disunity between these two groups of Sindhi Muslims was exacerbated, however, by the desire of some groups and individuals in the small Hindu community to exploit differences among the Muslims in order to keep them weak, and thus less of a threat to the minority Hindus.[6]

Factionalism as a form of disunity was a feature that characterized the Muslim leadership within Sindh League circles, but the strife which divided them stemmed less from ideological differences than from competition for personal power. The infighting among the League leaders assumed the appearance of individuals grabbing for power, but in most cases the struggle to secure political power was really an effort to elevate one's family or clan or caste to a high level of political influence.[7] These factional tendencies gathered strength in the aftermath of the Sindh separation movement when the Sindhi Muslim leadership enjoyed an advantageous position, but declined later in the period as the leaders came to realize that the singular pursuit of political ambition returned only minimal gains, while it served generally to weaken their own political position as well as that of their community.

The second major factor militating against the League's rapid growth and development in Sindh lay in the tension, and conflict inherent in the League's province-centre relationship. This relationship was constantly in flux as new developments continued to alter the leaders' perspectives at both the provincial and national levels, making it difficult at any time for the organizations at the two levels to bring their views into close proximity. In addition, the Muslim majority provinces, and the

Muslim minority provinces had different objectives which worked to undermine a congruence of outlook on the part of the leadership in the two blocs of Muslim provinces.[8] However, there was one important area of agreement between the elites of the two blocs: both looked upon the Hindu element in their respective provinces with fear and suspicion. Thus, there was some affinity in the views of the Sindhi Muslim leadership and the Muslim leaders in the Muslim minority provinces. This bode well for the development of close, cooperative relations between the provincial and central League organizations. During the mid-thirties, the Sindhi Muslims adopted a strong pro-Sindhi outlook, and virtually ignored all-India issues as part of the legacy of the Sindh separation movement. But as time passed, the leadership moderated their dominant Sindhi stance, and became more open to all-India considerations in the interest of bolstering their political position.

A similar change took place in the case of the two themes of disunity and province-centre relations. As the period progressed, the Sindhi Muslim leaders demonstrated less of their penchant for personalized politics, and more of an awareness of the need to unify themselves. Likewise, in terms of province-centre relations, they altered their earlier, one-sided emphasis on provincial issues, and gradually evolved a more balanced outlook that incorporated concerns of both local and national importance. The outcome of these changes helped the establishment of the League in Sindh and by 1941, the party had set down a solid foundation upon which to build a strong organization. The early years of provincial autonomy in Sindh were, in effect, a period of political apprenticeship for the League leadership in Sindh, during which they learned to restrain their political ambitions and at the same time free their political outlook from a narrow and limited provincial framework. Once they had learned to accommodate political principle and party discipline with their desire for political power, and to integrate local needs with national demands, they were able to make the League the dominant political force in Sindh until the creation of Pakistan in 1947.

The basis of this book was my Ph.D. dissertation, and research was undertaken in Pakistan between April 1974 and February 1976. In addition, I spent approximately two and a half months in England both before and after my visit to Pakistan. During this period abroad, I was supported by a Fulbright Doctoral Dissertation Research Fellowship, and a special two-month grant from the American Institute for Pakistan Studies (AIPS).

In Pakistan I owe debts of gratitude to many. I am obligated to Mr M. Siddiqi of the National Archives, Karachi who assisted me in using the materials housed there, and who was particularly helpful in procuring microfilms of *Gazettes* and newspapers. For the extensive use of the documents at the Muslim League Archives in Karachi, I am much indebted to Dr Riazul Islam and Mr Aqueel-uz Zafar especially for allowing me to consult unbound volumes. Mr Atique Zafar Sheikh was also very helpful in providing complete access to the Jinnah correspondence at the Quaid-i-Azam Papers Cell Islamabad, despite the rather rigid restraints of working there. I would also like to thank Mr Khalid Hasan for granting me the courtesy of visiting his home to use the Jinnah letters in his possession.

In true keeping with proverbial Sindhi generosity there were many in Sindh who assisted me in ways both great and small. I am grateful to Dr Hamida Khuhro, and Dr Ghulam Ali Allana of the Sindh University's Department of Sindhology, for their gracious cooperation in granting me free use of the valuable library located at the Jamshoro campus. Also, I am very much indebted to the following persons who allowed me to see and use the private family papers in their possession: Daulat Hidayatullah, for the correspondence and letters of her father, Haji Abdullah Haroon; Khan Mohammed Panhwar, for the private papers and books of Sheikh Abdul Majid Sindhi; M. H. Saiyid, for his collection of Jinnah's letters; Agha Sadruddin Durrani, for his brother's books and papers; Ghulam Mohammed Khatri, for his late uncle's virtually complete run of *Alwahid;* and Inayatullah Suleman, for his father's papers and newspaper clippings. I am specially grateful to those persons who were active in the period and gave generously of their time for interviews but who have since passed away: Mohammed Ayub Khuhro and Pir Illahi Baksh, both Sindh Leaguers and former Chief Ministers, Hatim Alavi, a confidant of Jinnah's, and Mazhar Alavi, Ghulam Ali Allana, Pir Ali Mohammed Rashidi, Kazi Fazlullah, Khair Mohammed Ohidi, all of whom were principal League workers during the period covered by this book.

In England, most of my time was spent at the India Office Library where Martin Moirer and Mr R. Bringle were of particular assistance in leading me to seemingly inaccessible files and documents.

I began my dissertation work under Dr Ainslie T. Embree while he was still at Duke University, and I have benefited from his suggestions and encouragement even after his departure. But my largest debt of gratitude at Duke University is to Professor Ralph Braibanti. I first heard of Dr Braibanti and Duke University years ago in India when I happened to attend the same boarding school as his children. Little did I realize then that one day I would attend Duke and study under Dr Braibanti. While I was abroad, Dr Braibanti was instrumental in securing for me the special AIPS grant that I needed to complete my research. I have also profited greatly from his guidance, advice and encouragement while writing the dissertation, and without his assistance and support this study may never have reached completion. I also wish to express my sincere appreciation to Dr Philip Calkins for the time he took to read the draft, and for his criticisms and helpful suggestions. Finally, I wish to thank my friend and erstwhile colleague, Keith Sipe, who, from his own interest in and study of Sindh, was able to furnish valuable insights and comments that helped considerably in the improvement of the dissertation.

NOTES

1. The following works are primary examples illustrative of this emphasis: Abdul Hamid, *Muslim Separatism in India: A Brief Survey, 1958-1947* (Lahore: Oxford University Press, 1967); Ram Gopal, *Indian Muslims:*

A Political History, 1958-1947 (Bombay: Asia Publishing House, 1964); P. Hardy, *The Muslims of British India* (Cambridge: At the University Press, 1972); Hafeez Malik, *Moslem Nationalism in India and Pakistan* (Washington, D.C.: Public Affairs Press, 1963); Anil Seal, *The Emergence of Indian Nationalism* (Cambridge: At the University Press, 1968); I.H. Qureshi, *The Struggle for Pakistan* (Karachi: University of Karachi Press, 1969); and I.H. Qureshi, gen. ed., *A Short History of Pakistan,* vol. 4: *Alien Rule and the Rise of Muslim Nationalism* by M. A. Rahim, M. D. Chugtai, W. Zaman and A. Hamid; 4 vols. (Karachi: University of Karachi Press, 1967). For one of the rare exceptions to this trend, see S.M. Ikram, *Modern Muslim India and the Birth of Pakistan* (Lahore: Sheikh Muhammed Ashraf, 1965).

2. The situation has since changed, aided, in part, by steps taken by the Pakistan government to provide scholars access to the Muslim League Archives formerly at the University of Karachi and to the Quaid-i-Azam Papers Cell at the Ministry of Education in Islamabad.

   In the mid-seventies several Americans graduate students—Steve Rittenberg and Robert Gandre from Columbia University and Emily Datta and David Gilmartin from the University of California, Berkeley completed research in Pakistan which focused on the Pakistan movement in one or another of the majority provinces. In addition the author also met a number of Pakistani scholars who were also working with an emphasis on the provinces of Pakistan.

3. Comparatively few studies have been undertaken specifically on the All-India Muslim League; the following works are the major ones. Lal Bahadur, *The Muslim League: Its History, Activities and Achievements* (Agra: Agra Book Store, 1954); Mohammed Noman, *Muslim India: Rise and Growth of the All-India Muslim League* (Allahabad: Kitabistan, 1942); A. B. Rajput, *Muslim League Yesterday and Today* (Lahore: Sheikh Muhammed Ashraf, 1948); Khalid bin Sayeed, *Pakistan: The Formative Phase* (London: Oxford University Press, 1968), and W.C. Smith, *Modern Islam in India* (Lahore: Ripon Press, 1954). All of these books view the Muslim League from an all-India perspective; only Rajput's begins where Noman's leaves off, in 1942. Rajput's book is also heavily biased towards the Muslim communal viewpoint whereas Lal Bahadur's is strongly pro-Hindu in outlook. Smith's work represents a Marxist interpretation; Noman's was written while the League movement was developing; but Sayeed's, the best all-round account, offers a balanced, systematic and comprehensive analysis of the growth and development of the All-India Muslim League.

4. Interview with M. A. Khuhro, Karachi, 28 January 1976. Khuhro was a Sindh Cabinet minister at the time of partition. In 1947, the exchange value of the Indian rupee was 1 shilling, 6 pence in English currency which worked out to Rs 3.308 per one U.S. dollar. Francis Low, ed.,

The Indian Year Book 1947 vol. xxxiii (Bombay: Bennett, Coleman & Co.), p. 25, 1947.

5. Interview with Hatim A. Alavi, Karachi, 8 September 1974. Alavi, a former Karachi mayor stressed this point, arguing that had not Sindh been separated from Bombay, it was unlikely Pakistan would ever have come into existence.

6. The outcome of the Sindh separation movement heightened the anxiety of some of Sindh's Hindus for their future well-being in Sindh, but from a constitutional standpoint, the Hindu community was not as weak as its minority status would appear to dictate. In fact, under the terms of the Communal Award which determined a community's allotment of seats in the various provincial legislatures, the Hindus in Sindh were given more seats by weightage which significantly increased their influence in the Assembly. See Chapter Two, p. 63.

7. For a general discussion of the relationship of factionalism to lineage group and caste loyalties in Indian politics, see Myron Weiner, *Party Politics in India: The Development of a Multi-Party System* (Princeton, N.J.: Princeton University Press, 1967), pp. 238ff.

8. See K.K. Aziz, *The Making of Pakistan: A Study in Nationalism* (London: Chatto and Windus, 1967), pp. 205-206. Syed Ghulam Murtaza Shah (G.M. Sayed), a prominent landlord and *Matiari Saiyid* stressed the differences between the two Muslim blocs in the author's interview with him in the village of Sann, Dadu district, 16 February 1976.

1. Sind Administrative Committee.
Front Row L to R: K.B. Kaula, Haji Abdoola Haroon, Sir Hugh Dow, Dewan Hiranand, M.A. Khuhro
Back Row: H.T. Lambrick is first from left

2. The 1938 session of the Muslim League
L to R: Mohammed Ayub Khuhro, Pir Ali Mohammad Rashdi, Allahbaksh Gabole, Mohammad Hashim Gazdar (standing), Haji Abdoola Haroon, M. A. Jinnah (reading newspaper), Mir Ayub (profile), G. H. Hidayetullah, Mir Bandee Ali Talpur

3. M.A. Jinnah and leaders in procession through Karachi streets. Muslim League
Session, 1938

4. The Sind Conference, 1932.
Front Row: M.A. Khuhro (2ND from left), Shahnawaz Bhutto (4TH from left) A.F.L. Brayne (5TH from left), Haji Abdoola Haroon (1ST from right)

1

THE EARLY POLITICIZATION OF SINDHI MUSLIM LEADERSHIP 1885–1935

Sindh, a region located in the western part of the Indian subcontinent, was one of the last areas to be added to Britain's Indian empire. In the early 1840s, the British army marched into Sindh and vanquished the ruling Talpur dynasty which, during its eighty-year reign, had achieved little except the political unification of the region.[1] British interest focused on Sindh at this time partly because the province was situated close to the frontier of India but mainly because the important Indus river flowed through the middle of Sindh. Indeed, the mighty Indus had been Sindh's chief feature throughout its long and turbulent history, attracting various peoples from different places at different times to its fertile and potentially prosperous valley. Thus, in the mid-nineteenth century, the British joined the invaders and conquerors who had gone before—the Mughals, the Persians, the Afghans and most recently, the Baluchis—in seeking to wrest from Sindh, and its river, strategic, military and economic advantages to strengthen and consolidate their imperial rule in India.

In area, the province of Sindh was relatively small by Indian standards—just over 46,000 square miles.[2]—and despite its rich soil and riverine tract, Sindh had only a sparse population scattered throughout the province.[3] By the beginning of the 1930s, the population of Sindh reached a total of 3,887,077[4], of which the overwhelming majority—82%—were rural-based, while the remaining 18 per cent resided in the towns and cities.[5] In 1931, the Hindus numbered 1,015,225 or 28 per cent of the total population while the Muslims, by far the largest community, totalled 2,830,800 or 70 per cent of the population (see Table 1.1).[6] The rural-urban settlement patterns in Sindh tended to follow along communal lines.

Table 1.1: Sindh's Population by Religion and District

District	Hindus	Muslims
Karachi	162,111	465,785
Hyderabad	198,684	460,920
Nawabshah	115,899	377,746
Larkana	113,040	577,899
Sukkur	177,467	440,148
Thar Parkar	218,850	245,964
Upper Sindh Frontier	29,174	262,338

Source: Census of India, 1931, complied by H.T. Sorley, Vol. VIII, Part I, Chapter XI, Subsidiary Table II, p. 368.

Table1.2: Hindus per 100 Muslims in Urban and Rural Areas by District

District	Urban Areas	Rural Areas
Sindh (overall)	129	25
Karachi	96	9
Hyderabad	180	28
Nawabshah	235	26
Larkana	105	15
Sukkur	155	22
Thar Parkar	272	86
Upper Sindh Frontier	101	8

Source: Census of India, 1931, Vol. VIII, Pt. I, Chp. II, Section II, Statement No. 24, p. 51.

Thus, the Hindu populace, particularly the upper castes, was concentrated in the cities, towns and larger villages of Sindh while the vast majority of Sindhi Muslims lived in small villages in the rural areas (See Table 1.2.) On the average, the Hindus in the towns outnumbered the Muslims by 29 per cent while in sharp contrast, in the rural areas there were three times as many Muslims as there were Hindus. Only in the urban areas of Karachi, Larkana and Upper Sindh Frontier districts did the two communities approach parity in population; in all of the other urban and rural sectors of the districts a marked imbalance existed, with one community far outnumbering the other.

Despite its minority status, the Hindu community in Sindh enjoyed a high socio-economic position, a fact which was related to their general dominance in the urban centres of the province. As town dwellers, the Hindus had access to English education which enabled them to enter government service and pursue careers in the middle class professions of medicine and law. In addition, the towns were the appropriate setting for some of the Hindu castes, such as the *Bhaibunds,* to follow their traditional occupations of trade and commerce. 'In almost all of Sind's towns all large business was in the hands of Hindu merchants and traders.'[7] During the British period in Sindh, the Sindhi Hindus also began to assume control and virtual ownership of land-holdings, an avenue of economic gain that had been closed off to them under the Talpurs.[8] The Hindus, especially the *bania* class, often managed their incursion into the rural landed sector by functioning as money-lenders, advancing loans to Muslim *waderas* or large landlords and then taking possession of the land when their debtors were unable to pay them back.[9] Of the total Hindu community, the majority (76 per cent) were members of the advanced and intermediate castes and of these the *vaisya* or *bania,* named *Lohano* in Sindh, constituted the most important element, particularly the sub-castes of *Amil*[10] and *Bhaibund.* The *Amils* figured prominently in government service having served earlier as the Talpur's administrative elite while the *Bhaibunds,* mostly merchants and traders, were concentrated chiefly in Hyderabad city, though they also had communities in Karachi, Sukkur, Nawabshah and other towns of the province.[11]

The other major community in Sindh, the Muslims, contrasted sharply with the Sindhi Hindus not just in numbers and in patterns of settlement but also in terms of social progress and economic development. The Sindhi Muslims were an essentially backward community, still retaining many of the traits of a former feudal social order. Dispersed throughout the countryside, the bulk of the Muslims were land tenants or cultivators called *haris*[12] who laboured under the autocratic control of a few *waderas* who possessed large land estates, usually several thousand acres in area.[13] Distance from the towns and cities of Sindh, combined with a reliance on village-based, religious *Mulla* schools, resulted in Sindhi Muslims losing the opportunity to pursue channels leading to social and economic advancement under the British *Raj*.[14] Thus, during the British period in Sindh the Muslims generally accomplished little in altering or improving the traditional agricultural livelihood that had been the lot of most of their community for generations.

The vast majority of the Sindhi Muslim population—roughly 70 per cent—comprised of *Pukka* Sindhis, persons belonging to the *Jat, Sammat* and *Sumro* tribes which had existed in Sindh since ancient times.[15] The category of *Pukka* Sindhis also included certain *Rajput* tribes and clans[16] which had migrated from the east at various times, both prior to and following the Arab conquest which first ushered Islam into Sindh, and India in A.D. 711 Virtually the entire cultivator class of Sindh as well as those having such ancillary occupations as blacksmiths, carpenters, washermen and dyers belonged to this indigenous stock.

In addition to the sons of the soil, Sindh's Muslim population comprised certain important outside elements. Most numerous among these alien peoples were the fierce Baluch tribes who left their barren mountain fastnesses in the west and came to the fertile Indus valley, mostly as shepherds and nomads, but some as soldiers.[17] Another group, much fewer in number, but nonetheless significant because of their high religious and social status were the various *Saiyids*, most of whom took refuge in Sindh following the Mongol invasions in Central Asia in the twelfth and thirteenth centuries.[18] The *Saiyids* of Sindh have been subdivided into two categories, the *Hasani Saiyids* and the *Hussaini Saiyids*[19] of which the latter were more numerous by two and a half times.[20] Among the *Hussaini Saiyids,* the *Matiari* and the *Lakiari* branches were the largest and most influential; the former settled in the village of Matiari in Hyderabad district, and the latter near the Lakhi pass in western Sindh. The *Saiyids,* favoured by previous rulers such as the Talpurs, became landowners as well as religious teachers and because of their special religious standing, some came to be regarded as *Pirs* or saints by the peasantry who held them in enormous veneration.[21]

Another small but important segment of the Sindhi Muslim population were the trading classes of *Memons, Khojas* and *Bohras,* called by Ansari the *Shaikh Nao* Muslims, which means new converts to Islam.[22] Some of these Muslim were comparatively recent converts from Hinduism—the *Memons,* for instance, were originally Cutchi Hindus who embraced Islam and migrated to Sindh during the seventeenth century[23]—and it was they who constituted virtually the entire, though tiny, Muslim middle class of Sindh. Most of them were concentrated in the cities so they could easily manage their commercial enterprises.

Once Sindh was added to the rest of British India, the object of British rule became to establish a peaceful and stable administration in the province, as part of the government's policy of securing a safe and defensible western frontier. Apart from maintaining law and order in Sindh, the major task of the British administration in Sindh was to ensure that revenue from the land was properly assessed and collected. To aid them in this undertaking, the British officials fostered close relations with the rural landed aristocracy which, by and large, meant the Sindhi Muslim elite. The British won the full support of this class by recognizing their *jagirs* of former times, [24] by awarding liberal grants of land[25] and by periodically holding *durbars* at which leading *zamindars* and *waderos* and tribal *sardars* were awarded swords or titles in return for pledges of loyalty or meritorious service. But toward the close of the nineteenth century, a few of the more progressive minded of the Muslim leadership began to realize that, whereas British rule had brought to Sindh a measure of peace and security, little was being done to promote the political, social and economic welfare of their backward community. So, with the encouragement of all-India Muslim leaders, Sir Syed Ahmed Khan and Syed Amir Ali, a group of leaders formed a branch of the National Mohammedan Association in Karachi in 1884, under the presidentship of Khan Bahadur Hassanally Bey Effendi, a Karachi lawyer.[26] The purpose of the Sindh Mohammedan Association (SMA) was to ensure that the Muslim community received its fair share of the benefits accruing from British rule, specifically in 'getting fair treatment for Mohammedan representation in Municipalities and District Local Boards and in the Legislative Councils.'[27] Apart from the fact that its membership comprised members of the Muslim landed elite—'waderos, Pirs and Mirs'[28], little is known of the Association. However, it was the first time that leading Sindhi Muslims got together to protect the interests of their community.[29]

The early years of the twentieth century witnessed a marked upsurge in the level and intensity of nationalist activity in India. This was also a period of Hindu revivalism and certain campaigns such as the effort in Bombay to ban cow slaughter, and the move to promote the use of the Hindi language in the United Provinces, took on a distinctly communal cast which created a sense of fear and insecurity in the Indian Muslim community.[30] In addition, the increase of political agitation, some of which took a violent form, especially in eastern India, produced considerable uneasiness among Indian Muslims. This anxiety, heightened by the outrage over Bengal's partition as well as the imminence of constitutional reforms, compelled the Indian Muslim leadership to form a new nationalist political organization to promote their community's interests. Thus, Muslim leaders from all over India met in Dhaka in December 1906, and in an atmosphere of underlying apprehension and tension, brought into existence the All-India Muslim League.

The All-India Muslim League, similar to the National Mohammedan Association, adopted a loyalist stance toward the government of India and included among its members Muslim noblemen and landed aristocrats. However, the League differed significantly in also attracting to its ranks members of the new, rising Muslim middle and professional classes. In the months and years that followed the establishment of the All-India Muslim League, as political consciousness among Indian Muslims continued to grow, interest in the League increased and branch organizations were formed in a number of the Indian provinces.[31] In Sindh, the League developed a following mainly among the urban-centered middle class Muslims, but it also included among its membership a few of the more enlightened *zamindars* of the *mofussil.*[32]

During the years of the League's early growth in Sindh and the rest of India, the *Khilafat* movement also served to further politicize the Indian Muslim community. This movement, precipitated by British hostility toward Turkey during the First World War, was an effort to bring pressure on the British to help maintain the Caliphate's authority, threatened by the post-war treaty settlements. In Sindh, one aspect of the *Khilafat* movement, the *hijrat* and its related *Tahrik Reshmi Roomal,* found significant support owing primarily to the presence of certain influential religious figures such as Hafiz Mohammed Siddique of Bharchundi and Moulana Abdul Hassan Amroti.[33] During the *Khilafat* period, a branch of the All-India Khilafat Conference was established in Sindh, and among its leadership were Sheikh Abdul Majid Sindhi, a Hyderabad journalist, and Abdullah Haroon, a Karachi merchant, both of whom played a prominent role in the province's subsequent political affairs.[34]

Following the decline of the *Khilafat* movement in the early 1920s, the focus of attention among politically conscious Sindhi Muslims turned to another issue—the separation of Sindh from the Bombay Presidency. The Muslims of Sindh favoured Sindh's separation from Bombay largely because they would then become the majority community in the province. Owing to the issue's immediacy and close relevance to their lives, the separation movement elicited from the Muslim community, particularly its leadership, a much deeper, more widespread commitment than the earlier *Khilafat* movement.

The Origins of the Muslim League in Sindh

In 1907, the year following the All-India Muslim League's birth in Bengal, the League leadership decided to hold the organization's first session in Karachi. Aside from the consideration that Sindh was a Muslim majority area, this decision was most likely made to manifest symbolically the League's all-India character, for Karachi, located in the western-most part of the Bombay Presidency, was situated at the opposite end of India from Bengal.[35] Thus, the League came to Sindh very early in its history, though only in a limited way, for once the session was over no effective organization remained to provide an institutional presence in the province.

However, despite the failure to establish a full-scale League branch in Sindh at this time, a beginning had been made. Mr A.M.K. Dehlavi, a Hyderabad barrister[36] who gave the welcome address at the Karachi session, mentioned in his remarks that he had been asked to be the League's local Secretary in Karachi. Dehlavi said he accepted the post but with hesitation 'because he did not know whether the line of action he had to take in Sindh would be consonant with the line of action which the League had in view now.'[37] The reason for the Secretary's reluctance is significant because it provides some explanation for why the League failed to gain a foothold in Sindh at this time, and also casts some light on the nature of the province—centre relationship within the League.

In Dehlavi's subsequent remarks, he alludes to the struggle within the League leadership between two different schools of thought. One, the older, moderate group favoured using methods such as petitions and representations to induce political change while the second, a newer faction of mostly younger Leaguers, pressed for adopting tactics of agitation and open opposition to the government to achieve political ends.[38] The mild language and loyalist posture of the League's goals established at the Dhaka inaugural session[39] indicated that the moderates held the dominant position in 1906, but some Leaguers, including Dehlavi, felt that the situation had changed by the following year, and that the radical group might pose a challenge equal to if not greater than the strength of the moderates. Dehlavi gave his view of which approach he favoured in his suggestion that the League might emulate the mode of politics in Sindh. He observed 'the Muslim League was a new institution in India but ...if it carried on work in that quiet and calm manner which was characteristic of the political methods in Sind, it would grow into a most powerful and effective political force.'[40] Thus, at the very outset of the League's involvement in Sindh, the whole question of the relationship between the provincial level leadership and the leadership at the centre emerged as an important issue, and in retrospect, it helps to explain more fully the dynamics of the League's early formation. Particularly in Sindh, the conflict between opposing factions at the all-India level undermined the centre's capacity to provide a clear policy direction for the provincial branch, which, in the end, seriously militated against the establishment of a branch organization in Sindh, in these very early years.

In addition to ideological ferment at the centre undermining the League's establishment in Sindh, a further explanation may be gained from a close look at the actual organizational structure of the central League. The structural formation of the All-India Muslim League (AIML) took shape during the first years of the organization's existence, but the principal landmark in this developmental process was the League's annual session at Aligarh in 1908, when the League's first office-bearers were elected.[41] It was also at this session that the membership of the Central Committee (later called the Council) of the AIML was determined, with a result that areas such as Agra and Oudh (later the UP or United Provinces) emerged with a position of strong representation, while other regions such as Sindh, the North West Frontier Province (NWFP) and Balochistan were accorded a much smaller and presumably weaker representation. (See Table 1.3). This outcome did not bring into question the League's claim to an all-India Muslim organization, for all Muslim regions were represented, but it did raise the issue of how equitable was the representation apportioned to each province. Instead of basing the criterion for representation on a province's proportionate Muslim population, which would have been the most democratic standard for the whole Indian Muslim community,[42] an alternate basis was selected which determined a province's representation according to the League's strength in that province. It was decided at the Aligarh session that the award of seats for the Central Committee should be 'in proportion to the number of members allotted to each province under Rule 5.'[43] By an undisclosed method, Rule 5 fixed the maximum number of members of the AIML to be taken from the various provinces, and in each case the membership from each province equaled ten times the number from each province on the Central Committee.[44] (See Table 1.3).

Table 1.3: Composition of the AIML and the AIML Central Committee (AIMLCC), 1908.

Province	Maximum Number of Members in AIML	AIMLCC Member according to Rule 5	AIMLCC Members after Aligarh
Agra and Oudh	70	7	8
Punjab	70	7	7
Bombay (including Sindh)	40	4	4
Madras	25	2½	2
NWFP and Balochistan	15	1½	1
Upper Bengal, Bihar and Orissa	70	7	7
Eastern Bengal and Assam	70	7	7
Berar, Central India and Ajmer	15	1½	1
Burma	10	1	1
Native States	15	1½	1

Thus, the minor place accorded to Sindh on the Central Committee is reflective of the few Sindhi League members and the minimal interest in the League in Sindh and provides a further explanation of the League's failure to establish itself there.

A third reason for the League's early failure in Sindh lies in the emergence of the leaders from the United Provinces as the real power brokers in the central League. During the Aligarh session, they demonstrated their strength and political influence at the third sitting when a discussion took place to determine how the Central Committee's fractional seats should be apportioned.[45] A Madras member sought to have his province's two and a half seats raised to three but he was blocked by the UP members, and Madras was left with only two.[46] A move was also made by the Punjabi lawyer, Mohammed Shafi, to increase NWFP and Balochistan's fraction to a full two seats, but a counter measure by the UP representatives favoured the Berar group. The outcome deprived NWFP of its fraction, and gave Berar a full two seats. This left one seat to be allotted. Shafi argued that it should go to the NWFP bloc which had lost in the first round[47] but the UP leadership, including one of the League's founders, the venerable Nawab Viqarul-mulk, maintained it should be given to Agra and Oudh because the League's 'centre of operations for the present is the United Provinces and it would help the conducting of ordinary business to have enough members in this part of the country to secure easily the presence of a quorum at the ordinary meetings of the Central Committee.'[48] Shafi conceded on the condition that this would only be a temporary arrangement. Thus, in the final apportionment of seats for the League's Central Committee, the UP leadership clearly played the dominant role and consolidated their position by scoring a victory on each of the points under discussion. By securing a position of unassailable strength, the UP leaders were free to use the League organization to advance their own particular interests and, as the discussion revealed, they could afford to show indifference to the League's involvement in such areas as NWFP and Sindh. Therefore, it can be concluded that whereas there was little local interest in the League generated in Sindh, neither was there much help forthcoming from the centre, which might have led to the establishment of a League branch in Sindh.

The effects of the League's early failure to gain a foothold in Sindh persisted for some time, and it was not until four years after the Aligarh session that initial steps were once again undertaken to organize a League branch in Sindh. In January 1912, a Karachi lawyer, Mir Ayub Khan, sent a letter to the central League office expressing interest in starting a League branch in Sindh and requesting the necessary documents and authorization.[49] It is noteworthy that Mir Ayub wrote this letter in his capacity of Honorary Secretary of the Sind Muhammadan Association which suggests this Association, at least certain of its more progressive minded members,[50] sought to establish rapport and possible alignment with the League in an effort to promote the interests of Sindh's Muslims. Mir Ayub's letter might indicate that the impetus for establishing the League in Sindh came from the local level, but a later letter revealed a different source. The Aga Khan, the Bombay-based spiritual leader of the *Khoja* sect, as well as a former League president, had indicated the need to start a League branch during a recent Karachi visit.[51] A reply from the central League office was sent to Mir Ayub the same month, expressing pleasure with the new League interest in Sindh and enclosing AIML Rules and Regulations but giving no word about affiliation.[52] Subsequently, communication between the two parties ceased and consequently Mir Ayub's initiative ended without success.

The central League's failure to affiliate the Sindh branch may be explained as continued indifference at League headquarters, but a more plausible interpretation would be that the central leadership saw no reason for a separate branch in Sindh, when Sindhis could logically be and indeed were members of the Bombay Presidency Muslim League (BPML). Ghulam Mohammed Bhurgari, a Hyderabad barrister and *jagirdar,* and Sayed Allahdano Shah, a *Matiari Saiyid* landlord and Honorary Magistrate from Nawabshah, were both registered BPML members when they were elected to represent Sindh in the Bombay Legislative Council following the Morley-Minto

Reforms of 1909.[53] Bhurgari and Shah were also among the seven listed as the Sindh contingent on the BPML membership rolls for 1916-1917.[54] The others were Ghulam Hussain[55] and Mohammed Hafiz, both, like Bhurgari, Hyderabad lawyers, two landlords from Hubli in Thar Parkar district, Hayat Khan Sahib and Mehboob Ali Khan Nawab, the latter a Talpur Mir, and Ghulam Ali Chagla, a businessman and, interestingly, the only member from Karachi.[56] This listing provides some idea of the people who, in terms of socio-economic status, were attracted to the League in the early days. These few members indicate that the League following comprised a virtually even mix of three urban-based professionals and three rural landlords with the seventh, Bhurgari, as both a lawyer and a *jagirdar,* fitting easily into both camps. Bhurgari's ability to represent the interests of both these groups was likely a major factor in his emergence as Sindh's premier Muslim leader during the late teens and early twenties.

Following the collapse of Mir Ayub's 1912 initiative, five more years passed before steps were once again taken to establish a League branch in Sindh. In 1917, renewed interest in the League developed among the Sindhi Muslim elite largely in response to the creation of the high level Montague-Chelmsford Inquiry into Indian constitutional reforms. The appointment of this inquiry had the effect of polarizing the SMA and League-minded Sindhi Muslims who formerly had appeared to be on good terms. In a letter to the central League in September 1917, Ghulam Ali Chagla requested the necessary documents to establish a League branch, and then went on to charge that the SMA was 'falling into the hands of reactionaries' evident from their intention 'to present an address to the Viceroy against Home Rule.'[57] The Karachi businessman continued, 'The thinking portion of the community' are not for this; we 'do not want puppets to be spokesmen' for Sindhi Muslims. It was clear that the pro-League segment of Muslim opinion in Sindh was displeased with the loyalist, pro-government posture of the SMA, and they sought to establish a League branch in order to ensure that their appositional views received a respectable hearing equivalent to the SMA's[58]

This new campaign of the pro-League Sindhi Muslims to secure formal ties with the AIML ended in frustration as before but this time they decided not to wait any longer on the central organization and went ahead, in early November, to form a branch which they called the Sindh Muslim League.[59] Of the four office-bearers appointed by the branch, three were Karachi businessmen indicating that Karachi-based urban, particularly commercial, interests were emerging as the ascendant element in Sindh League circles, thus altering the earlier image of a Hyderabad-centered League in which rural and urban interests were evenly balanced.[60] This trend continued, and in 1920 when a new slate of office-bearers were appointed, Karachi again claimed three of the four[61] but even more illustrative of this tendency was the Sindh League list of ninety-three registered members in which the names of Karachi's Muslim traders and merchants—Moosajis, Alibhoys, Karimjis, Memons and Mandviwalas—predominated.[62]

The 1917 branch also established among Sindhi Leaguers a pattern of preoccupation with all-India issues. One of the first actions of the Sindh branch was to request permission from the central League to 'represent Montague asking 1/2 Indian seats on executive councils for Muslims.[63] The all-India outlook of the Sindh Muslim League was even more evident later when, at a 1920 meeting, three resolutions were passed, all of which pertained to concerns of national prominence and none contained any local, Sindhi content.[64]

The holding of meetings and the passage of resolutions, as well as the existence of office-bearers, a council and a registered membership amply demonstrated that by 1920 the Sindh Leaguers had established a coherent branch organization in the province. It was also in 1920 that the Sindh League, after trying for eight years, finally secured affiliation with the AIML but only after the secretary, A. Ahmad, threatened 'to write either directly to the president or (to) advise the Council of the Sind Muslim League to declare itself an independent body.'[65] Because of their early initiative on the issue of affiliation, it is likely that the Karachi element was chiefly responsible for this virtual ultimatum to the central League but it was also most probable that Bhurgari, the branch's president, concurred wholeheartedly with the strong stand taken. Bhurgari, an active member from Sindh on the Bombay Legislative Council and, at times, an outspoken critic of government policy,[66] took considerable interest in the work of the League, particularly its propaganda. He eschewed the common use of propaganda 'to rouse mass feelings' and instead stressed its positive potential 'to improve the mental and natural conditions' and to increase the political consciousness of Indian Muslims.[67] Bhurgari was active in promoting the League's cause not just in Sindh but in Bombay and other parts of India as well as abroad, and in recognition of his service to the Indian Muslim community he was selected president of the League's Annual Session held in Lucknow in 1923.[68]

The following year, Bhurgari died and with his demise the first phase of League activity in Sindh came to an end. The loss of Bhurgari's dynamic leadership proved a temporary setback for the Sindh League and interest revived in 1925. As reflected in a letter from the Sindh League secretary to the League headquarters, part of the impetus for the League's revitalization came from the growing sentiment during the mid-1020's among Sindh Muslims, for the separation of Sindh province from Bombay. Writing in February 1925, Nur Mohammed informs the central League office that in addition to enrolling new members, the Sindh League will soon request the AIML Council to recognize the 'Sindh Muslim League as a Provincial League as separate from the Bombay Provincial Muslim League and enjoying all the rights of a Province in the Constitution of the All-India Muslim League.'[69] This represented a significant new development; formerly all-India issues had provided the focus of concern for League-minded Sindhi Muslims, but now a local issue had emerged to command their political attention. The movement for Sindh's separation dominated Sindhi politics for the remainder of the nineteen-twenties and thirties, posing an important challenge for the League leadership at both the provincial and all-India levels.

The Sindh Separation Movement

The sentiment and desire for Sindh's separation from Bombay, which first emerged in the early twentieth century, gathered force during the nineteen twenties and thirties until it became embodied in a widespread political movement. This movement, whose chief support came from the Sindhi Muslim leadership, played a major formative role in helping shape the political outlook and behaviour of the Muslim leadership in Sindh during the subsequent period of provincial autonomy. In addition, the movement had a bearing on the two major themes of Muslim factionalism and provincial-centre relations.

The whole issue of Sindh and its relationship with the Bombay Presidency had a long history that extended back to the early days of British rule in Sind[70]. Sir Charles Napier, after he had conquered Sindh for the British *raj* in 1843, served as the Governor of the province until 1847. When he retired, Sindh was annexed to the Bombay Presidency and placed under the rule of a Commissioner-in-Sindh. At the time, little consideration was given to the disparities of religion, language and culture between the two regions, though there was some comment in the press as well as some thought in official circles that Sindh might be more suitably joined with the Punjab, a province with which it had greater affinity.[71] It was not until 1913, however, that the idea that Sindh be separated from Bombay was first raised in a major political forum.[72] A prominent Sindhi Hindu, Harchandrai Vishindas, Chairman of the Reception Committee of the Indian National Congress's annual session in Karachi, alluded to the notion of separation in his speech by stressing that Sindh, 'possesses several geographical and ethnological characteristics of its own, which give her the hallmark of a self-contained, territorial unit.[73] Implicit in this speech was the idea that Sindh should be constituted a separate province. Thus, Vishindas used a national platform to publicize and marshal support for a local issue. It was not his intention to raise the issue to the level of an all-India demand; the notion of separation was still novel to many Sindhis, and it would have been premature to inject it into the arena of national politics.

The separation issue lay dormant for a few years and then re-emerged in 1917 and 1918, at the time of the Montague-Chelmsford Report, which for the first time committed India to the evolution of a parliamentary system of government.[74] Prompted by the far-reaching effects of some of the reforms embodied in the Report, some of Sindh's political leaders and organizations began to consider what Sindh's position should be under India's political order. The leaders of Sindh's two major communities, H. Vishindas and G.M. Bhurgari, voiced a common theme in raising the separation issue once again. They furnished a new argument to justify Sindh's separation from Bombay, and to give it greater force, they made it consistent with the liberalizing spirit of the Montague-Chelmsford Report. Departing from the earlier notion of Sindh's cultural and territorial discreteness as sufficient grounds for Sindh's separation, Vishindas and Bhurgari now focused on the oppressive and autocratic rule of the Commissioner-in-Sind as symbolic of Sindh's evil connection with Bombay.[75] If the reforms of Montague and Chelmsford were to have any meaning in Sindh, they argued, the Commissionership should be abolished as a first step toward the eventual dissolution of Sindh's link with Bombay.[76]

The issues of separation and Sindh's Commissioner elicited a less uniform response from Sindh's major political organizations at this time. Only the Sind Political Provincial Conference, a branch of the Congress, took a strong position favouring separation (at its annual session in 1918).[77] The Sind Muslim League did express interest in the separation idea by demanding annulment of the commissionership and supporting constitutional reform, but its stance was less forceful than Congress, while the more conservative Sind Muhammadan

Association expressed its satisfaction with the present system of government and wished no change, but if change were inevitable, then it would support separation.[78]

The reforms of the Montague-Chelmsford Report which became a formal part of India's government structure with the passage of the Government of India Act, 1919, produced no changes in Sindh. However the operation of the more liberal aspects of the Act in Bombay served to sustain interest in the separation issue among the Sindhi leadership, many of whom were in the Bombay Legislative Council. Up to this time, the Hindu leadership of Sindh had generally taken the initiative in the separation issue, and if it had not been for the singular leadership of Bhurgari in the early years, it is doubtful that the Sindhi Muslim community would have given it much support considering its preoccupation with all-India issues. Following Bhurgari's death in 1924, Sindhi Muslim interest in Sindh's separation seemed destined to decline, but an able political lieutenant of Bhurgari's, Sheikh Abdul Majid Sindhi, emerged to continue the work his mentor had begun. Significantly, however, Majid decided to adopt a different tactical approach; aware of the relative lack of interest among Sindhi Muslims for Sindh's separation, he concluded it would first be necessary to make the separation issue an all-India demand before Sindhi Muslims would give their support to it.[79] Consequently, in December 1925, Majid attended the annual sessions of Congress, the All-India Khilafat Conference and the All-India Muslim League to introduce resolutions calling for Sindh's separation from Bombay.[80] Majid met with conspicuous success at the League meetings; his resolutions were passed by both the Council and the Annual Session, unanimously in the case of the latter.[81] Majid's resolution included both premises cited earlier— Sindh's cultural distinctiveness and its detrimental connection with Bombay—as reasons justifying Sindh's separation.

As the resolution's substance makes clear, the All-India Muslim League's support for Majid's resolution can be explained in part by the League's wish to demonstrate its solidarity with the Sindhi Muslim's case for separation. But of greater interest to the League was its intention to make the separation issue one of several all-India Muslim demands as the basis of a platform to secure adequate representation of the Muslim minority in India's present and future constitutional order. The question of Sindh's separation did become an all-India issue as is clear from the evidence that between 1925 and 1927, the Congress, the All-India Hindu Mahasabha and a high level meeting of Hindu and Muslim legislators all confronted the demand in their proceedings.[82]

As the separation demand became an issue of all-India politics, in vindication of Majid's tactics, it began to have a wider following among Sindhi Muslims. In 1926 and 1927, largely in response to the national political attention Sindh now commanded, Sindhi Muslims began to agitate for the provinces's separation by pamphleteering, holding public meetings and organizing conferences. In order to give direction and guidance to this increasing political activity, a new group of leaders emerged from the Muslim community. Two of these leaders were Mohammed Ayub Khuhro and Sayed Ghulam Murtaza Shah (G.M. Sayed) who were both young, members of the Bombay Legislative Council and influential landlords in rural Sindh. They represented a new breed of leadership: rural-based, progressive minded, less obsequious to the British and militantly pro-Muslim.[83]

In 1927, an incident occurred in Sindh which served to further crystallize Muslim sentiment in favour of Sindh's separation. Communal rioting broke out in Larkana, Khuhro's home ground, over the forcible abduction of women and children for purposes of conversion.[84] The Muslims, Khuhro in particular, charged that the Hindus who started the trouble 'did not scruple to institute false prosecutions against innocent Muslims which cost their community several *lakhs* of rupees for securing justice.'[85] The Muslims also held the British authorities partly responsible for aiding and abetting the Hindus.[86] The Muslim leadership concluded the British and the Hindus were acting in collusion to protect their own interests, at the expense of Sindh's Muslims. Thus, the Larkana riots helped to reinforce the Muslim desire for Sindh's separation, for once Sindh became an independent province, they reasoned, the Muslims would become the majority community, and would then be in a better position to end their oppression by the British, and their exploitation by the Hindus.[87]

The impact of the communal rioting in Larkana was not limited to the Muslim community alone. Following the trouble, a section of the Sindh Hindu leadership announced their opposition to Sindh's separation. This group of leaders were in a minority, but they had close ties with the All-India Hindu Mahasabha which partly explained their stance on the separation issue.[88] These Sindhi Hindus found an articulate spokesman in a Delhi economics professor, Dr H.L. Chablani, who wrote a pamphlet in 1927 opposing Sindh's separation on racial, political and economic grounds.[89] Chablani's most forceful argument was that Sindh would be unable to survive financially as an independent province. Although the validity of this position was questionable, it emerged as the primary point of debate. In reality, the Hindu position was a direct consequence of the Larkana trouble. It was apparent to Hindu political leaders that an independent Sindh would potentially threaten their community's overwhelming economic position as the province's business class.

The influence of this group of Hindus, and the strength of their economic argument was revealed the following year at the level of all-India politics. The Congress' 'Nehru Report', which formulated a framework for India's future constitution, conceded the Sindh separation demand. However, a few months later in August 1928, an All-Parties Conference was convened in Lucknow to discuss the Report. The Conference altered the Report's position of support for separation in line with the wishes of the anti-separationist Sindhi Hindus: that Sindh's separation should be granted only after certain financial and administrative conditions had been met.[90]

This attachment of conditions to the separation demand represented a setback to hopes for an early creation of a Muslim majority Sindh province. The Muslims reacted with anger and dismay, but also with renewed efforts to secure the separation demand. The All-India Muslim League leader, Mohammed Ali Jinnah, declared heatedly at the December meeting of the All-Parties National Convention in Calcutta that: 'The *Mussalmans* feel that (conditional separation) is shelving the issue and postponing their insistent demand until doomsday and (they can not agree to it).'[91] Also at the Calcutta meeting, the Sindhi Muslim leadership led by the wealthy Karachi merchant, Abdullah Haroon, submitted a representation urging that the linkage of conditions to the separation demand be ended and that separation be undertaken as the majority of Sindhis 'have already so desired it.'[92]

Jinnah's position was challenged the same year by the Simon Commission which observed that the separation demand was not particularly strong among the Sindhi cultivator class to which most Sindhi Muslims belonged.[93] This finding suggests that the Sindhi Muslim elite were speaking on behalf of their own community, in order to mask their real motive in agitating for Sindh's separation which was to ensure that they subsequently received the largest share of political power in Sindh. The Simon Commission also put forward the view, strongly reinforced by Sir Muhammed Iqbal's famous League address two years later, that the separation demand had its greatest backing 'among leaders of Hindu thought all over India, to whom the idea of a new Muslim province, contiguous to the predominantly Muslim areas of Balochistan, the Northwest Frontier Province and the Punjab naturally appeals as offering a strong-hold against the fear of Hindu domination.'[94] In any case, despite the dissimilar purposes of the local and national Muslim elites in supporting the separation demand, the fact that they both favoured separation provided some basis for harmonious relations between the two levels of leadership.

By 1929, the Sindhi Muslim leadership was virtually unanimous in its support of the separation demand with one important exception. In May, a committee report of the Bombay Legislative Council, prepared for the Simon Commission, released its views on the issue of the separation of Sindh. The six-man committee included two Sindhis, one of whom was Sir Shah Nawaz Bhutto, a member of Sindh's rural landed aristocracy, and a minister in the Bombay Governor's cabinet, who served as committee chairman. The committee's majority report reflected the opinion of the Bombay government and predictably opposed the separation demand. It maintained that from the financial as well as the administrative viewpoint, the separation 'proposal (was) impractical.'[95] in addition, the report argued that Sindh would benefit most from the future extension of full provincial autonomy to the Bombay Presidency. Bhutto opposed the separation demand at this stage firstly, because he placed his ties of loyalty to the British and to the Bombay government above his commitment to the Sindhi Muslims and secondly, because separation would end his close association with Bombay's Muslims. Bhutto clearly viewed Bombay politics as a stepping stone to national prominence, and he feared separation would quickly end his ambition by relegating him to the political backwaters of Sindh.[96] Thus, by mid-1929, Bhutto was the only major Sindhi Muslim leader who voiced opposition to Sindh's separation; the other Sindhi on the Bombay committee, Sayed Miran Mohammed Shah, a member of the Bombay Legislative Council from Hyderabad, submitted a minute of dissent which favoured separation.[97]

Bhutto continued to oppose the separation demand until shortly before the British government came out in favour of separation at the Round Table Conference held in London in 1931. The British government had called the Round Table Conference chiefly to rectify the major failings of the Simon Commission to achieve any progress on the issue of India's future constitution, caused largely by the boycott of the major Indian nationalist organizations.[98] These organizations had denounced the Simon Commission because of its exclusively British composition and so, in an effort to avoid making the same mistake twice, the British government invited the leaders of the leading political parties to London to participate in the shaping of future constitutional advances for India.

At the Round Table Conference, the question of Sindh separation was examined by a sub-committee chaired by Lord Russell which ended its deliberations with the following opinion:

> The sub-committee with two dissentients (Dr Moonje and Raja Narendra Nath) are impressed by the strength of the arguments in favour of separation, and they have come to the conclusion that the principle of separation should be accepted.[99]

Sir Shah Nawaz Bhutto and Sir Ghulam Hussain Hidayatullah spoke before the sub-committee of behalf of Sindhi Muslims, as did M.A. Jinnah as the All-India League's spokesman, and among their arguments, the sub-committee cited those which were most impressive and persuasive:

> The racial and linguistic differences between the inhabitants of Sindh and those of the Presidency of Bombay proper, the geographical isolation of Sindh from Bombay, the difficulties of communication between the two and the insistency with which separation has been advocated.[100]

The sub-committee noted further in its conclusion the Bombay government's opposition on administrative grounds but decided they were not 'insuperable'.

The recognition of the need to separate Sindh from Bombay by the high-level Russell sub-committee did not finally resolve the issue of separation, however, for the financial side of the question remained open. The sub-committee had refrained from taking a position on Sindh's economic outlook because 'no detailed examination of the financial consequences of separation has been made.'[101] Accordingly, the sub-committee recommended that an expert Indian committee be formed to look into the question of Sindh's economic viability as an autonomous province, adding that if the investigation revealed that separation would leave Sindh with a deficit, 'the sub-committee thinks that the representatives of Sindh should be asked to show satisfactorily how the deficit be met before the province is set up.'[102] Thus, the Russell committee focused on the same aspect of the separation issue as the anti-separatist Hindus had chosen but, by strongly implying[103] that financial considerations would not present a major obstacle to Sindh's separation, the sub-committee's conclusion served to co-opt and undermine the position of those who opposed separation.

Despite the Russell committee's apparent support for separation, the issue remained unresolved, and during subsequent months the two groups representing the two sides of the issue marshalled their forces in an attempt to pressurize the British government into conceding their respective claims. The anti-separatist, Mahasabha-leaning Sindhi Hindus, in spite of their small numbers,[104] were able to mount a persistent campaign for their cause primarily because of their vocal spokesman, Chablani, and their control of certain influential news papers, in Sindh, such as the *Sind Observor*. These Hindus grouped themselves into the Anti-Separation Conference and proceeded to hold meetings in Sindh, at which speakers voiced opposition to the demand for separation. One such meeting was held in Hyderabad in June 1932, presided over by a prominent Punjabi, Sardar Sampuran Singh of Lyallpur.[105] Singh, in his speech, reiterated the claim of Sindh's financial inability to survive as an autonomous province, which remained the corner-stone of the anti-separatist's position. Subsequent Sindhi speakers raised further arguments which gave a certain communal hue to the anti-separatist stand. Hirand Khemsingh, a prominent Hyderabad barrister and a member of the Bombay Legislative Council, asked how the Muslims, who were only 0.3 per cent English-educated would manage to run a government, and a Karachi physician, G.T. Hingorani, complained that Muslim dominance would lead to excessive taxation of Hindu landed and middle class interests.[106]

The strong and effective campaign of the anti-separatists served to further politicize the Muslim community and reinforce unity in the ranks of the Sindhi Muslim leadership. Unlike the Hindus, there was no division among the Muslim elite over the issue of separation once Bhutto joined the cause, but similar to their opponents in the Hindu camp, Sindhi Muslim leaders formed their own informal organization, called the Sind Azad Conference early in September 1932,[107] to provide a platform for the cause of Sindh separation. This formation of an exclusively provincial level organization on the part of the Sindhi Muslim elite was significant in at least two ways. One, it provided a basis for Sindhi Muslim strength and unity by bringing together the landed aristocracy and the emergent Muslim middle classes on the single issue platform of separation. Two, it also reflected among them a growing sense of a regional, largely Muslim, Sindhi identity which was reinforced by the arguments they chose to advance their cause of separation. They continued the old arguments of Sindh's cultural discreteness and the unjust Bombay connection, but they also evolved new arguments to counter the thrusts of the Hindus. They sought to satisfy financial doubts by claiming that Sindh could be made self-supporting through administrative retrenchment, the development of the Sukkur Barrage irrigation scheme, and the tapping of new and equitable sources of taxation.[108] They went on to argue that even if Sindh were to have a deficit, that burden should be more properly borne by the Indian government rather than the Bombay government.[109] The Muslim leaders attempted to refute the arguments of Khemsing and Hingorani by, in the first place, pointing to the great Sindhi Muslim leaders such as the Aga Khan, G.M. Bhurgari and M.A. Jinnah as well as the respectable record of the Sindhi Muslim legislators in the Bombay Legislative Council, and secondly, by emphasizing that Muslims were not opposed to Hindu interests but stressed Muslim needs as they were truly the most backward community as a result of Sindh's long link with Bombay.[110]

The emergence of the Sind Azad Conference was also noteworthy in another sense for it had a bearing on the theme of provincial, all-India relations. The Sindhi Muslim elite were compelled to form their own provincial organization chiefly because, for reasons noted above,[111] the national Muslim organizations had failed to provide any leadership at the provincial level. But despite the All-India League's inability to furnish organizational leadership for the Sindh separation cause, it continued to support the issue at its meetings as did the other Muslim national organization, the All-India Muslim Conference.[112] Thus, the pattern of harmonious local-centre Muslim relations, established in the 1920's and based on a common allegiance to the goal of separating Sindh from Bombay, continued into the 1930's and the final years of the separation movement.

While the pro-separatists and the anti-separatists continued their respective campaigns to secure their opposing claims, two investigations instead of the one recommended by the Round Table Conference were undertaken to determine Sindh's financial outlook as an independent province. The report of the first, the Miles Irving Committee, concluded in 1931 that Sindh, as an autonomous province, would face a burdensome initial deficit of Rs. 110.42 *lakhs*.[113] This Committee had declined to determine ways in which Sindh might meet its deficit as such a task had been outside its terms of reference.[114] The question of a deficit was, however, included in the scope of the Brayne Committee, constituted the following year, to investigate further the financial aspects of the separation of Sindh. The Brayne Committee produced a lower initial deficit of Rs. 80.5 *lakhs* and determined that the deficit could be met by 1944-5 by tapping additional sources of revenue through new taxation but chiefly through increased revenue accruing from the new Sukkur Barrage lands.[115] Thus, by projecting a favourable financial picture of an autonomous Sindh province, the Brayne Committee anticipated the final resolution of the Sindh separation issue several months later.

On 24 December 1932, the Secretary of State for India announced the definite decision of the British government to separate Sindh from the Bombay Presidency and establish an independent, autonomous Governor's province in Sindh.[116] While there can be little doubt that the findings of the Brayne Committee played some part in determining this outcome, it should also be noted that the British government, in reaching this decision, was equally if not more influenced by the principles of self-determination and provincial autonomy which were given a prominent place in its new Constitution for India, the Government of India Act, 1935, intended to finally satisfy the insistent Indian demand for greater constitutional advances.[117] Under the authority of the 1935 Act, Sindh was constituted a separate province on 1 April 1936, thus bringing victory to the Sindhi Muslims who had waged a long and bitter struggle to secure the goal of an independent and autonomous Sindh province.

Disunity and factionalism characterized early Muslim political organizations in Sindh as well as at the national level, though the nature of dissension at the provincial level differed markedly from the form the conflict took within the all-India League body. Disunity among politically organized Sindhi Muslims was reflected in differences in class outlook as represented by the conflict of interests between the Sind Muhammadan Association and the League-minded Sindhis. By contrast, at the national level, factionalism occurred within the all-India League organization itself based on the competing interests of the regional blocs comprising the central League leadership.

The existence of divisions within the central League had a bearing on the nature of province-centre relations, with particular reference to the all-India League organization. The persistent infighting among the central League leadership weakened the national organization, and consequently undermined efforts to establish a League branch organization in Sindh. But the breakdown in province-centre relations reflected in the failure to establish a Sindh branch, was restored to the degree of achieving a consonance of views, though not an organizational linkage, during the movement for Sindh's separation. The expression of local-centre solidarity in support of the movement revealed, however, a dissimilarity of motives which pointed to the potential for frustration rather than harmony in subsequent province-centre relations.

Upon the conclusion of the Sindh separatist movement, the Sindhi Muslim leadership appeared to have reached a pinnacle of political success: they had achieved a broad measure of unity among themselves, they had established close relations with the all-India Muslim leadership, and they stood to become the new power brokers in the new, autonomous province of Sindh. The question now was: would the Muslim leadership in Sindh manage to maintain and consolidate their position of political strength or would they prove unequal to the task of shouldering the burden of leadership and responsibility?

NOTES

1. H. T. Sorley, *The Gazetteer of West Pakistan: The Former Province of Sind (Including Khairpur State)* (Lahore: Published under the Authority of the Government of West Pakistan, 1968), p. 172.
2. Government of India, *Census of India, 1931,* complied by J.H. Hutton, Vol. I, Part I, Chapter I, (Delhi: Manager of Publications, 1933), p. 16.
3. In 1931 the average population density for all of Sindh was 81 persons per square miles (psm) which increased to the figure of 94 psm in 1941. In 1931 the district with the highest density was Larkana with 157 psm and lowest in Thar Parkar with 34 psm. Maneck B. Pithawalla, *An Introduction to Sind: Its Wealth and Welfare* (Karachi: Sind Observor Press, 1951), p. 43.
4. *Census of India, 1931,* p. 16.
5. *Census of India, 1941,* Vol. XII: Sind, compiled by H.T. Lambrick, (Delhi: Manager of Publications, 1942), p. 2.
6. Ibid., p. 26. The remaining communities were very small in number; next in size were the Christians (15 133), followed by the Parsees (3537), then the Jains (1144) and finally the tribals (204).
7. *Census of India, 1931,* Vol. VIII, Pt. I, Chp. II, Sec. II, p. 53.
8. The Talpurs prohibited Hindus from holding land, but under the British, the Hindus were attracted to the land following the introduction of Civil Courts in 1866, which made land liable for debt. The lightness of assessment as well as the security of life and property also made land a valuable commodity. Sorley, *The Former Province of Sind,* p. 540.
9. A Government report in the mid-1920's showed that 31 per cent of the total occupied area in Sind was largely in Hindu hands. S.H. Covernton, *Report on the Subject of Legislation to Restrict the Alienation of Land in Sind by Members of the Agricultural Classes* (Karachi: The Commissioner's Printing Press, 1972), p. 19.
10. The *Amils,* particularly the urban members of the community, later claimed *brahman* status. Keith Sipe, '*Karachi's Partition-Related Migration*' (Ph.D. Dissertation, Duke University, 1967), p. 83.

11. *Census of India, 1931,* Vol. VIII, Pt. I, Chp. XI, Appendix F, p. 499. See also Sorley, *Former Province of Sind* p. 256, E.H. Aitken, *Gazetteer of Province of Sind* (Karachi, Mercantile Steam Press, 1907), pp. 180ff.

12. The 1931 Census declines to report a proper enumeration for *haris* because no official classification had been made of them. They could be categorized as either rent receiver, tenant cultivators or agricultural labourers. Ibid., Chp. V Sec. II, p. 232. Aitken in 1907 classified them as landed labourers and gave their number as 1,262,695 or 40 per cent of the total population. Aitken, *Gazetteer of Sind,* p. 190. For a description of the harsh lives they led as well as a critique of Sind's zamindari land system see M. Masud, *Hari Report: Minute of Dissent* (Karachi: Printed at the Government Press, 1948).

13. In the Sind Legislative Assembly in 1938 the large landholders were identified as those who paid a land assessment of over Rupees 1000 and of these there were a total of 1,301 as compared with a total of 223,451 who paid an assessment between Rs. 25 and Rs. 1000. Government of Sind, *Proceedings the Sind Legislative Assembly,* Vol. V, Book 10, May 30, 193 p. 27 (Hereinafter cited as PSLA). The largest landholder in British India resided in Sind: the *Sardar* of the Baluch tribe of Chandio owned over 300,000 acres located west of Larkana town. *History of Alienations in the province of Sind Compiled from the Jagir and other Records in the Commissioner's office* 2 vols., (Karachi: Printed at the Commissioner's Press, 1886) 1:232.

14. In 1928 a Muslim representation listed the replacement of Persian with a Hindu-Sindhi script, the exclusive expenditure of landholder cesses on municipal schools, the absence of educational facilities for rural Muslims and the breakdown of the *Mulla* school system as reasons explaining the low educational status of Sindhi Muslim. Noor Mohammed, *The Backwardness of Sind Mussalmans in Education* (Poona: Scottish Mission Press, 1928), pp. 1-2, 4, 10.

15. These tribes were the most numerous; Sadik Ali in his authoratative work gives the names of eleven such tribes in all. Sadik Ali Ansari, *A Short Sketch Historical and Traditional of the Musalman Races Found in Sind, Balochistan and Afghanistan* (Karachi: Sind Government Press, 1954), p. 1.

16. The Sammat were believed to be descendants of the Yadur Rajputs. Sorley, *Former Province of Sind,* p. 238.

17. In 1941 the Baluch numbered 23 per cent of the total Muslim population. *Census of India, 1941,* p. 25.

18. Ansari, *A Short Sketch of Races in Sind,* pp. 2-7; Sorley, *Former Province of Sind,* p. 246.

19. So named because of their claim of descent from either *Imam* Hasan or *Imam* Hussain, both grandsons of the prophet Mohammed (PBUH).

20. This is a 1901 Census citation quoted in Sorley, *Former Province of Sind*, p. 246.
21. For a discussion of some of the cults surrounding the *Saiyids* and *Pirs* of Sind see M. Mujeeb, *The Indian Muslims* (London: Allen Unwin and Co., 1967), p. 12. See also J. Parsram *Sind and its Sufis (Madras: Theosophical Publishing House, 1924)*, and Peter Mayne, *Saints of Sind* (London: John Murray Publishing Co., 1956).
22. Ansari, *A Short Sketch of Races in Sind*, pp. 64-69.
23. *Census of India, 1931*, Appendix F, p. 575. For a useful discussion of the *Memon* and *Khoja* communities see K. Sipe, 'Karachi's Refugee Crisis,' pp. 93-108.
24. *Jagirs* were free grants of land usually given as rewards for military service. See Hamida Khuhro, '*The British Administration of Sind, 1843-1865*' (Ph.D. dissertation, University of London, 1965), pp. 73, 99-100, 123, 148.
25. Sorley, *Former Province of Sind*, p. 383.
26. Sir Syed's influence was revealed in the establishment of the Sind Madressah-tul-Islam, a school started by the Association and patterned after Sir Syed's Aligarh institution. Khawaja Ali Mohammed, 'History of the Sind Madressah-tul-Islam,' *The Sind Madressah-tul-Islam Platinum Jubilee Book 1885-1960* (Karachi: Ehsan Baduwi, 1960), p. 53.
27. Ibid.
28. Ibid., *Mir* was the title used by members of the former ruling family of Talpurs.
29. See Matiur Rahman, *From Consultation to Confrontation: A Study of the Muslim League in All-India Politics 1906-1912* (London: Luzac and Co., 1970), p. 3.
30. P. Hardy, *The Muslims of British India* (Cambridge: At the University Press, 1972) pp. 140-146.
31. See Chapter Three of A. Rahman's book, 'The Formation of Provincial Branches,' pp. 67-85.
32. The early activity of the League in Sindh will be discussed in greater detail later in this Chapter.
33. The *Hijrat* in this case was a religiously inspired mass migration from India to Afghanistan, and Sindh was one of the main areas from which the *muhajarin* or emigrants came. A.O. Niemeijer, *The Khilafat Movement in India* (The Hague: Martinus Nijhoff, 1972), pp. 102-104. *Tahrik Reshmi Roomal* means literally 'Silk handkerchief movement' and refers to the letters secretly written on silk handkerchiefs to foreign governments appealing for help. See Hussain Ahmed Madani, *Tahrik Reshmi Roomal* (Lahore: Classic, 1960) and Z. Faruqi, *The Deoband School and the Demand for Pakistan* (Bombay: Asia Publishing House, 1963), pp. 56-57.
34. For the meetings and resolutions of the Khilafat Conference in Sindh see K.K. Aziz, *The Indian Khilafat Movement 1915-1933: A Documentary*

Record (Karachi: Pak Publishers, 1972), pp. 183-185, and P.C. Bamford, *Histories of the Non-Cooperation and Khilafat Movements* (Delhi: Government of India Press, 1925), pp. 147, 160, 171, 204.

35. One historian suggests that Karachi was chosen because of Sindh's special place in the hearts of Indian Muslims as the first region of India to come under the influence of Islam. Lal Bahadur, *The Muslim League: Its History, Activities and Achievements* (Agra: Agra Book Store, 1954), p. 71.

36. Dehlavi originally came from Delhi and later represented Sindh on the Bombay Legislative Council. Interview with Kazi Fazlullah, Larkana, January 22, 1975. Also Lal Bahadur, *The Muslim League*, p. 240. At the 1908 League session in Aligarh, Dehlavi was the only member from Sindh to be elected to the League's forty man Central Committee. *Rules and Regulations of the All-India Muslim League* (Aligarh: Institute Press, 1909), p. 2.

37. Syed Sharifuddin Pirzada, ed., *Foundations of Pakistan: All-India Muslim League Documents: 1906-1947*, 2 vols. (Karachi: National Publishing House, 1970), 1:11.

38. For a fuller discussion see Matiur Rahman, *From Consultation to Confrontation*, pp. 34-35.

39. The League's goals were included in Resolution No. 1 and were stated as follows:
    (a) To promote among the Musalmans of India, feelings of loyalty to the British Government, and to remove any misconception that may arise as to the intention of Government with regard to any of its measures.
    (b) To protect and advance the political rights and interests of the Musalmans of India, and to respectfully represent their needs and aspirations to the Government.
    (c) To prevent the rise, among the Musalmans of India, of any feeling of hostility towards other communities, without prejudice to the other aforementioned objects of the League.' Pirzada, *Foundations of Pakistan*, 1:6.

40. Ibid., p. 16.

41. Ibid., pp. 22ff.

42. The most ideal arrangement would have had equal representation for all the provinces but this standard along with the one above were possibly deemed as impractical for, as a general rule, the regions where the Muslims were the most populous were also the areas where they were the most backward, ill-educated and least politically conscious.

43. Karachi, University of Karachi, Muslim League Archives. Annual Session at Aligarh, March 1908, Volume 5, p. 14. (Hereafter cited as MIA, Aligarh Session, 1908, Vol. 5, p. 14.)

44. *Rules and Regulations,* Clause 5, pp. 14-15.

45. The final outcome is given in Table 1.3, Column 3.

46. This account is based on the Archives record, MLA, Annual Session at Aligarh, Vol. 5, pp. 15ff.

47. Shafi is seen here speaking for the interests of the Muslim majority areas, thus providing an example very early in the League's history of tension between Muslim majority area interests and Muslim minority area interests.

48. Ibid., This reason might be interpreted as a thinly-disguised excuse to mask the UP leaders' desire to maintain a firm, controlling grip on the League. See Rahman, *From Consultation to Confrontation,* p. 59-60; also F. Robinson, *Separations Among Indian Muslims: The Politics of the United Provinces' Muslims, 1860-1923* (Cambridge: At the University Press, 1974), pp. 148-150.

49. MLA, Sind Provincial Muslim League, 1912-1938, (1), Vol. 241, Mir Ayub Khan SMA Honorary Secretary to Honorary Secretary of the All-India Muslim League, Aligarh, 20 January 1912 p. 1.

50. Mir Ayub Khan was a member of the traditional ruling Aliani family of Las Bela, a native state west of Karachi, but his westernized legal training accounted for his liberal outlook. Karachi. Sindhi residence, Papers of Sheikh Abdul Majid Sindhi (Hereinafter PSAMS), 'A Tribute to Mir Ayub Khan,' by Sheikh Abdul Majid Sindhi, n.d. Also, Abdul Hameed Aliani, 'Memorable Mir Ayub Khan,' *The Sind Madressah-tul-slam Platinum Jubilee Book* pp. 38-42.

51. MLA, Sind Provincial Muslim League, 1912-1938, (1), Vol. 241. Hafizula Shahabuddin Baba to H.A. Ansari, AIML Secretary, Lucknow, 2 February 1912, p. 3 (Hereinafter MLA, SPML 1, p. 3). The Aga Khan was the president of both the Aligarh (1908) and Delhi (1910) sessions. Pirzada, 1:23,87.

52. Ibid., AIML Secretary, Aligarh to Mir Ayub Khan, 24 January 1912, p. 2.

53. M. Rahman, p. 157. Bhurgari, as the only Sindhi office-bearer, was elected one of the first vice-presidents of the BPML in April 1909. Ibid., p. 69. For further background on Shah, see Ziaullah G. Ghulamally, 'Some Historical Personalities of Sind,' (Hyderabad, 1970). Copy in Sindhology Library, University of Sind, Jamshoro, Sind. (Typed manuscript).

54. MLA, AIML Membership and Subscriptions, 1916-1917, Vol. 254, pp. 60A-61.

55. This was most likely Ghulam Hussain Hidayatullah who later was elected to the Bombay Legislative Council, was knighted and became Sindh's first prime minister in 1937.

56. Chagla was later elected the first President of the Karachi Municipality. Behram Sohrab H.J. Rustomji, 'A Short Historical Survey of the Beginnings of the Corporation of Karachi,' *Proceedings of All Pakistan History Conference* (Karachi: Times Press, 1951), p. 399.

57. MLA, SPML, 1, Chagla to AIML Secretary, Lucknow, 24 September 1917, p. 8.

58. In a December 1917 representation to the Viceroy, the Sind League (which had been formed by this time) stated that the SMA which had wrongly expressed 'satisfaction with the present system of administration' was ill-suited to represent 'fearlessly the wishes and feelings of the community' dominated as it was by an 'oppressed and intimidated *zamindar* class, fearful of officialdom, and burdened by heavy taxation and debts to moneylenders.' n.a., *Some Features of Bureaucratic Administration in Sind* (Hyderabad: The Sind Publishing House, 1918), pp. 63-74.

59. Chagla informed the League headquarters by telegram that a branch had been formed in Karachi on 1 November and that affiliation with the central League was sought. MLA, SPML, I, Chagla to AIML Secretary, Lucknow, 3 November 1912, p. 11.

60. Yusafali Alibhoy, Chagla and Abdullah Haroon were respectively the branch's president, honorary secretary and treasurer and all three were prominent in Karachi's commerce. See Abbassi, p. 41. The only non-Karachite was Ghulam Mohammed Bhurgari who was appointed vice-president.

61. A Haroon, vice-president, A.H. Ahmad, Secretary and Tayabali Alibhoy, treasurer, were all from Karachi but their numerical strength was offset by the influential Hyderabad lawyer, G.M. Bhurgari, who occupied the president's chair. MLA, SPML, I, A. Ahmad to AIML Secretary, Lucknow, 27 February 1920, p. 12.

62. Ibid.

63. Ibid., Chagla to AIML Secretary, Lucknow, 5 November 1917, p. 12. This demand was included in the Sind League representation in December. *Some Features of Bureaucratic Administration*, p. 63.

64. The resolutions supported the AIML position on cow sacrifice, the acquisition of the Jallianwala Bagh and expressed solidarity with the Manifesto of the All-India Khilafat Conference. MLA, SPML, 1, Minutes of the Sind Muslim meeting, 4 March 1920, p. 23.

65. Ibid., A. Ahmad to AIML Secretary, 27 February 1920, p. 17. The Sind League was affiliated by the AIML Council on 18 July 1920. MLA Council Meetings, 1920 (1), Vol. 144, p. 63. The agenda of the Council meetings for this period reflect an AIML preoccupation with such issues as the *Khilafat*, Muslim holy places, and the Government of India Act, 1919, which worked to push such matters as Sind's affiliation into the background. Ibid., pp. 44ff. See also Pirzada, I: VIII ff. and Lal Bahadur, pp. 140ff.

66. See his evidence in Government of Bombay, *Report of the Committee Appointed to inquire into the advisability of extending the period of Settlement in Sind from 10 to 30 years* (Bombay Castle: Government of

Bombay, Revenue Department, 1917) pp. Iff. For his evidence before the Royal Commission on Public Services in India, see *Some Features of Bureaucratic Administration*, pp. 2-62.

67. MLS, SPML, 1, G.M. Bhurgari to Zahur Ahmed 9 April 1922, p. 28.

68. MLA, Annual Session at Lucknow, 1923, Vol. 101, Letter from M.A. Jinnah to Zahur Ahmed, 7 March 1923, n.p.

69. MLA, SPML 1, Nur Mohammed to the AIML Secretary, Lucknow, 22 February 1925, p. 30.

70. For contemporary accounts of the conquest and early years of British rule in Sind, see J. Outram, *The Conquest of Scinde-A Commentary* (Edinburgh: C.W. Blackwood and Sons, 1846); W.F.P. Napier, *The Conquest of Sind* (London: Boone, 1845); and W.F.P. Napier, *History of General Sir Charles Napier's Administration of Sind* London: Chapman and Hall, 1851). For more recent accounts, see Robert A. Huttenback, *British Relations with Sind, 1749-1843, An Anatomy of Imperialism* (Berkeley: University of California Press, 1962); and P.N. Khera, *British Policy Towards Sind, up to its Annexation, 1843* (Delhi: Ranjit Printers and Publishers, 1963).

71. Muhammad Irfan, 'A Brief History of the Movement of the Separation of Sind,' in *Alwahid Special Issue Number*, 1 April 1936, p. 52.

72. By contrast, Sind's commercial community, particularly Karachi's, had shown an interest in separation from Bombay as early as 1866. Herbert Feldman, *Karachi through a Hundred Years: The Centenary History of the Karachi Chamber of Commerce and Industry, 1860-1960* (Karachi: Oxford University Press, 1960), p. xiv. This factor may account indirectly for the early effort led by Karachi's Muslim businessmen for a separate League branch discussed previously above.

73. Quoted in Alhaj Mian Ahmad Shafi, *Haji Sir Abdoola Haroon: A Biography* Karachi: Pakistan Herald Press, n.d.), p. 70.

74. R. Coupland, *The Indian Problem, 1833-1935* (Oxford: At the Clarendon Press, 1968), p. 54.

75. Ghulam Hyder Pir, 'A Glimpse into the History of Sind Separation,' in *Alwahid*, 1 April 1963, pp. 49, 50. For a discussion of the gradual increase and expansion of the powers of the Commissioner-in-Sind after 1847, see Chapter VI of *A Handbook of the Government Records lying in the Office of the Commissioner-in-Sind and in District Offices* (Karachi: Commissioners Printing press, 1933), pp. 36-46.

76. This argument was contained in a memorandum submitted to Montague-Chelmsford in 1917. Shafi, *Haji Sir Abdoola Haroon*, pp. 70-71.

77. Interview with Hatim Alavi, Karachi, 28 September 1974.

78. Irfan, p. 53. The SMA did later join the cause for Sindh's separation. Hamida Khuhro, 'The Separation of Sind and the Working of an Autonomous Province: An Analysis of Muslim Political Organization in

Sind, 1843-1938,' pp. 1-2. Paper presented at the 'Sind Through the Centuries' Seminar, Karachi, 23-25 March 1975.

79. Irfan, 'A Brief History of Sind's Separation', p. 53.

80. In organizational terms, the Congress and the Khilafat Conference had already recognized the separation principle in forming Sindh branches. Ibid., Also, Note by the Secretary of the All-India Congress Committee, *Report of the Committee, All Parties Conference, 1928,* Allahabad, 1928, p. 31.

81. MLA, Annual Session at Aligarh, December, 1925, Vol. 135, p. 111.

82. In 1925 the Mahasabha conceded the probability of separation as part of a larger communal settlement, and in 1927 the Congress endorsed the separation claim. Irfan, 'A Brief History of Sind's Separation', p. 53; M.A. Khuhro, *A Story of the Sufferings of Sind: A Case for the Separation of Sind from the Bombay Presidency* (Karachi: Bharat Printing Press, 1930), p. 45. For Mahasabha Politics at this time, see Barbara Flynn, 'The Communalization of Politics: National Political Activity in India, 1926-1930' (Ph.D. Dissertation, Duke University, 1974), pp. 58ff.

83. interview with Pir Ali Mohammed Rashidi, Islamabad, 21 May 1974. Rashidi, a *Lakiari Saiyid* by birth and a journalist by training, proved a useful informant because of his close association with political events in Sindh throughout the period under study.

84. Flynn, *'The Communalization of Politics'* p. 73.

85. Evidence of Khan Bahadur Mohammed Ayub Khuhro M.L.C. on Behalf of the Sind Separation Conference taken before the Joint Parliamentary Select Committee on Indian Constitutional Reform, 19 July 1933 (Bombay: Appeal Press, 1933), p. 5. (Hereinafter cited as *Minutes of Evidence).*

86. Interview with Rashidi, 21 May 1975.

87. In the case of the Hindus, in particular, the Muslims were not simply concerned with Hindu economic dominance, but with the fact that they were steadily reinforcing this position of strength. Covernton's 1927 report concluded 'Mohammedan agriculturalists are already losing their land to Hindus of the non-agricultural classes to an extent which is disturbing.' Covernton, *Report on Legislation to Restrict Land Alienation,* p. 19. Also, *Minutes of Evidence,* p. 5; p. 45, (Table III); p. 46, (Table IV). This fear was also expressed by a Sindhi *zamindar* in the early thirties. *Daily Gazette,* 18 May 1934, p. 5.

88. The Mahasabha's position on separation was based on the premise that 'no new Province should be created with the object of giving a majority therein to any particular community.' Thus, the Madaabha opposed separation because Sindhi Hindus were against it and, secondly, because Sindh would be a deficit province. See the Mahasabha's Evidence in *Proceedings of the Round Table Conference, 12 November, 1930, to*

19 January, 1931, 1st Session (London: His Majesty's Stationery Office, 1931, p. 416.

89. The title of Chablani's pamphlet was *Financial Aspects of the Separation of Sind from the Bombay Presidency,* Flynn, *'The Commualization of Politics,'* p. 161.

90. All-Parties Conference, 1928. *Report of the Committee appointed by the Conference to determine the principles of the Constitution for India* (Allahabad: General Secretary, All-India Congress Committee, 1928), p. 162.

91. All-Parties Conference, 1928. *The Proceedings of the All-Parties National Convention.* Allahabad, Rafi Ahmad Kidwai, Secretary, All-Parties National Convention, (1929).

92. Khuhro, *A Story of the Sufferings of Sind,* p. 53.

93. Great Britain, *Parliamentary Papers,* (House of Commons and Command), Cmnd. 3568 and 3569, 'Report of the Indian Statutory Commission,' Vol. I, (London: His Majesty's Stationery Office, 1930), p. 58. (Hereinafter cited as The Simon Commission *Report*).

94. Ibid. For Iqbal's speech see, Pirzada, 2: 153.

95. Simon Commission *Report,* 4:36.

96. Interview with Rashidi, Islamabad, 21 May 1975, and with Hatim Alavi, Karachi, 25 September 1974.

97. Simon Commission *Report,* 3:68ff.

98. The appointment of the Simon Commission created a split in the All-India Muslim League into two factions; the Shafi group which favoured cooperation with the Commission and the Jinnah group which did not. This split in the League persisted for three or four years and does much to explain the League's failure to provide any leadership in Sindh for the separation movement. Noman, *Muslim India,* p. 255-260.

99. Government of India, *Indian Round Table Conference, 12 November 1930—19 January 1931 Proceedings of Subcommittees,* Vol. IX, [Sub-Committee No. IX (Sind)], (Calcutta: Government of India Central Publication Branch, 1931), p. 91.

100. Ibid.

101. Ibid.

102. Ibid.

103. This implication was made clear by the sub-committee's mention of how the issue would be resolved should the deficit prove insoluble.

104. Most of the Sindhi Hindus were in favour of separation and demonstrated their support by signing a Sindh Hindu-Muslim Pact in 1928 which called for Sindh's separation. Ifran, p. 55; Khuhro, *Story of the Sufferings of Sind,* pp. 54-5.

105. Karachi, Jehanger Kothari Building, Papers of Inayatullah Suleman. (Hereinafter cited as PIS). File I on the Sind Separation, Newspaper clipping from the *Sind Observor,* 20 June 1922, p. 5.

106. PIS, File I, Newspaper clippings from *Sind Observor,* 22 June 1932, pp. 4, 5 and 9 July 1932, pp. 5, 8.

107. At the first meeting, Sir Shah Nawaz Bhutto was appointed chairman, M.A. Khuhro, vice-chairman, Sheikh Abdul Majid, secretary and Abdullah Haroon, treasurer. Interestingly, all were also AIML Councilmen at this time. MLA SPML I, pp. 40ff. *Daily Gazette,* 2 September 1932, p. 5.

108. *Minutes of Evidence,* pp. 11ff.

109. M.A. Khuhro, 'Note for the Sind Conference' which appears as an appendix to his *Minutes of Evidence.*

110. Ibid.

111. Division within the AIML Council continued into the thirties with Muslim majority province Leagues opposing those from the Muslim minority provinces. In September 1933, Abdul Aziz and his group from Punjab, Bengal, and Madras split off charging the Delhi leaders with gathering power to themselves and ruling in an arbitrary manner. Clipping from *Statesman,* 23 September 1933, in MLA, Council Meetings Register, 1931-43, Vol. 221, p. 22.

112. The All India League passed resolutions supporting Sind's separation after 1925 at the Delhi annual session in 1926, the two sessions in Calcutta and Lahore in 1927, at Allahabad in 1930 and again in Delhi in 1931. MLA Annual Session at Delhi, Vol. 50, (1926), Resolution No. 2 introduced by M. Ehtishamuddin, M.A. p. 36; Pirzada, Foundations 2: 119, 129, 135, 174, 178, 184-5, and 189. Regarding the Conference, see Khuhro, *Story of the Suffering of Sind,* pp. 51-51; and Sultan Mohammed Shah, *The Memoirs of the Aga Khan* (London: Cassell and Co., 1954), pp. 229-230.

113. Miles Irving, *Sind as a Separate Province* (Simla: Government of India Press, 1931), p. 28. A *lakh* is 100,000 units.

114. Ibid., p. 1.

115. A.F.L. Brayne, *Report of the Sind Conference, 1932* Calcutta: Government of India Central Publication Branch, 1932), pp. 16-17, 25.

116. Great Britain, India Office Records, Public and Judicial Series 9, File 59 (Hereinafter cited as IOR, P/J/9/59) File Entitled 'Sind: Question of Constitution as a Separate Province,' Extract from Secretary of State for India's Speech, 24 December 1932, p. 12.

117. Evidence of this was the Act's indication of these two principles in other reforms undertaken, namely the separation of Burma from India, the formation of another new province, Orissa and the elevation of the NWFP to a full-fledged Governor's province. See: Great Britain, Laws, Statutes, etc., *Government of India Act,* 1935, 25 GEO 5, Ch. 2, Sections 46, 289, 290. (Hereinafter cited as *Government of India Act,* 1935).

2

THE FORMATION OF MUSLIM POLITICAL PARTIES

During the mid-1930's, as the certainty increased that Sindh was soon to become an independent, autonomous province, the Sindhi Muslim leadership began to look ahead to consider what its political position would be once Sindh achieved its new status. The Sind *Azad* Conference (SAC), the informal umbrella body that Muslim leaders had constituted during the days of the separation movement, provided the nucleus for a political organization but it suffered from a communal image; all of its members had been Muslims. Whereas the separation victory had engendered in Sindhi Muslims a deep sense of pride and accomplishment, their triumph also produced among them a spirit of magnanimity which compelled them to relegate to the past the ugly communal feelings the movement had unleashed. Therefore, as Sindhi Muslims began to contemplate their future political standing, they decided, at an August 1935 meeting of the SAC to convert that body into a new political party based 'on democratic lines and non-communal grounds to safeguard the interests of the agriculturalists in particular, and the whole province in general.[1]

A short while later, however, these plans were threatened by the emergence of a personal dispute between two SAC leaders. G.M. Sayed claimed that the August meeting had lacked legitimacy as there had been no quorum and furthermore, he charged Mohammed Ayub Khuhro with attempting to make of the proceedings a bid for personal supremacy in the conference.[2] This incident effectively killed the initiative to transform the

SAC into a political party but more importantly, it represented the first fissure in Sindhi Muslim solidarity since the separation movement. Most significantly, however, it foreshadowed the predilection among the Sindhi Muslim leadership for infighting and struggles for personal power which was to become the hallmark of Muslim political activity during the post-separation period of political party formation.

The Sind Azad Party

The failure of the Sindhi Muslims to maintain intact their position of political unity resulted in the development of three separate Muslim political parties in the period following the separation movement and just prior to the 1937 elections. The first political party to take shape was the Sind Azad party, principally, because it was built upon certain Muslim organizations which were already in existence. The party was established at a joint meeting of the Karachi Khilafat Committee, the Sind Hari Association[3] and the Sindh Branch of the *Jamiyyat al-ulama-i-Hind*[4] held in Karachi in September 1935.[5] At the meeting, some structural form was given to the party by constituting a working committee of fifteen men and organising a general body of forty-five. In addition, a provisional committee was created to enroll 5,000 members by the end of the year, and the Hyderabad editor, Sheikh Abdul Majid Sindhi, was elected the party's provisional leader. It was also decided at the meeting to convene a conference after enrolment to elect a permanent general and working committee, approve the party programme and devise strategy for the elections.

The final business of this founding meeting of the Azad party (SAP) was to draft an outline of the party's tentative platform— a significant statement in the sense that it embodied a vision of Sindhi Muslim aspirations for themselves and their province upon the conclusion of their successful struggle for separation. The party programme included such items as retrenchment of administrative expenditure in Sindh, revision of the land revenue system, equitable distribution of water for cultivation, the improvement of the economic position of peasants and landlords, the protection of agriculturalists from moneylenders, and medical relief and primary education in rural areas[6]—all vague points yet ones that revealed a bias in favour of the rural populace which by and large meant the Sindhi Muslim community.

Prominent among the leadership of the new party were Pir Illahi Baksh, a well-educated, small land-owner from Dadu district;[7] Hakim Fateh Mohammed Sehwani, a Karachi physician who had close connections with the Congress party; and two landlords who were also tribal chieftains, *Rais* Ali Mari and *Rais* Ali Mohammed Khero.[8] The principal leader, however, was Sheikh Abdul Majid Sindhi. Majid was a Hindu convert. He was born into the influential Lilaram family of Thatta, a former capital of Sindh, on 7 July 1889, but during his youth he converted to Islam. Forced to leave his family because of his beliefs, he moved to Hyderabad where he became the editor of G.M. Bhurgari's newspaper *Al-Amin*.[9] As an editor and associate of Bhurgari's, Majid became involved in Sindhi as well as all-India political affairs. Movements and organizations with which he became associated included the Khilafat Conference, the Non-Cooperation movement, the Khudam-e-Kaaba Society, the Muslim Conference, the Muslim League and the Indian National Congress.[10]

During the *Khilafat* period Majid established his political reputation as an effective organizer and spell-binding orator. As the secretary of the Khilafat Conference of Sind, he was instrumental in establishing district committees in each of the eight district headquarters beneath which was spread a network of 178 subordinate committees throughout the province.[11] He was a moving speaker; at a *Khilafat* Day celebration in Hyderabad he gave a 'beautiful speech which made Hindus and *Mussalmans(sic)* weep.'[12]

The SAP's party manifesto, in addition to its pro-Sindhi Muslim bias, also revealed a preoccupation with provincial Sindhi concerns as virtually no all-India Muslim demands were included.[13] This reflected the desire of the party leadership, particularly Majid, that the SAP, consistent with Sindh's new status, maintain an independent posture, with few if any all-India organizational ties. This trend in Majid's thinking was also evident in his dealings with the Muslim League of which he was a member at this time.

In 1935, Majid attended a Karachi meeting of the League called by Mazhar Alavi, a United Provinces barrister, who had come on his own to organize the League in Sindh[14] At this meeting, attended by about 200 Karachi Muslims, Majid expressed his opinion that the League in Sindh should not be called 'a branch of the All-India Muslim League but the Sind Azad League so that it may remain unfettered in its activities and not subject to the control of the centre.'[15] Thus, it was probable that Majid was working to bring the Sindh Muslim League in line with his own party in anticipation of merging the two organizations.

During the following months, however, Majid began to shift his ground and became more receptive to the idea of an organizational linkage with the all-India body. Factors that likely accounted for his change in outlook included his party's need of outside help in the approaching 1937 elections, and the new, all-India League policy of recruiting members from all classes, not just those of the upper classes.[16] In May, 1936, Majid was among those named by the All-India League president, Mohammed Ali Jinnah[17] to serve on the League's Election Board for Sindh[18] and in June, he went to Lahore to attend the Board's first meeting.[19] Jinnah's selection of Majid, Sehwani, Moulvi Khadda and Mohammed Gazdar to comprise Sindh's Board did not receive unanimous support from those in Sindh's League circles. Hatim Alavi, a prominent Bohra businessman, wrote to Jinnah criticizing his choices.[20] He informed the AIML president that Majid had just joined the Congress amidst much fanfare[21] and that there was much bad blood between Majid and Gazdar eliminating any possibility that the two could work together. In addition, Alavi was critical of the fact that all four were Karachites, and he raised the question of who would represent the interior, rural Sindhi Muslim interests. He also wondered why Sehwani was chosen, as he had no respect in Karachi.

Alavi's sharp attack on the Board's selection most likely stemmed from a combination of jealousy and disappointment at not having been chosen. Alavi was already a bitter enemy of Gazdar's, having lost an election contest to him in 1934[22] and he must have thought, if he could succeed in besmirching the names of the others, Jinnah would be compelled to place him on the Board instead.[23] Alavi's behaviour provides an example of the kind of personal self-interest and motivation which became common in this early period of Sindhi politics. The keen desire for a large measure of personal and political power and influence among Sindhi Muslim politicians was often the chief cause of rivalry and intrigue among them, which does much to explain the chronic disunity from which they suffered.

Before departing for Lahore, Sheikh Abdul Majid announced that the immediate objectives of his party would be to 'help prepare a programme for the Assembly and support the best possible candidates for election.'[24] With a view toward the election, the SAP planned to contest in all of the Muslim constituencies (thirty-three of sixty) but particular interest was shown in the Assembly seats from Karachi and Larkana.[25]

When Sheikh Abdul Majid returned from Lahore he set to work organizing his party. Certain that the SAP was the best party to meet the needs of the new province, he lashed out at the new, rival Sind United party which had recently been formed by Haji Abdullah Haroon. He described Haroon's party as 'a frantic effort on the part of some well-known Muslim reactionaries to secure their own position in the future government,'[26] and claimed that Muslim progressive elements judged the record of service of the new party's supporters 'as most detrimental to the interests of the country and the Muslim community.'[27] Majid charged, furthermore, that the United Party was attempting the impossible in planning to run non-communal candidates in communal electorates. His party, Majid stressed, was not guilty of such pretensions; it would work within the communal context for the time being, but it would also strive for an all-India Hindu-Muslim settlement to replace the inadequate Communal Award of 1932.[28]

Haroon issued a rebuttal to Majid in the *Daily Gazette* two days later[29] which revealed, significantly, the strong Sindhi emphasis of his new party's outlook. The United party leader denounced Majid's charges as 'unjustified and uncalled for criticism.'[30] He stated that when Majid first began the SAP he failed to get a good response so he went for shelter to Jinnah's Muslim League, which Haroon implied, was an unwise choice because the League's all-India programme of work did not suit the peculiar conditions in Sindh where the agriculturalist class suffered under the burden of direct and indirect taxation and needed immediate relief. Haroon emphasized the non-communal character of the Sind United party (SUP) and reiterated his party's intention to support both Hindu and Muslim candidates in Sindh's up-coming elections. This was imperative, Haroon maintained, because the real work would begin in the Assembly when Hindus and Muslims, whose interests in Sindh were almost identical, would work in complete harmony for ameliorating the lot of the toiling *haris* and the petty agriculturalists. He charged that Majid's attempt to set up a communal party in the future Assembly to follow the All-India Muslim League line would prove disastrous for Sindh.

The work of organizing the Azad party continued and by early July 1936, twenty branches had been organized with ten in upper Sindh and ten in lower Sindh.[31] Within a month, sixteen more branches had been formed bringing the total to thirty-six.[32] Localities where the party was thought to be strong were Sukkur, Nawabshah, Thar Parkar districts and Karachi city. In Sukkur district, ten branches had been formed, in both Nawabshah and Thar Parkar there were plans to run candidates successfully in all constituencies (five in Nawabshah and three in Thar Parkar). In Karachi city, fifty prominent citizens had signed the pledge and joined the party. The outlook was also good for the SAP in two other districts: Dadu and Larkana. There was no branch in either of these two districts, but a public meeting in Dadu had drawn good support, and one was planned for Larkana, where

Sheikh Abdul Majid was to visit the district and organize it. The party was weak in the two remaining districts, Hyderabad and Karachi, where only two branches had been organized in each district.

With these latest efforts at organization, the Azad party, for the first time attracted the attention of the government authorities in Sindh. The Sindh Chief Secretary in his *Fortnightly Report* to Simla mentions that the Sindh Azad party has been formed under Majid with forty branches organized to date.[33] In addition, he notes the party's ties with the All-India Muslim League Parliamentary Board.

In August 1936, Majid issued a press statement which embodied the all-India goals of his party: the full attainment of responsible government for India, inter-communal unity, and the social, economic and general uplift of Indian Muslims.[34] Two months later, in October, the SAP's working committee took a stand on two issues confronting the Sindh government.[35] These two statements taken together reflect a subtle shift in Majid's position. He had two purposes in mind. First, he wished to respond to the new challenge posed by Haroon's party by indicating that his party had a position on all-India as well as Sindhi issues. Second, he sought to strike a more independent posture in relation to the central League. Of the three planks in his all-India position, only one bore any resemblance to the Central Parliamentary Board's platform.[36]

This independence was borne out during the Central Parliamentary Board's review of the work of the Muslim League in September.[37] Affiliations to the Board were accepted from the Punjab, U.P., Madras, Bombay, Bengal and Assam and it was noted that the League had made much progress in Bombay, Madras and Assam but less that satisfactory progress in the UP and the Punjab. But in Sindh (as well as in the North West Frontier, Bihar and Orissa) no progress was noted at all.

A further indication of the Azad party's growing independence from the League was a press report in early November that the party had been 'superseded' by the Muslim League.[38] The report stated a Sind Muslim League Parliamentary

Board would be affiliated to the All-India League Board and it would open branches in the province. The report added that the 'Azad Party (would) cooperate fully' with this scheme but the implication in the report was that this action had been taken without the SAP's consultation. In fact, this report provided a hint of the power struggle that was going on behind the scenes between Majid and Jinnah.

Mazhar Alavi refers to this struggle in his *Reflections*.[39] He wrote that he went along with Sheikh Abdul Majid and used his party's name—Azad—for the party organization except in his correspondence with Jinnah. He claimed that Jinnah insisted the party must be called the Sind Muslim League, a branch of the All-India Muslim League. Jinnah wrote to Mazhar Alavi that unless the word Azad was dropped, he could not allow its affiliation with the AIML. What was at issue between Majid and Jinnah was not a mere word but a principle. Majid wanted to maintain ties with the All-India Muslim League, but above all he wanted to ensure his party's independence and autonomy. Jinnah desired that the Azad party end its independent identity and turn instead to the League organ for its authority and *raison d'être*.[40]

Majid found himself in a difficult position. He realized that in order for his party to do well in the elections it would need the prestige and assistance of the All-India Muslim League. He was aware that, otherwise, Haroon's party would take away a lot of votes from the SAP.[41] But while he still hoped to exploit the League connection, Majid did not yield on his position.

Majid's firm resolve to hold to his position was evident from some of his correspondence at this time. He dictated a letter to Mazhar Alavi to be sent to Jinnah which stated the 'League's Parliamentary Board (in Sindh) will also be the Executive Committee of the Sind Azad Party as well.'[42] Alavi finished the letter in a defensive tone: 'This may look a bit odd that we have branches without the Provincial body but Mr Abdul Majid thought it advisable to work from the bottom up and have the Provincial organ in the end.' What was implicit in this letter was a reiteration of Majid's stand which amounted to a direct contradiction of Jinnah's position. What Majid was saying here was that the Azad Party was formed before the Muslim League and, therefore, in Sindh, the League derived its legitimacy from the Azad Party.

Majid's stand was further made clear in his own correspondence with Jinnah. Majid sent two telegrams to Jinnah concerning a conference scheduled for December to establish a Provincial Parliamentary Board to approve candidates for the elections. In the second telegram, Majid stated an 'Azad party conference (has been called) *under whose auspices* the Sind League Parliamentary Board will be established.'[43] In order to mollify Jinnah, he added that the Sind Azad Party 'has adopted from the very beginning the constitution, programme and resolutions of the League and those of the League's Central Parliamentary Board.' And at the end of the telegram, Majid requested Jinnah to accept the presidentship of the conference. Majid's choice of words in this telegram may be interpreted as a clear defiance of Jinnah's point of view. The import of Majid's words were not lost on Jinnah, however, who refused to reply to Majid despite a telegram from the Azad party leader four days later to 'kindly reply (to) my two wires.'[44]

Instead of replying to Majid, Jinnah corresponded with Alavi, the secretary of the Azad party.[45] Alavi throughout had been striving to serve as mediator between the two leaders and trying, as well, to bring the Azad party more closely within the League fold.[46] In his letter (the one dictated by Majid), Alavi informed Jinnah of the agenda for the proposed conference[47] and invited the League president to preside over the conference. Jinnah's reply ignored the other points in the letter and addressed himself to the request to preside. He wrote 'I regret very much to say that it is very difficult for me to leave Bombay just now and I suppose it is not possible for you to wait, because you must form your board.[48] He went on to issue guidelines for the formation of the Board and in them he held fast to his position: 'I therefore suggest that you proceed with the conference and please form the Board, but I request you to call it the All-India Muslim League Parliamentary Board for Sindh and adopt the policy and programme defined by the All-India Muslim League Central Board.' He concluded by saying he was mailing a few copies of the League's policy and programme and that he would try to visit Sindh after the selection of the candidates.

The strained relations between the SAP leadership and the AIML, especially Majid and Jinnah, failed to improve, and as a consequence the conference that had been planned was never held. Nonetheless, Jinnah did visit Sindh in late 1936 in an effort to persuade Sindhi Muslim politicians to contest the 1937 elections on the League ticket, but he was given a cold reception when he arrived in Karachi. Hatim Alavi wrote that in arranging a dinner in Jinnah's honour, he issued invitations to leading Sindhi Muslims but 'none of them was willing to allow his name to be included in the list of hosts as they thought it would annoy the Hindus and prejudice their chances of election.'[49] Commenting further on the political attitudes of the Sindhi Muslim elite at this time, Hatim Alavi noted, 'Their outlook was so narrow and selfish that they could think only in terms of the immediate prospects of their individual election and had no conception of the great and vital issues with which Muslim India was going to be faced.'[50]

Thus, the Muslim politicians in Sindh were clearly preoccupied with their own personal political fortunes and, insofar as they were still inspired by the spirit of the separation movement, with the welfare of the new autonomous province. The propensity of the Muslim leaders to put their own political interests as well as those of Sindh first had resulted, in the case of the SAP's involvement with the League, in the breakdown of province-centre relations. The prospect for a restoration of these relations by the other Muslim parties, the SUP and the Sind Muslim Political Party, was even dimmer for, unlike the SAP, these parties exhibited a virtually complete absorption with Sindh concerns in their political programmes.

The Sind United and Sind Muslim Political Parties

The first public mention that a Sind United Party (SUP) was to be formed was made in a *Times of India* article on 20 May, 1936, entitled the 'Political Situation in Sind.'[51] The article disclosed that the prominent Karachi merchant, Haji Abdullah Haroon, was founding a political party in Sindh patterned along the lines of Fazl-i-Husain's non-communal, agrarian-oriented Unionist party in the Punjab.[52] The newspaper report stated further that 'invitations and constitutions' marked 'strictly confidential' had been sent out, so labeled because of the known personal political rivalry between Sir Ghulam Hussain Hidayatullah and Sir Shah Nawaz Bhutto.[53] It was commonly thought in Sindh's political circles that Hidayatullah would not join hands with both Haroon and Bhutto but that he might broaden his political base by choosing to side with Haroon alone.

Abdullah Haroon had been among the leadership of the Muslim League when it was formed in Sindh in the early twenties[54] but, during the late twenties and the early thirties, he gradually lost interest in the League as the central organization became increasingly plagued by internal factions and an absence of forthright leadership.[55] Instead, Haroon became involved in the work of the All-India Muslim Conference. This Conference, which grew out of the All-Parties National Convention, met on 1 January 1929 under the presidentship of the Aga Khan.[56] Two years later, a Karachi branch of the All-India Muslim Conference was started, with Haroon as president[57] and in 1934, the Aga Khan appointed Haroon the Conference's secretary at the organization's meetings in February.[58] The difference between the Conference and the League was negligible[59] in terms of issues, but the Conference was considered to be the premier Muslim organization in India at this time on account of the moribund state of the League.[60]

At the same time that Haroon was involved with the Conference, he also took a leading part in the movement for Sindh's separation. After the movement was over, he was one of those concerned with the communal feelings the movement had aroused. He was convinced that if provincial autonomy in Sindh was to work to its fullest potential, there must be full cooperation between the two major communities.[61] Haroon's strong desire for harmonious communal relations precipitated his break with the Muslim League. When the Central Parliamentary Board published its manifesto, Haroon interpreted it to be too communal for him, and he tendered his resignation.[62]

While Haroon severed his League ties on his own, his action was likely part of a larger design, engineered by the Aga Khan and Fazl-i-Hussain, to undermine Jinnah's efforts to create a strong Board.[63] The Aga Khan and Husain wished to see parties organized in the Muslim majority provinces based on allied, inter-communal, agrarian interests. Thus, while there was outside support for the formation of a Sind United party, there was also support from inside Sindh, too. At one of the last meetings of the Sindh Azad Conference a call was issued for establishing a non-communal party in Sindh.[64]

The first public report that a Unionist-type party was to be formed in Sindh alluded to the Azad Conference. In an article in the *Daily Gazette* in early June, mention was made that Haroon, as one of the elected members of the Sind Azad Conference sub-committee was attempting to form a Unionist party by 'bridging the gap between Sir Ghulam Hussain and Bhutto and between himself and the other two.'[65] With this end in view, Haroon called an informal meeting at his residence and among those attending were Sir Ghulam Hussain, Sir Shah Nawaz, M.A. Khuhro, Allah Bux Umar Soomro, Miran Mohammed Shah and Hatim Alavi[66] They discussed the party programme for three hours and all present appeared to agree to it. It was decided to release the programme to the press and to meet with Hindu leaders to discuss it. The other matter of business at the meeting was the selection of candidates for the approaching Assembly elections. Four names were mentioned as probable candidates for Karachi District: *Wadero* Mohammed Usman Soomro and Mr Mouledina Abbasi (to contest Thatta and Karachi *talukas* respectively) and *Rais* Mohammed Gaho and Mohammed Yusaf Chandio, to contest in the remaining

Talukas. Except for Abbasi, the three were leaders of their respective tribes and large landlords in the district.[67] The only other constituency mentioned was Ratodero *Taluka* of Larkana district where the Unionists knew the SAP leader, Majid, was slated to contend. Bhutto was the obvious candidate of the Unionists as his ancestral lands were located in Larkana and he had represented that district in the Bombay Legislative Council since 1923. He was expected to defeat Majid easily. This selection of candidates made clear two features of the Unionist party: it was a party of the Sindh Muslim elite and its base was Karachi with little support in the outlying districts of Sindh.

The creed, objectives, platform and proposed rules of the SUP were released to the press on 9 June 1936.[68] The underlying theme which emerged from the various statements of the new party was that the major issues of the day were economic rather than political in nature. The key point of the five part creed reflected the party's emphasis on economic issues: 'the acceptance of the community of economic interests as the true basis of political parties, irrespective of caste, creed or residence.'

Similarly, the platform of the party was inspired more by economic than political considerations. Most of the important planks of the eighteen point platform were directed at improvements in the agricultural sector, such as adjusting land revenue assessments, decreasing rural underemployment, and protecting the small landholder; others called for overhauling the educational system, ending corruption in administration and creating a favourable climate for commerce and industry. The weakness of the platform was that the goals of the party were vaguely stated. The SUP isolated the major problems in the province, but it failed to prescribe effective solutions for their remedy.

What was significant, in addition to the economic theme, was the division of the creed and platform along provincial, all-India lines. Some consideration was given to all-India demands but the major focus of attention was directed at Sindh issues, which clearly established the SUP as a provincial party. Two of the five points in the creed concerned all-India issues: the early attainment of Dominion status and honourable status for overseas Indians. Only four of the eighteen planks in the platform related to all-India issues: the development of national self-respect, economy at the centre, the reduction of military expenditure, and more income tax revenue returned to the provinces.

The proposed rules of the party outlined the organization of the party, regulations governing membership and the functions of the branches including a model programme of work for the branches. The party was to be organized with a central body, a branch for every constituency of the Sindh Legislative Assembly and sub-branches for all important towns and villages located within a constituency. Membership was open to all Sindh residents who accepted the creed and paid the subscription fee (higher for those who paid land revenue or income tax, four *annas* for those who paid none).[69] The model programme reflected the agrarian orientation of the party: crop rotation, more efficient marketing through weights and measures reform, alleviating rural unemployment through cottage industries, relieving rural indebtedness by familiarizing tenants with their legal rights, ending corruption and bribery and the use of lectures on education, health and related fields to raise the quality of life in the rural areas.

The Sind United Party was inaugurated on 9 June 1936, at a reception at Haroon's residence for the Governor, his advisers and the Muslim and Hindu members of the Sind Advisory Council.[70] The presence of the Governor, and Kirpalani, the Chief Secretary and Ridley, the Revenue Commissioner, reflected the party's close ties with the official establishment as well as its elitist character. Speeches were given by Haroon, Sir Shah Nawaz Bhutto and Sir Ghulam Hussain Hidayatullah. Haroon stressed rural indebtedness and oppression, corruption, and an inequitable tax burden as the chief evils in the province and he proclaimed the SUP was created to tackle and uproot them. The theme of speeches by Sir Shah Nawaz and Sir Ghulam Hussain was the same; they both labeled communalism as the chief problem in Sindh.[71] Shah Nawaz noted the absence of communal bickerings in the villages, and stressed that communalism was only a problem among the town-bred and educated who became jealous over securing political power or government positions. Sir Ghulam Hussain observed the rural movement in the Punjab was a success because all the communities were rural-based; in Sindh the different communities were divided not just by religion but by rural-urban interests as well.

Despite this show of interest and unity by the top Sindhi Muslim leadership at this inaugural meeting, the subsequent growth of the SUP was slow and irregular. One cause was the rivalry between Bhutto and Hidayatullah. The *Daily Gazette* observed they were 'playing a game of chess with each other' and were staying aloof as both had aspirations to be Prime Minister and neither wanted to restrict themselves.[72] Another reason was the poor reception of the party programme by the Sindh Muslim leadership. In his *Fortnightly Report* for the first half of August, the Sindh Chief Secretary wrote that the SUP met on 15 August, to discuss 'certain modifications to be made to suit the special needs of Sindh, particularly with regard to agriculture and rural reconstruction.'[73] This meeting followed a report in the press that the Unionist party had ceased to function because it had not been well received.[74] The report went on to say a move had been made to form a new United party in Sindh. This new party would differ from the old one in two significant respects: it would be exclusively a regional party with no all-India ties, and it would be a communal party.[75]

Despite the serious troubles besetting his party, Haroon remained optimistic and a few days later issued a statement intended to bolster the image of the party. He said the SUP was receiving support from all over the province and despite some changes, the party would remain the same.[76] A note in the same article on Haroon's statement mentioned political observers did not think the party would survive as Haroon's one-man show; in order to survive, both Bhutto and Hidayatullah would have to be included at some point.

These two leaders showed indifference to the SUP for a time, but after a month they were ready to support the new party.[77] Others expected to give their support included Gazdar,[78] Hatim Alavi (Gazdar's rival), Ghulam Nabi Shah, Allah Bux Soomro, Miran Mohammed Shah, Yar Mohammed Junejo, Syed Maherali Shah and G.M. Sayed. The latter names were significant because they suggest new support from influential landlords in the countryside.[79] At this time a draft manifesto of the party was circulated. It is interesting that this manifesto differed only in form and not in substance from the initial programme, thus contradicting the later report of a new SUP programme. It retained the plank that the SUP was open to all communities and moved the all-India planks from the beginning of the manifesto to the end where they were added together and not separately to diminish their visibility.[80]

This latest newspaper report shed more light on the difficulties of the Sind United Party and provided a clearer understanding of why the party was unable to establish itself as a strong, dynamic party. First of all, the various reports about the party's programme were confusing and inconsistent. But the programme itself was not what was important; it was important only in serving as a foil for the political manoeuvrings of Bhutto and Hidayatullah. At this stage, these two leaders were the real power brokers in Sindhi Muslim politics by virtue of their long experience in the Bombay legislature, their knighthoods and their close ties with the Sind Governor, Sir Lancelot Graham.[81] Until they decided what their respective courses of action would be, the Sind United Party could do little to organize itself because its elitist character made it dependent on them.

Governor Graham, in a letter to Linlithgow, India's Viceroy, disclosed the ongoing, covert manoeuvres of Bhutto and Hidayatullah, precluding the consolidation and stabilization of the United Party.[82] Graham mentions he was aware of the ill feeling between the two stemming from their Bombay Council days[83] but, nonetheless, he was hopeful that the two would issue a joint manifesto and divide the election candidates between them. But then Haroon's party had emerged to disrupt this scenario, and now the task was somehow to bring them both into the same party. Hidayatullah, Graham stated, was shy of the SUP, but he agreed to support the SUP after Haroon established an electioneering fund of Rs. 50 000 and disavowed in writing, any desire for a cabinet seat. Hidayatullah's joining the SUP would then prepare the way for Bhutto's inclusion as well, for the Larkana politician had made his support contingent upon Hidayatullah's.

The conditions for an agreement between Bhutto and Hidayatullah were apparently met for the second inauguration of the SUP, which took place at Haroon's Karachi residence at the end of October 1936, and was attended by the two former political foes.[84] Haroon's opening speech struck a buoyant note; the SUP would make Sindh 'safe' from communal strife and would insure that 'the communities would work and live in peace.[85] Haroon's optimism, however, was to prove short lived; not because of friction between the two communities, but because of the persistent problem of disunity within his own community.

Division within the leadership of the SUP was revealed in the first official act of the new party—the election of office bearers. In a meeting on 1 November, the SUP elected Haroon as the party's leader; Bhutto, Hidayatullah and Miran Mohammed Shah as deputy leaders; Gazdar and Khuhro as secretaries and H. Alavi and Meharali Shah as joint secretaries.[86] Upon the election of Miran Shah as a third deputy leader, however, Hidayatullah announced he was resigning from the SUP and forming his own party, to be named the Sind Muslim Political Party. He stated, furthermore, that M.A. Khuhro, Mir Bandeh Ali Talpur, and Noor Mohammad were also leaving the SUP to join his new party. Hidayatullah in a later press statement[87] justified his defection by claiming that Shah's election violated a prior SUP pledge to have just two deputy leaders, but most observers believed Hidayatullah was merely using the incident as a pretext to leave the SUP.[88]

Haroon defended the outcome of the party election in a press statement two days after the meeting.[89] He supported the choice of Miran Shah by saying he had been in the forefront of organizing and canvassing for the party while Hidayatullah had kept aloof and only offered to join the SUP in return for a prominent place in the party leadership. He stated further that the proposal for three deputy leaders had been endorsed by the party meeting.

The SUP leaders Bhutto and Haroon held out hope that Hidayatullah would return to the party fold[90] but the secessionist leader insisted on going his separate way. On 3 November, Hidayatullah announced in the press the aims of his new party which included working the new Constitution and cooperating with any party having similar goals.[91] He readily confessed his party was a communal one, but found justification in the Hindu decision to form their own party, the Sind Hindu Sabha, which ended Sindhi Muslim hopes for a common party, and left them with no alternative but to form their own party.[92] In addition, Hidayatullah issued his party's manifesto which differed from the SUP's only in its brevity.

Despite its late formation, the Sind Muslim Party (SMP) claimed to have won strong support within a short period of time, especially in upper Sindh where the influential Junejo, Jatoi and Khuhro families had pledged their backing.[93] In addition, the party sought to strengthen its ties with the local administrative establishment and gain support among the District Local Board members, particularly in Sukkur district of upper Sindh. These similarities in the two parties made it clear that the splinter SMP was not inspired by any ideological differences but rather by personal competition among the Sindhi Muslim leadership for political power and the spoils of office.

In May 1936, as political parties began to take shape in Sindh, the *Daily Gazette* published an editorial, 'Principles before Politics,' which portrayed Sindh's politicians 'putting the cart before the horse' by founding parties without first finding common principles.[94] As a result, parties dissolved as they were formed as there was nothing to hold them together. The editorial further characterized the politicians as inspired by the vision of opportunity before them but lacking in the knowledge of how to reap the harvest of that vision. A few months later, the *Gazette's* chief rival, the *Sind Observer,* struck a similar theme:

> Marooned in the backwaters, we in Sindh have no clear cut political alignments, we seem to be living remote from all-India politics. The development of a healthy political life with its sharp outlines and ringing banners is a far-off divine event which will take Sindh many years to realize. In the meantime, little men with their little programmes have their way.[95]

These editorials aptly characterized the mood as well as the behaviour of Sindh's politicians in the period between the separatist movement and the 1937 elections. Upon the successful conclusion of the separatist movement, the Sindhi Muslim leaders had stood as a strong and unified bloc at an apex of political power, but within a period of just a few short months they had fallen from their high position and found themselves in a divided and weakened state, absorbed with infighting and personal struggles for power. Instead of perpetuating the solidarity they had achieved during the long, hard-fought separation struggle, they split into three separate, competing political parties. The two larger parties, the SUP and the SMP, which attracted most of the Sindhi Muslim elite and which had the closest ties with Sindh's officialdom, reflected most clearly the leadership's propensity for feuding and division; indeed, the SMP was the product of this very kind of traditional political behaviour. In addition, both of these parties manifested an almost complete preoccupation with their own provincial affairs to the exclusion of outside interests. Only the smaller SAP had all-India ties, but even these were of a tenuous nature primarily because the SAP, too, was influenced by the legacy of the separation movement. Thus, on the eve of the 1937 elections, the leaders of the Sindhi Muslim community had lost their position of pre-eminence and had lapsed into a time of political disunity, absorbed with the stakes of power within Sindh and oblivious to the currents that swept the larger stage of all-India politics.

NOTES

1. *Daily Gazette* (Hereinafter *D.G.*), 20 August 1935, p. 14.
2. *D.G.*, 3 September 1935, p. 1.
3. This Association, founded to secure rights for Sindh's *haris*, had recently been established. Hassan Nasar, 'History of the *Hari* Movement in Sind,' Communist Party of India Document, Copy in Foreman Christian College Library, Lahore. (Typed manuscript.)
4. For the origins of this association see W.S. Smith, *Modern Islam in India, a Social Analysis* (Lahore: Minerva Book Company, 1947), pp. 276-280, and P. Hardy, *Partners in Freedom and True Muslims* (Lund: Student litteratur, 1971), pp. 21ff.
5. *D.G.*, 10 September 1935, p. 5.
6. The thirty-seven point party manifesto of the SAP which included these items as well as others was published in a special issue of the Sindhi daily, *Alwahid,* published on 1 April 1936, the day Sindh officially became a separate province. The manifesto appeared on pages 80 and 81.
7. Pir Illahi Baksh, who held an Aligarh law degree, was not a real *Pir*; he simple borrowed the title. Interview with Pir Illahi Baksh, Karachi, 15 January 1975.
8. Baksh and Marri also had ties with the *Jamiyyat. D.G.,* 10 June 1931, p. 5. *Rais* is a Baluchi tribal title.
9. Details of Majid's life are found in G.M. Sayed, *Janab Guzarim Ginse* [Those with whom I have spent my life] 2 vols. (Hyderabad: Sindhi Abadi Board, 1967), 1: 165ff. (Sindhi); M.H. Bhutto, 'Role of Sind in the Awakening of Indian Muslims 1843-1947,' *Sind University Research Journal: Art Series, Humanities and Social Sciences,* 3 (1963), 49-50, and the 'Sheikh Abdul Majid,' *Sindhi Publications,* 4, (1975), 17-21. (Sindhi).
10. *Alwahid,* 1 April 1936, p. 77; Bhutto, 'Role of Sind' p. 57. *The Khudam-e-Kaaba* Society aided Muslim pilgrims.
11. *Report of Sheikh Abdul Majid, Secretary, Jamiat Khilafat of Sind* (Karachi: Alwahid Printing Press, n.d.), pp. 13-15, quoted in Bhutto, p. 49.
12. Karachi, Seafield House, Papers of Daulat Hidayatullah. (Hereinafter cited as PDH). *The Khilafat Day in Sind: The Presidential Address of Seth Haji Abdullah Haroon Sahib and a Brief Report of the Proceedings of some of the Important Meetings,* (Karachi: Mr Mohammed Khan, Secretary, Sind Provincial Khilafat Committee, n.d.), p. 28.
13. *Alwahid,* 1 April 1936, pp. 80-81.
14. Interview with Mazhar Alavi, Karachi, 23 January 1976.
15. Karachi, Mahmudabad, Papers of Mazhar Alavi, (Hereinafter cited as PMA) Mazhar Alavi, 'Reflections,' 12 vols. (unpublished manuscript) 12:11.

16. Majid's dislike of privileged, upper class Muslims became clear later during the 1937 elections. For the League's new policy, see Choudhry Khaliquzzaman, *Pathway to Pakistan* (Lahore: Longmans, Green and Co., 1961), p. 144.

17. Jinnah was authorized to form a League Central Parliamentary Board at the 24th Annual Session of the AIML held in Bombay in April 1936. Pirzada, *Foundations of Pakistan*, 2: 262-263.

18. The others were Hakim Fateh Mohammed Sehwani, *Moulvi* Mohammed Sidiq Khadda, a prominent Karachi religious leader, and Mohammed Hashim Gazdar, a Karachi contractor. Jamil-ud-din Ahmad, ed., *Historic Documents of the Muslim Freedom Movement* (Lahore: Publishers United Ltd., 1970), p. 195.

19. The purpose of the meeting was to grant formal approval of the establishment of the Provincial Parliamentary Boards and to review the Central Board's fourteen point election manifesto. Khaliquzzaman, *Pathway to Pakistan*, pp. 144-146., and *All-India Muslim League Central Board: Policy and Programme* (n.p., 1936), pp. 1-16.

20. Islamabad, Ministry of Education, *Quaid-i-Azam* Paper Cell, File 208, Alavi to Jinnah, 2 June 1936, pp. 1-2 (Hereinafter QAPC, with F for File).

21. There is no press evidence to support this allegation though Majid was known to have been in the Congress at one time. See p. 56 above.

22. It is interesting that *Moulvi* Khadda escaped criticism in Alavi's letter. In 1934 *Moulvi* Khadda had awarded his Karachi Municipal Corporation seat to Alavi but Gazdar challenged the legitimacy of this action and won, forcing the election which Alavi then lost. *D.G.*, 13 February 1934, p. 5. H. Alavi and Gazdar also came from rival business communities, the Bohras and Silawatas respectively. Interview with Shaukat Ali Gazdar, M.H. Gazdar's son, Karachi, 23 September, 1975.

23. In order to bolster his position, Alavi enclosed with his 2 June letter to Jinnah a clipping from the *Times of India* for 20 May 1936, which included an article entitled 'Political Situation in Sind.' The article portrayed Alavi as the most prominent of Sindh's pro-League leaders and suggested that Alavi and the brainy, young men around him–G.M. Sayed, Miran Mohammed Shah and Syed Noor Mohammed Shah (all landlords and Matiari Saiyids)–could well emerge as a key force in the new Sind Legislature. QAPC, F 208, pp. 1-2.

24. *D.G.*, 6 June 1936 p. 4.

25. This reflects Sheikh Abdul Majid's thinking as he subsequently ran in both cities. His residence was in Karachi so it made sense to run there, but there is evidence to suggest that he ran in Larkana because of earlier political strife with the Bhutto family. There is a newspaper report in 1932 that Sardar Nabibux Bhutto along with other Larkana Muslim leaders 'repudiated the representative character of Abdul Majid, that he

was neither a leader of the Sind Muslims nor was he their nominee to the Allahabad Conference.' No further explanation is given why there was this animosity. *D.G.,* 30 January 1932, p. 5.

26. *Alwahid,* 18 June 1936, p. 1.

27. Ibid.

28. On account of the failure of the Indian communities to reach an agreement on communal representation, the British government announced its own scheme known as 'The Communal Award of 1932' which was later incorporated in The Government of India *Act,* 1935. For the terms of The Award, see Great Britain *Parliamentary Papers* (Commons), (1931-32, Vol. 18 (Accounts and Papers, Vol. 5) Cmnd. 4147, 'Communal Decision.'

29. *D.G.,* 17 June 1936, p. 4. Majid's attack had been published in the *D.G.* on the 15th.

30. Ibid.

31. *D.G.,* 9 July 1936, p. 4.

32. *Alwahid,* 6 August 1936, p. 1.

33. '*Fortnightly Reports* from Local Governments and Administrations on the Political Situation for the first half of the month of August 1936.' Kirpalani, Chief Secretary, Government 24 August 1936. (Hereinafter cited as FR for August 1936 (1), Kirpalani to Hallett, 24 August 1936).

34. *D.G.,* 24 August 1936, p. 4.

35. The working committee passed two resolutions; the first protesting the Sind government's decision to include Municipal populations with Local Boards for the purpose of distribution of seats, the second, denouncing as unfair and unjust the Hindu demand for 50 per cent recruitment in all departments and stressed that recruitment should be on a population basis ensuring 73 per cent recruitment for Muslims. Both resolutions had clear communal overtones. *D.G.,* 8 October 1936, p. 11.

36. See Khaliquzzaman, *Pathway to Pakistan,* p. 417.

37. *D.G.,* 22 September 1936, p. 6. The meeting was held in Bombay; for a discussion see Noman. *Muslim India,* pp. 332-3.

38. *D.G.,* 5 November 1936, p. 9.

39. Alavi, *Reflections,* 1:11.

40. Jinnah's position was based on Resolution No. 9 of the 1936 Bombay Session which stated that 'Muslims should organize themselves as one party' under the aegis of the AIML and its Central Election Board. Pirzada, 2:262-263.

41. The Sind Chief Secretary reports that since the formation of the Sind United Party and the Sind Muslim Party (a smaller, more recent party organized by Sir Ghulam Hussain Hidayatullah) the SAP has 'gone into the background'. FR for November 1936 (2), Kirpalani to Hallett, 4 December 1936.

42. QAPC, F 1215, from Mazhar Alavi to Jinnah, n.d., p. 1.

43. My italics. QAPC, F 514, Sheikh Abdul Majid to Mohammed Ali Jinnah, 8 December 1936, pp. 37-8.

44. QAPC, F 514, Majid to Jinnah, 12 December 1936, p. 40. G.M. Syed supports the contention that a rift occurred between Majid and Jinnah at this time. Interview with G.M. Sayed, Sann, Dadu district, 8 April 1975.

45. This is a further indication of Jinnah's pique with Majid. Normally he would correspond with the president of the party (Majid) rather than the secretary.

46. An example of this is the compromise position Alavi offered in a letter written to the *Daily Gazette* to 'correct' the report of the Azad party's supercession by the League. See p. 67, n. 1 above. He stated that the Azad party had not been superseded, and that it would continue to remain in existence. However in matters of legislative policy and election strategy it would adopt the programme of the Central League's Parliamentary Board. *D.G.,* 17 December 1936.

47. Alavi included in his outline the following items: the formation of a Provincial Parliamentary Board, the approval of candidatures of district party nominees, the running of candidates wherever necessary, the dissemination of propaganda and any other work that Jinnah might suggest. QAPC, F 1215 Alavi to Jinnah, 16 December 1936, p. 2.

48. Alavi, 'Reflections,' 1:10.

49. Hatim Alavi, 'The Leader I Knew Best,' in Jamil-ud-Din Ahmad, ed., *Quaid-i-Azam as Seen by His Contemporaries* (Lahore: Publishers United Ltd., 1966), p. 59.

50. Ibid., p. 60.

51. QAPC, F 208, Alavi enclosure to Jinnah, 2 June 1936, p. 3.

52. For some months the Aga Khan, Fazl-i-Husain and Abdullah Haroon had been preoccupied with the political future of the Indian Muslim community. In late 1935, the Aga Khan drafted his views into a statement which Fazl commented upon and Haroon consulted. PDH, Aga Khan to Haroon, 25 December 1935; Haroon to Fazl-i-Husain, 3 January 1936, and Husain to Haroon, 9 January 1936. This conferring by these three leaders, according to Haroon's biographer, 'quickened the birth of the Sind United Party.' Shafi, *Haji Sir Abdullah Haroon*, p. 121. For the origins of the Unionist party of the Punjab, see Azim Husain, *Fazl-i-Hussain* (Bombay: Longmans, Green & Co., 1946), pp. 249, 381-3.

53. The personal feud between Hidayatullah and Bhutto extended back to the days when both represented Sindh in the Bombay Legislative Council. While Hidayatullah was Bhutto's senior in age and political experience, he lacked Bhutto's eminence as a member of one of Sindh's most powerful political families. Hidayatullah, born in Kashmir and a Hindu convert, was a self-made man politically as his knighthood attested to but his political ambition suffered a setback when in the early 1930's, the Bombay Governor passed him over to select Bhutto to serve as his close

adviser. Since that time the two became political enemies. This information is based on interviews in Karachi with Daulat Hidayatullah, daughter-in-law of Ghulam Hussain, and M.A. Khuhro, a long-time political associate of Hidayatullah's, on 25 February 1976, and 23 January 1976.

54. Haroon had been elected the Sindh League's vice president in early 1920. MLA, SPML, I, A. Ahmad to Zahur Ahmed, 27 February 1920, p. 17. See n. 2, p. 27 above.

55. Two rival sessions of the League were held in two years, 1928 and 1933, and no Annual Sessions were held from 1933 to 1936. See Pirzada, *Foundations of Pakistan*, 2: 107-237.

56. Sayeed, *Pakistan: The Formative Phase*, p. 71.

57. *D.G.*, 17 June 1931, p. 6.

58. *D.G.*, 16 February 1934, p. 1.

59. The Aga Khan attempted to unify the Conference and the League but his efforts failed. M.H. Saiyid, *Mohammed Ali Jinnah: A Political Study*, 4th edn., (Karachi: Elite Publishers, 1970), p. 158.

60. The Conference's policy positions echoed those of Jinnah and the Muslim League and focused on various constitutional safeguards for the minority Indian Muslims such as the continuation of separate electorates, a guarantee of Muslim representation in the services and reserved seats for Muslims in the central legislature. Ibid.

61. *D.G.*, 21 January 1936, p. 3.

62. Noman, *Muslim India*, pp. 331-332.

63. Z.H. Zaidi, '*Muslim Politics in Sind 1937-1940—Darbari Politics?*' Paper presented at the International Seminar on Sind Through the Centuries, Karachi, March, 1975. Also Interview with Rashidi, Islamabad, 3 June 1975.

64. See n. 3, p. 73.

65. *D.G.*, 6 June 1936, p. 4.

66. G.M. Sayed has stated that neither Hussain nor Bhutto attended Haroon's meeting but he may be talking of a different meeting as he includes no date. But the rest of his account does corroborate the press report that a draft programme and constitution were agreed to. G.M. Sayed, *Struggle for a New Sind* (Karachi: Sind Observer Press, 1949), p. 4.

67. Abbasi, *Some Colourful Personalities of Sind*, pp. 30, 35. Mouledino Abbassi, a leader, was a former Congress Member. *D.G.*, 2 February 1935, p. 4.

68. They were published in the *Daily Gazette* issue for 9 June 1936, on page 4. The SUP's platform was also presented in a slightly modified form later by Allah Baksh Soomro in a no-confidence motion against him in the Sindh Assembly. PLSA, Vol. 6, Book 7, 12 January 1939, pp. 73-74.

69. There were sixteen *annas* to a *rupee*, Low, *Indian Year-book, 1947*, p. 26.

70. *D.G.,* 10 June 1936, p. 4. The tenure of the Council was for one year beginning on 1 April 1936. It lapsed in April 1937 when the Sind Legislative Assembly held its first Session.

71. Communalism was also a common theme in their respective messages to the province when Sindh officially became separate and autonomous. *Alwahid,* 1 April 1936, pp. 6-7, 9.

72. *D.G.,* 6 July 1936, p. 3, and 19 August 1936, p. 4.

73. FR, for August 1936 (1), Kirpalani to Hallett, 24 August 1936.

74. *D.G.,* 14 August 1936, p. 4.

75. Apparently the earlier party had had some success in attracting Hindus. Syed mentions in his account that R.B. Hotchland, Chandumal, Rewachand and Dingo Thadani were Hindu supporters who attended party meetings. Syed, *Struggle for a New Sind,* p. 5.

76. *D.G.,* 20 August 1936, p. 4.

77. *D.G.,* 24 September 1936, p. 4.

78. Gazdar was mentioned earlier as a Sindh Azad party leader; his anticipated defection here indicated the disarray in that party.

79. All were mostly large *zamindars* in their respective districts; Ghulam Nabi, Junejo and Maherali Shah in Nawabshah, Allah Bux in Sukkur, Mohammed Shah in Hyderabad and G.M. Sayed in Dadu.

80. *D.G.,* 24 September 1936, p. 4.

81. Bhutto was the Governor's Adviser, Hidayatullah the Chairman of the Sind Advisory Council. IOR. Linlithgow Papers, Mss Eur F 125/112, Graham to Linlithgow, No. 1, 16 October 1936, p. 1.

82. Ibid.

83. See n. 3, p. 73 above.

84. *D.G.,* 30 October 1936, p. 1.

85. Ibid.

86. *D.G.,* 2 November 1936, p. 4.

87. *D.G.,* 6 November 1936, p. 4.

88. Hidayatullah was against Shah's election primarily because it meant the exclusion of his supporters, Mir Bandehali and Noor Mohammed from the SUP leadership. *D.G.,* 3 November 1936, p. 3.; Sayed, *Struggle for a New Sind,* p. 5; F R for November 1936 (1) Kirpalani to Maxwell, 23 November 1936.

89. *D.G.,* 4 November 1936, p. 1.

90. Bhutto had in his possession a letter from Haroon resigning the party's chairmanship to him but he refrained from publicly disclosing the letter in the hope that Hidayatullah would return. IOR, MSS Eur F 125/112, Graham to Linlithgow, No. 3, 16 November 1936, p. 3. The text of the letter can be found in Shafi, *Haji Sir Abdoola Haroon,* p. 122. Bhutto and Haroon do change places owing to Haroon's pressing business obligations. F R for November 1936 (2), Kirpalani to Hallett, 4 December 1936.

91. *D.G.,* 3 November 1936, p. 1.
92. The SUP, despite professions to the contrary, was essentially a communal party. It did have a sprinkling of Hindus among its membership but it elected no Hindu office bearers nor did it run any candidates later in the non-Muslim constituencies. *D.G.,* 2 November, 1936. For a brief period in May 1936 a non-communal organization called The Political Club, did come into existence. Its membership included prominent Hindus and Muslims, but its chief purpose was to provide a stage for image-building rather than a platform of political principles and it quickly passed into oblivion. *D.G.,* 5 May 1936, p. 4.
93. *D.G.,* 10 November 1936, p. 10, and 17 November 1936, p. 4.
94. *D.G.,* 5 May 1936, p. 4.
95. Quoted in *Alwahid,* 6 August 1936, p. 7.

3

THE ELECTIONS OF 1937

Elections were held in Sindh in early 1937 to elect representatives to the new sixty seat Sindh Legislative Assembly. These elections were the first to be conducted in Sindh since the new province was constituted a separate and autonomous province in April 1936. Prior to 1936, Sindh had sent thirteen representatives to the Bombay Legislative Council; of these nine represented rural seats while the remaining four occupied urban seats.[1] However, the Government of India Act, 1935 under which the elections of 1937 were held, greatly extended the franchise[2] by lowering property qualifications.[3] As well as augmenting the number of Indian voters, the 1935 Act also greatly enlarged representation which, in the case of Sindh, resulted in a sixty seat Assembly with seats distributed as follows: nineteen General (including one for women), thirty-four Muhammadan (including one for women), two European, two Commerce, two Landholders and one Labour.[4]

For the purpose of elections, the Government of India Act, 1935, had incorporated the Communal Award of 1932,[5] therefore, two of its principal features were separate electorates and weightage for minority community representation. Thus, in Sindh, separate electorates meant primarily two kinds of seats— Muhammadan and non-Muslim or General, as they were called. Because the Muslims were the majority community, they received the largest number of seats in the Assembly, in fact a majority (thirty-four of sixty), but because of weightage given to the minority communities, chiefly the Hindus, the number of Muslim seats were less than they would have been had a community's population percentage been the criterion used for seat allocation.[6]

Weightage as it occurred in Sindh can be illustrated by the fact that the average Muhammadan constituency contained 87,353 persons while the average General constituency included a considerably smaller population of 58,001.[7] The contrast between the two types of constituencies become even sharper when one considers the average size of the General constituency was twice that of its Muhammadan counterpart (3,089 and 1,495 square miles respectively, but the average number of voters in a General constituency was just over half the average number in a Muhammadan constituency (6,569 and 12,699 respectively). By using these figures, then, it was possible to determine how many seats should go to each community in each district and it was, in this way, that Sindh came to have a sixty seat Assembly (see Table 3.1).

In September 1936, the Sindh Congress party announced its plans to contest in twenty of the sixty Assembly constituencies.[8] This announcement came soon after the issuance in Bombay of the Congress Working Committee's manifesto for the elections which declared that, while Congress would contest the elections, afterwards the party would attempt to defeat India's new 1935 Act from within the provincial legislatures. But in Sindh, disputes over seats and differences over goals weakened the Congress' prospects as did the decision of Congress Muslims to stand as independent candidates.[9] As a result, the Sindh Congress changed its plans and decided in the end to contest only fifteen seats or one quarter of those in the Assembly.

The Sindh Congress counted a few Muslims among its membership but it was predominantly a Hindu party. The only avowedly Hindu party in Sindh during this period was the Sindh Hindu Sabha and it adopted a stance in direct opposition to that of Congress. The Sabha attacked the Congress for its 'constitution wrecking tactics' and furthermore, denounced its rival for having harmed Sindhi Hindu interests by supporting the separation movement, which, the Sabha implied, demonstrated that there was little Congress would do for Sindhi

Table 3.1: Assembly Seats by Community and District in Sindh, 1937

District	Muhammadan(M) population	Seats (M) due	Seats (M) allotted	General (G) population	Seats (G) due	Seats (G) allotted
Karachi	417,576	4.86	5	165,179	2.84	3
Dadu	286,839	3.35	3	51,555	.83	1
Upper Sindh Frontier	234,086	2.73	3	25,611	.44	1[a]
Larkana	367,542	4.28	4	81,085	1.38	1
Sukkur	440,127	5.13	5	183,393	3.44	3
Nawabshah	377,746	4.41	5[a]	118,849	2.04	2
Hyderabad	460,920	5.28	5	201,954	3.47	4
Thar Parker	245,964	2.86	3	222,068	3.81	3[a]
Total:			33[b]			18[b]

[a]These irregularities are explained in the below cited *Report*, pp. 22-23.
[b]The women's seats are not included in these totals.

Source: *Report of the Sind Provincial Delimitation Committee*, published in the *Daily Gazette*, 10 August 1935, pp. 1, 19-21.

Hindus in the future.[10] The Sabha had close ties with both the All-India Hindu Mahasabha to which it gave its support on all-India issues[11] and the Sindh Hindu Association which had been formed in the aftermath of Sindh's separation to protect Sindhi Hindu interests.[12]

In contrast to Congress, the Sabha declared it would work the 1935 reforms and would cooperate with other parties to improve the condition of the people of Sindh. In its party manifesto, the communal outlook of the Sabha was made clear; it promised mass education for Hindus and the protection of Hindu lives and property. In addition, it called for increased Hindu representation in the services, reduced administrative expenditures and increased spending in Sindh's nation building departments.[13]

In an editorial at the end of November 1936, the *Daily Gazette* projected the outcome for the three Muslim parties.[14] In the case of the SUP, the editorial noted the party workers claimed they would carry Hyderabad and Sukkur districts, and share seats in Larkana and Nawabshah districts. The SAP was expected to make its strongest showing in Thar Parkar district, share the Karachi district seats and perhaps win one or two urban seats in Hyderabad district. The SMP was anticipated to win only a few scattered seats on account of its late emergence as a party. Pre-election attention focused on Larkana district because it was there that leaders of the three Muslim parties were contesting seats[15] and the outcome there was expected to have an impact on which party gained supremacy in the Assembly.

Educated political opinion in Sindh held that the province's Legislative Assembly would become a battleground between the 'highly organized and intelligent urban interests and the unorganized and mostly ignorant rural interests.'[16]

This view bode ill for the new province's communal relations because the urban-rural dichotomy also reflected closely the division between Sindh's Hindus and Muslims. In every urban area except Karachi, the Hindus predominated, and in the rural areas the Muslims far outnumbered the Hindus. The Hindus exceeded the Muslims in fifteen of Sindh's towns, and in another seven they comprised thirty-three to fifty per cent of the population.[17] The economic dominance of the Hindus in the province as well as their electoral weightage indicated that they would become a considerable, if not a major force in the Assembly.

Table 3.2: Number of Muhammadan Candidates by Constituency and by District in Sindh in the 1937 Elections.

District	Total Seats	Constituency by number of Candidates	Number of Candidates
Karachi	5	4	2
		1	4
Dadu	3	1	2
		1	3
		1	4
Hyderabad	5	1	1
		2	2
		2	3
Sukkur	5	1	2
		2	3
		2	4
Larkana	4	3	2
		1	4
Thar Parkar	3	1	4
		1	3
		1	4
Upper Sindh Frontier	3	1	2
		2	3
Nawabshah	5	4	2
		1	4
Women's Muhammadan urban	1	1	3

Source: Abstracted from the following issues of the *Sind Government Gazette*, Part 1: 7 January 1937, p. 19; 14 January 1937, pp. 40-47, 51-52; 15 January 1937, p. 59; 18 January 1937, p. 61.

The elections were held on 1 February 1937. The percentage of those who could vote and did was only 54.3, just below the average—54.55 per cent—for all the Indian provinces.[18] Perhaps surprisingly, the figures show greater interest and participation in the rural areas than in the urban centers. In both the General and Muhammadan rural constituencies, voting percentages were higher (58.8 and 55.7 respectively) than in the General and Muhammadan urban constituencies (42.5 and 48.5 respectively).[19] In Karachi, only 44.5 per cent of the electorate voted, almost ten points below the provincial average.[20]

In the Muhammadan constituencies, ninety-one candidates contested the thirty-four seats. Most of the constituencies in which there were three or more candidates per constituency were located in the upper Sindh region comprising the districts of Sukkur, Larkana and the Upper Sindh Frontier. (See Table 3.2.)

In just over one half of the Muhammadan constituencies (eighteen) there were only two candidates;[21] of the remaining 16 constituencies, nine had three candidates, six had four candidates and one had five. The location of constituencies with three or more candidates followed a pattern; most of them were in the upper Sindh region, in Sukkur and Upper Sindh Frontier districts especially,[22] with only a few in the middle and lower Sindh regions, particularly in Hyderabad, Nawabshah and Karachi districts. (See Table 3.2).

The upper Sindh region, in addition to having the greatest concentration of multi-candidate (three or more candidates) constituencies, also exhibited the greatest uniformity in terms of voter percentages (the percentage of voter to elector); all were close to one another and either near or above the provincial average. (See Table 3.3). Thus, in this area, there appeared to be a correlation between a large number of candidates and high voter percentages in the respective constituencies. This finding, which suggests this region had a high degree of political consciousness, may help to explain why this area later became the scene of intense political attention and activity.[23]

The pattern of electoral participation pertaining in the upper Sindh region did not apply to the rest of the province. In fact, in terms of the correlation between the number of candidates and voter percentages, the opposite seemed to be true: there were proportionately more two candidate constituencies with the voter percentages exceeding the provincial average than there were in the multi-candidate constituencies. Furthermore, in contrast to the fairly even set of voter percentages in the upper Sindh region, the voter percentages elsewhere in Sindh varied from uniform to extreme, including the lowest (38 per cent in Hyderabad South Rural) and the highest (85 per cent in Dadu North Rural). Thus, in 1937 no clear pattern emerged to explain electoral behaviour for the whole province. In most constituencies there were specific factors, such as the enmity between a leading landlord and a tribal chieftain or the alliance between a *wadero* and an influential *pir* that usually determined how many candidates a constituency had or how many electors turned out to vote.[24]

The electorate in the 1937 election was largely illiterate so the use of symbols or labels in voting to identify a candidate was a significant factor in the elections.[25] Mention is made here of the symbols to provide some insight into the nature of the Muslim party organizations. In all, thirteen different symbols were used. The most common were the horse (twenty-two), the sword (sixteen), the crescent (twelve), the flag (twelve) and the tree (eight).[26] Of these five, only the crescent and the sword could be said to be clearly Islamic symbols; the rest took their meaning from Sindhi culture and society. Thus, while the wide variety of labels used probably did work to defuse the communal colouring of the campaign, the frequency with which the Islamic symbols were used indicated that a communal tinge was nonetheless present.

The number of symbols clearly exceeded the number of political parties contesting the election which provides an immediate indication that the parties did not issue directives for their candidates to use the same symbol, or if they did, the directives were ignored. In the case of the Sindh United Party, which fielded the largest number of candidates—there was no

Table 3.3: Muhammadan Constituencies by Number of Candidates and by Voter Percentages

Constituency	Number of Candidates	Percentage of Voters to Electors
Thar Parkar North Rural	5	53
Dadu North Rural	4	85
Sukkur Southwest Rural	4	62
Sukkur Southeast Rural	4	54
Karachi City North Urban	4	53
Larkana West Rural	4	50
Nawabshah East, Rural	4	49
Women Muhammadan Rural	3	72
Sukkur Northwest Rural	3	71
Upper Sindh Frontier East Rural	3	63
Dadu South Rural	3	62
Upper Sindh Frontier Central Rural	3	57
Sukkur Central Rural	3	52
Hyderabad Northwest Rural	3	52
Thar Parkar West Rural	3	48
Hyderabad South Rural	3	38
Hyderabad Southwest Rural	2	70
Upper Sindh Frontier Rural	2	70
Karachi East Rural	2	64
Nawabshah North Rural	2	63
Thar Parkar South Rural	2	62
Nawabshah West Rural	2	61
Larkana North Rural	2	59
Karachi North Rural	2	59
Karachi South Rural	2	58
Sukkur Northeast Rural	2	57
Nawabshah Northwest Rural	2	56
Larkana East Rural	2	55
Dadu Center Rural	2	53
Nawabshah South Rural	2	47
Hyderabad East Rural	2	45
Karachi City South, Urban	2	44
Larkana South Rural	2	27

Source: *Elections Return,* pp. 114-117.

one symbol used to identify the party's candidates. This was even true of the party's leaders: Haroon used the horse; Bhutto, the bullock cart; Gazdar, the elephant and Miran Mohammed Shah, the flag.[27] The experience of the Sind Azad party candidates was similar to the Sind United Party's though they had more success adhering to one label. Five candidates including Majid in Karachi City, (North Urban) used the crescent, but Majid himself in Larkana North used the wheel instead of the crescent.[28] What has been said about the other two parties can also be said about the Sind Muslim Political Party; no one symbol was used to identify the party's candidates. Three symbols the Sind Muslim Political Party used were the flag, the horse and the sword;[29] the latter two had also been used by Sind United Party candidates. Another symbol, the crescent, had also been used by candidates in two parties, the SUP and the SAP.

The use of the same symbols by different parties made futile any efforts by a party to use its chosen symbol as a means to strengthen party coherence or create a distinctive party image. The symbols remained as personal labels selected by the candidates themselves to aid voters in distinguishing them from among the other candidates in the constituency. The fate of these symbols provides added insight into the nature of party politics in Sindh during the election campaign. The parties had been started with little time before the elections. They had not had time to evolve a strong party organization comprised of individuals committed to the party's ideals. Instead, the parties represented collections of men of wealth or power in the province who were interested more in what added prestige they could derive from association with the party than in what sacrifices they could make to ensure their party's success.

Table 3.4: Results of 1937 Elections, by Muslim Party

Party	Official (GOS)[1]	Official (GOI)[2]	Press Version[3]
Sind United Party (SUP)	21	17	23
Sind Azad Party (SAP)	3	1	3
Sind Muslim Party (SMP)	3	15	3
Independent	7	NA	NA
Total	34	33	29

Source: [1]Government of Sind (GoS), *Sind Government Gazette*, (various issues, ser no.34).
[2]Government of India (GoI), *The Return showing the Results of Elections in India, 1937*
[3]*Daily Gazette*, 13 February 1937, p.1.

The absence of a well-defined party system made it difficult to determine the precise standing of the parties in the election results (see Table 3.4).[30] A press version of the results published on 18 February 1937, gave the SUP twenty-three seats, the SAP three seats, and the SMP two seats.[31] Coupland, in his study, gives fewer to the SUP, only eighteen, the same three to the SAP, but two more to the SMP to give it a total of four.[32] The official publication, *The Return showing the Results of Elections in India 1937,* gave almost as many seats to the Sind Muslim Political Party (fifteen) as it did to the Sind United Party (seventeen)[33] It gave only one seat to the Sind Azad Party and listed one seat as 'doubtful'. The most accurate results which were later accepted as the official results and served as the basis for the formation of government, were the official results of the Government of Sindh, published in the *Sind Government Gazette* and cited in the Chief Secretary's *Fortnightly Report.*[34] These results show that the Sind United Party won twenty-one of the twenty-eight seats it contested, the *Azad* party, three of the twelve it contested, and the Sind Muslim Political Party three of the ten seats it sought.[35] This left a remainder of seven Muslims who were elected as Independents without party labels. Thus, the Sind United Party, by the wide margin of seats it won, emerged as the clear winner among the Muslim parties, and it seemed destined for a dominant role in Sindh politics.

The United Party won in a majority of constituencies in six
of Sindh's eight districts.[36] In Larkana, the SUP broke even
taking two of the four seats but in Sukkur district the SUP
managed to win only two of the five seats and one of these seats
was also claimed by its rival, the Sind Muslim Political Party.[37]
The Sind Azad Party's seats were spread out over the province,
one each in Larkana, Karachi and Nawabshah districts. The
Sind Muslim Political Party also won a seat in Larkana district,
won by deputy leader Khuhro; its other two seats were in Dadu
and Sukkur districts.

Though the United party won a clear majority of the Muslim
seats, it was significant that its position was weakened in the
two key districts of Larkana and Sukkur by the success of the
other two parties, particularly its chief rival, the SMP which
won a seat in both districts. Thus, with a foothold in these two
key districts, the SMP, despite its meagre standing of only three
seats, could expect to play a role in subsequent political
developments. Though the SMP made inroads into SUP strength,
it failed to deliver the most significant setback to the SUP's
political fortunes. That triumph went to the Sindh Azad party in
the person of its leader, Sheikh Abdul Majid Sindhi. Sheikh
Abdul Majid defeated SUP leader, Sir Shah Nawaz Bhutto, in
the latter's native Larkana in one of two stunning upsets for the
Sind United Party. In the second upset the other SUP leader,
Abdullah Haroon, was defeated on his home ground in Karachi
and Majid played a role in the contest, too.

Majid and Bhutto were the only two candidates in Larkana's
North Muhammadan Rural constituency. Of 11,328 electors, 6,702
or 59 per cent voted.[38] Majid polled 3,691 votes to Bhutto's 2,091,
a wide margin of 1,600 votes. Some of the reasons given in
interviews to explain the outcome in Larkana stressed Majid's
popularity and dislike for Bhutto. Majid had established a
considerable following throughout Sindh during the *Khilafat* days,
going to jail twice for his political beliefs.[39] The SMP leader,
M.A. Khuhro, and his political lieutenant, Kazi Fazlullah, a
Larkana lawyer, also assisted Majid in his campaign which
emphasized his convert status in order to create an impression

on communally conscious voters.[40] Majid's conversion was also highlighted to contrast with Bhutto's close ties with the British and his fondness for their culture. Bhutto was called *Nasara* for one who was 'English' and 'a Christian' and he was attacked as one who would levy taxes on beards and graveyards because he was anti-Islam.[41] Most observers thought, however, that more than any smear campaign, Bhutto was hurt by his own aloofness and overconfidence.[42] Bhutto apparently used to spend most of his time in Bombay where he held his Legislative Council seat. He spent the Christmas holidays preceding the election there, and returned to Larkana with only eight days left to campaign. Sir Shah Nawaz expected he would win handily, but he discounted the potential of Majid and the conspiracy of his family and opponents to defeat him.[43] Thus, one of the pre-eminent leaders of the Sindhi Muslim community lost the election on his own home ground, partly on account of his own overconfidence and negligence, but largely as a result of a strong campaign mounted against him.

The other notable election upset also involved one of the major figures in the Sindhi Muslim leadership, Abdullah Haroon, the prominent *Memon* sugar merchant of Karachi, who had recently been knighted.[44] In the Karachi City North Muhammadan urban constituency four candidates contested for the seat: Sheikh Abdul Majid (SAP), Adam Khan Mirza (independent), Abdullah Haroon (SUP) and Khan Sahib Allah Baksh Gabol (independent). Of the 14,217 electors in this constituency, 53 per cent or 7,559 voted.[45] The winner of the election was Gabol who polled 3,311 votes. Haroon followed with 2,559 votes, trailing by a margin of 712 ballots. Mirza and Majid marshaled only 666 and 78 votes respectively. 203 votes were rejected.[46]

Most observers of the election explained Gabol's success by his appeal to ethnic Baluch pride.[47] Gabol, a member of a distinguished *Mekrani* Baluch family which served in the Afghan war and the first World War, had been active in Karachi and Bombay politics since 1927. He represented Lyari quarter, a Baluch and Pathan worker colony in west Karachi, in the

Karachi Municipal Corporation, and this quarter constituted a significant portion of the Karachi City North urban constituency. In the 1937 campaign Gabol used the slogans *Garite Balochon, vote bide Gabolon* (A vote for Baluch is a vote for Gabol)[48] and *Himat Kaney Balochon, voton Madah Banaton* (Oh Baloch, you have your national honour, don't sell your honour by receiving money for your votes)[49] which helped to swing the Baluch voting bloc behind him.[50]

Haroon also had ties with the Baluch community in Karachi. In February 1936, he received a letter from one of the Baluch leaders requesting him to place before the Delhi Assembly two resolutions promoting Baluch interests in the army and the government services. The writer offered his thanks 'for the interest you have taken to make the Baloch cause (sic) a success... You are held as the champion of the Balochi's cause and your efforts will be shortly rewarded for you possess the joint cooperation and sympathy of the Baluch's youths (sic).'[51]

Haroon also took an interest in the welfare of the Lyari residents. At one point during his tenure as a Municipal Councillor in Karachi, from 1921 to 1934, he offered Rs. 175,000 to build a model village in the Lyari quarter, and later, contributed Rs. 8000 to a scheme to provide bathing *ghats* and drainage in Lyari.[52] But Haroon's money and his generosity became an issue against him in the 1937 election. The voters communicated the message to Haroon that unless he gave them money and more buildings, they would not vote for him.[53] But Haroon refused to be bought and the voters turned against him. Thus, his refusal to be bribed coupled with the fact that he was not Baluch, ensured Haroon's defeat.[54]

Majid also attempted to play a part in Haroon's defeat. He knew he could not outvote Haroon but he hoped by contesting the seat to take votes away from him. His strategy had been to run against the three Sindhi Muslims knighted by the British and defeat them to make room for a new generation of leadership: younger yet with experience, more nationalistic and independent, less pro-bureaucracy and pro-British.[55] He was successful against Bhutto, but his meagre seventy-eight votes in

Karachi indicate he had little influence on the outcome there. Majid was unable to contest against Sir Ghulam Hussain Hidayatullah, who won one of the two seats in the mixed electorate Landholder seat. Whereas his strategy was not a complete success, Majid was certainly shrewder than his opponents in gauging the mood and instincts of the voters in 1937. On the whole, the Sindhi Muslim electorate voted conservatively; they found their loyalties to kinship and religion as articulated by Majid and Gabol to be more compelling than the lofty, vague party promises of Bhutto and Haroon.

The electoral defeats of Bhutto and Haroon were the only significant surprises of the 1937 elections; in the majority of the Muhammadan constituencies the victors were, in most cases, influential *zamindars,* important *Saiyids* or *pirs* or powerful tribal *sardars.* In nine of the constituencies *Saiyids* or *pirs* were elected and in another eighteen, chieftains of tribal clans emerged as winners, including four who were scions of Sindh's former ruling house, the Talpurs.[56] Thus, a large majority of the Muhammadan seats in the Sindh Legislative Assembly (twenty-seven of thirty-four) were secured by the traditional elite of the Sindhi Muslim community, suggesting that these rural-centered power holders would come to play a significant, if not a dominant, role in the subsequent course of Assembly politics.[57]

The election of 1937 represented the first experiment in Sindh to elect representatives to the province's new Assembly, created under the reforms of the 1935 Act. As it was a novel experience for many of them, the Sindhi electorate behaved cautiously and responded to their fundamental loyalties of kinship, religion and economic dependence with the result that, in most cases, the traditional elite of the province, the landlords, the religious leaders and the tribal chiefs, were attracted to the SUP because its claim to be a non-communal, agrarian-oriented Sindhi party seemed to be just what Sindh needed as it embarked on its new course as an independent and autonomous province. But, in affiliating themselves with the SUP, the leadership were motivated more by self-interest than by party interest and, as a consequence, the SUP failed to become a strong, tightly-knit party, a fact reflected most sharply in the defeat of its two chief leaders.

The tactics used to upset the top SUP leadership, particularly Bhutto, bore witness to the primacy of personalized politics in Sindh at this stage; politics dominated by disputes and infighting stemming from personal pursuits of political power. Such political behaviour served to enlarge the scope for division among the Sindhi Muslim leadership rather than to resuscitate the solidarity that had once been achieved during the separation movement. But similar to the period of the separation struggle, the Muslim leadership in Sindh continued to hold a dominant Sindhi outlook which included little if any interest in outside affairs. The SAP, the only party with any semblance of all-India ties had failed, by its weak electoral showing, to restore a balance to provincial-centre relations. Thus, in the outcome of the 1937 election, the factors of Muslim disunity and a preoccupation with provincial concerns appeared destined to play a dominant part in shaping post-election provincial politics during the first phase of ministerial government in Sind.

NOTES

1. Of the rural seats, two were General (or non-Muslim) and seven were Muhammadan; of the urban seats there was one each for General, Muhammadan, Landholders (*Jagirdars* and *Zamindars*) and Commerce. Great Britain, Parliament, *Parliamentary Papers.* (Commons), *1935-36,* vol. IX (*Reports,* vol. 3), Cmnd. 5099, 'Report of the Committee appointed in connection with the Delimitation of Constituencies and connected matters,' Volume I—Report, p. 97. (Hereinafter DCC *Report,* I.)

2. The electorate in the Indian provinces increased almost sixfold in 1937, from five and a half million under the Government of India Act, 1919 to over thirty million under the 1935 Act. Coupland, *The Indian Problem,* pp. 62, 134.

3. For Sindh's voter qualifications under the 1935 Act, see Government of India Act, 1935, Sixth Schedule, Part XII, Sections 1-10.

4. DCC *Report,* I, p. 97.

5. See n. 3, p. 63, above.

6. Had population percentage been the standard, Muslims, comprising 70.7% of the province's population, would have been entitled to forty-two seats in the sixty seat house, an increase of nine which would have made for a comfortable majority. The diminution of Muslim representation has been used by some leaders to explain Muslim impotence and disunity in the Assembly during the period of provincial autonomy. Interviews with M.A. Khuhro, Karachi, 28 January 1975; G.M. Sayed, Sann, Dadu district, 8 April 1975, and Pir Illahi Baksh, Karachi, 15 January 1975.

7. *DCC Report*, II, Statement I, p. xi. The constituencies discussed here are rural constituencies. These average figures were arrived at by using the revenue division—the *taluka*—as the unit for both electoral and administrative purposes. *DCC Report*, I, p. 98.

8. F R for August 1936 (2), Kirpalani to Maxwell, 9 September 1936, p. 5.

9. F R for November 1936 (1), Kirpalani to Maxwell, 23 November 1936; *D.G.*, 3 October 1936, p. 4.

10. *D.G.*, 26 August 1936, p. 1;

11. Flynn, 'The Communalization of Politics,' p. 58ff; *D.G.*, 5 May 1930, p. 5.

12. In late 1935 there were plans to unite the Sabha and the association but they never reached fruition. *D.G.*, 26 November 1936, p. 4.

13. *D.G.*, 26 August 1936, p.1.

14. *D.G.*, 27 November 1936, p. 2.

15. The SAP leader, Majid, was standing against the SUP leader, Sir Shah Nawaz Bhutto, in the Larkana North Muhammadan Rural constituency; M.A. Khuhro, a SMP leader, was contesting in Larkana East Muhammadan Rural constituency. Government of Sindh, *Sind Government Gazette*, 14 January 1937, Part 1, p. 44. (Hereinafter cited as *SGG*).

16. *D.G.*, editorial for 1 September 1936, p. 6.

17. *Census of India, 1931,* Vol. VIII, Part 1, Chapter II, Section 2, p. 45. In Karachi there were 96 Hindus for every 100 Muslims, the Muslim population being swelled by the large migrant labour pool of Pathans and Baluchis in Lyari quarter. Ibid., p. 46.

18. The total number of voters in contested constituencies was 614,942 and the total number of votes polled was 333,589. (The total electorate was somewhat larger, 639,043, but some did not vote as 7 seats were filled without contest). For these figures as well as the provincial percentages see *Government of India, Return Showing The Results of The Elections in India, 1937* (Delhi: Manager of Publications, 1937), p. 5. (Hereinafter cited as *Elections Return*).

19. These figures show the greatest disparity between the General urban and General rural constituencies which suggests that the urban General voters were the most apathetic while the General rural voters were the most interested. The urban and rural Muslims both fall in between. The greatest

interest was shown in the Landholders constituency where 75.4 per cent voted and second, surprisingly, was the Women Muhammadan Urban constituency (72 per cent). The lowest percentage (27.2) was Labour. See *Election Returns*, p. 13.

20. F R for February 1937 (1), Kirpalani to Maxwell, 19 February 1937; *D.G.*, 2 February 1937, p. 1.

21. Actually one of these constituencies (Hyderabad North Rural) had only one candidate—Makhdum Ghulam Hyder Zahir-uddin who was elected unopposed, because he was a *Pir* with one of the largest followings in Sindh and was thought unbeatable. *SGG* Pt. 1, 21 January 1937, p. 87.

22. Larkana district was an exception, it fit more closely into the pattern for middle and lower Sindh.

23. See Chapter Six below.

24. Sayid Ghulam Mustapha Shah, *Towards Understanding the Muslims of Sind* (Karachi: Alwahid Printing Press, 1943) pp. 31, 135-138. Interviews with Hatim Alavi, Karachi, 18 September 1974, and M.H. Khuhro, Karachi, 28 January 1976.

25. A symbol was placed on the ballot beside the candidate's name to enable an illiterate voter to identify the candidate he wished to vote for. This material is taken from the *SGG*, Pt. 1, 7 January 1937, p. 19; 14 January 1937, pp. 40-47, 51-52; 15 January 1937, p. 59; and 18 January 1937, p. 61.

26. The numbers indicate how many candidates used each symbol. Other labels used were the tiger (six), the elephant (five), the bullock cart (three), a man's head (two), the scales of justice (one) and the wheel (one).

27. Other Sind United Party candidates used the tree (two), the crescent (three), the sword (seven), a tiger (one), and a man's hand (one). *SGG*, Pt. 1, 14 January 1937, pp. 40-47, 51-52.

28. And two other candidates used other symbols, the tiger and the sword. *D.G.*, 18 February 1937, p. 7. *SGG*, pt. 1, 14 January 1937, p. 44.

29. Ibid.

30. The point is well illustrated by the rival claims of the two chief Muslim parties. In the *Daily Gazette* of February 18, 1937, the Sind United Party claimed twenty-three of its candidates elected. In the next day's issue Khuhro, the Sind Muslim Political Party leader, countered by stating the Sind United Party had elected only eleven candidates and that seven of the others were in his party. *D.G.*, 19 February 1937, p. 1.

31. The standings of the non-Muslim seats will be given later as they are not particularly germane to this discussion. This press version was published in the *Daily Gazette* 18 February 1937, p. 7. *The Gazette*, an unofficial organ of the Sind United Party at this time (Haroon served as one of its directors) tended to maximize the United party's results and minimize those of its rivals.

32. Coupland, *The Indian Problem*, p. 65.
33. This report, published several months after the election, reflects the party situation in Sindh at the time of the formation of Ghulam Hussain's government rather than at the time of the election. *Elections Return*, pp. 115-117.
34. This material for the official Sind Government results was drawn largely from these two sources which corroborate each other closely. See *SGG*, Pt. 1, 7 January 1937, p. 19, 26 February 1937, pp. 330-331, 14 January 1937, pp. 40 to 42; 51-52, 18 February 1937, p. 250., 21 January 1937, p. 87, 15 January 1937, p. 58, 25 February 1937, pp. 319-320; 18 January 1937, p. 61; also FR for February 1937 (1), Kirpalani to Maxwell, 19 February 1937. Reference was also made to the *D.G.*, issues of 16 February 18 and 22 to supply confirmatory evidence.
35. The non-Muslim party position was as follows: Congress (eight), Sind Hindu Sabha (ten), Europeans (three), and Independents (twelve), for a total of thirty-three.
36. The SUP swept all three of Thar Parkar's seats, took four of Nawabshah's five, in both Karachi and Hyderabad won three of five and won two of the three seats in Dadu and the Upper Sind Frontier.
37. The disputed seat was Sukkur, Southeast Rural won by a Sukkur landlord, Abdus Sattar Pirzada. *D.G.*, 16 February 1937, p. 5. It is noteworthy that in Sukkur, the most politically conscious district, the party outcome was inconclusive. Two seats went to the United party, two to Independent's and one to the Sind Muslim Political Party.
38. *Elections Return*, p. 115.
39. Interviews with Jamal-ud-Din Bokhari, a former journalist, Larkana, 14 December 1975; G.M. Sayed, Sann, Dadu district, 8 April 1975; and Pir Illahi Baksh, Karachi, 15 January 1975.
40. Interviews with G.M. Sayed, Sann, Dadu district, 8 April 1975; K.B. Khalid, a journalist, Karachi, 4 April 1975; and Taj Mohammed Dakhan, a political worker, Dakhan village, Sukkur district, 15 December 1975. These three allege that financial village *mullahs* were employed by Khuhro to orchestrate an anti-Bhutto campaign. Khuhro denies this and stresses Bhutto's unpopularity for raising road taxes in Larkana and his uncle's opposition as factors explaining his defeat. Interview with Khuhro, Karachi, 23 January 1976.
41. Interviews with Pir Ali Mohammed Rashidi, Islamabad, 3 June 1975; Khalid, Karachi, 4 April 1975; Sayed, Sann, 8 April 1975; and Kazi Fazlullah, Larkana, 22 January 1975. Rashidi was Bhutto's campaign manager in this election.
42. Interviews with Hatim Alavi, Karachi, 7 October 1974; M.A. Khuhro, Larkana, 22 January 1975; Rashidi, Islamabad, 3 June 1975; and Sayed, Sann, 8 April 1975. This view was also corroborated by Governor

Graham. IOR, Linlithgow Papers, MSS Eur F 125/112, Graham to Linlithgow, No. 6, 18 February 1937, p. 6.

43. Rashidi claims that Shah Nawaz's two cousins, Nabi Baksh, the *Sardar* of Sindhi Bhuttos, and Khan Bahadur Ahmad Khan, who were entrusted with his campaign, colluded with the enemy forces of Khuhro and Fazlullah to ensure their relative's defeat. Interview with Pir Ali Mohammed Rashidi, Islamabad, 3 June, 1975. Also, in reference to Bhutto's defeat, Graham mentions 'a dirty trick played at the last minute by rivals.' IOR, Linlithgow Papers, MSS Eur F 125/112, Graham to Linlithgow, No. 6 18 February 1937, p. 6. Bhutto himself alluded to 'wilful calumny and political jealousy' in explaining his defeat. *D.G.*, 4 April 1937, p. 9.

44. Haroon, who had been elected to the Indian Legislative Assembly in 1934, was knighted in January 1937. Shafi, *Haji Sir Abdoola Haroon*, p. 123.

45. *Elections Return*, p. 115.

46. *D.G.*, 16 February 1937, p. 1. This was not the first time Haroon and Majid had faced each other in an election. In 1934, Haroon, Majid and Nabi Baksh Bhutto ran for two seats in the Indian Legislative Assembly. Bhutto and Haroon polled 9,328 and 8,353 votes respectively to win; Majid was defeated with 6,945 ballots. *D.G.*, 22 November 1934, p. 4. 12,880 of 24,017 electors (53.6 per cent) voted in the election. IOR Information Series 1, Vol. 546, File 308 (1934), 'Return Showing Results of General Election to Legislative Assembly in India, 1934,' p. 8.

47. Interviews with Kazi Abid, an editor, Hyderabad, 8 December 1974; Kazi Mujtaba, a political worker, Karachi, 8 December 1975; G.M. Bhurgari, a Hyderabad politician, Karachi, 28 September 1975; K.B. Khalid, Karachi, 4 March 1975.

48. Interview with Bhurgari, 28 September 1975.

49. Interview with Kazi Mujtaba (campaign worker), Karachi, 12 December, 1975. The reference to receiving money was from reports that the wealthy Haroon would try to buy votes in Lyari.

50. Apparently the Baluch voters had forgotten a very unpopular action of Gabol's in 1935. While serving as a District Magistrate in Karachi, Gabol had ordered a police firing on Pathan and Baluch workers. They were demonstrating following the funeral of a Muslim leader, executed for killing a Hindu in a court fracas. For an account, see *D.G.*, 20, 21 March and 10 April 1935.

51. PDH, Abdul Ghafar Khan, Dura Khan to Abdullah Haroon, 24 February 1936. Apparently Gabol had ties with the same family. He and Abdul's father Fakir Mohammed Durra Khan distributed a handbill earlier to the Muslim labourers of Lyari warning them not to be seduced by the sweet words of Congress. *D.G.*, 7 May 1931, p. 5.

52. Shafi, *Haji Sir Abdoola Haroon*, pp. 32–33.

53. Interviews with G. Allana, Karachi merchant and politician, Karachi, 1 October 1975, and G.M. Sayed, Sann, 8 April 1975.
54. Like Bhutto, Haroon may have also neglected his campaign but his reasons were different. In a letter to Bhutto resigning his SUP chairmanship, Haroon mentioned he had to be away from Sindh for several weeks on a business trip; an event that coincided with the last few weeks of the election. Text of letter in Shafi, *Haji Sir Abdoola Haroon*, p. 122.
55. Interview with G.M. Bhurgari, Karachi, 28 September 1975.
56. Not all tribal chiefs deigned to stoop to enter the Assembly but mindful that the new politics of provincial autonomy would have a bearing on their interests, they had members of their family elected to represent them in the legislature. The chiefs of the Chandio tribe and of the Manikani and Shahwani Talpurs were notable examples. Interviews with H.T. Lambrick, former I.C.S. officer in Sindh, Oxford, England, 24 April 1976, and Mir Ali Ahmed Talpur, Sindhi politician, Karachi, 26 February 1976.
57. For a list of the representatives in the Assembly see, PSLA, Vol. I, Book 1, 24 April 1937, p. 1.

4

THE FIRST TWO MINISTRIES IN SINDH

In the aftermath of the divisive election period, the leaders of the two principal Muslim parties issued high-sounding statements of conciliation, goodwill and commitment to campaign promises. These declarations, designed to put the best face on the election results, were essentially respective bids to become the party that formed Sindh's first ministry. On 20 February 1937, the acting leader of the SUP, Sayed Miran Mohammed Shah, issued a press statement which outlined the post-election position of the party. He stated the SUP was the party of all Sindhi communities which would work in unison to achieve the party's goals and, furthermore, he stressed that the SUP would ensure protection for the Sindhi Hindu community and would strive to do all it could to uplift and enlighten the province's *haris*.[1] Also, with a view toward forming the government, the SUP sought to bolster its position by revealing plans at a party meeting on 18 February to have the defeated Bhutto take the seat of Mohammed Usman Soomro, a party winner in the Karachi North constituency.[2]

Several days after Miran Mohammed Shah's statement, Sir Ghulam Hussain, the SMP leader, issued a statement similar in tone to the SUP leader's. 'We are quite ready,' Hidayatullah declared, 'to work in the legislature in cooperation with all communities, including my own, on the basis of principles and policies.'[3] He added, in a thinly disguised proffer for the Sindh chief ministership: 'I have asked the successful candidates from the various communities for their cooperation with my party.'[4]

No statement was forthcoming from the SAP. Despite its significant defeat of Bhutto, the SAP made a poor showing in the election. It had fielded twelve candidates but had won only three seats; a record which compared unfavourably with the other two Muslim parties. Even the Larkana victory was more a personal triumph for Majid than a victory for the SAP. The election outcome for the SAP was a disappointing one, considering its strong beginning. The SAP had been started before the other parties and it boasted a better organizational basis. It had also sought to strengthen itself by establishing ties with the All-India Muslim League but this strategy worked in the end to cause more harm than good. The strained relationship between Majid and Jinnah undermined what party coherence had been achieved, with the result that the SAP fought the elections essentially on its own.

Following the election the SAP secretary, Mazhar Alavi, ever committed to SAP-AIML solidarity, ignored the hiatus that had developed between Majid and Jinnah, and wrote to the AIML president informing him of the SAP's success and requesting guidance for the party's future course.[5] Jinnah likely learned the SAP's true standing in the election results from elsewhere, as there is no record of his reply to Alavi. The quiet demise of the Sind Azad Party might be said to date from this time because nothing was again heard of the party. In fact, the next time Majid emerged on the political stage, he was running for the Assembly speakership with the support of the SUP and Congress.[6] Thus, the brief liaison between the SAP and the Muslim League came to an end, a result which was consistent with the preoccupation of the Sindhi Muslim elite with the province's affairs in the period following the 1937 elections.

Once the elections were over, Governor Graham, whose task it was to select the head of Sindh's first cabinet, found himself in a difficult position. Before the elections took place, he had been pleased to see the SUP emerge with the province's three most powerful Muslim leaders—Bhutto, Hidayatullah, and Haroon—all within its fold.[7] But the Governor's hopes were dashed, first, when Hidayatullah defected from the SUP and, second, when Bhutto and Haroon were both defeated in the election.[8] Thus, the combination of one dominant Muslim party, and the prominent Muslim leadership of Sindh that Graham had so earnestly encouraged, failed to materialize. As he could not have both a leading party and a strong leader together, the Governor realized he was going to have to choose between the two.

Graham's correspondence with the Viceroy provides an idea of what his choice was to be. Immediately after the election, Graham informed Linlithgow of his impression of Sindh's political situation. He noted that the SUP won the majority of the Muslim seats but added 'the party label means very little, I shall have to do a lot more analysis before I decide whether to offer two seats in my ministry to (the SUP) or one to them and one to the SMP.'[9] It was clear from this letter that Graham was still thinking of making a choice by accommodating the parties, but by the time he next wrote to Linlithgow, that option no longer seemed realistic. In March 1937 he informed Linlithgow that 'the situation is (still) difficult in forming a government as there are *no parties* among the Muslim.' (Graham's emphasis)[10].

Apparently Graham reached this conclusion after the two Muslim parties, either by themselves or together, had been unable to offer a viable ministry. The two parties had met in early March and agreed to form a united front as a basis for the first ministry.[11] But this scheme for a united front collapsed when, according to Graham, Sir Shah Nawaz decided he could not accept Sir Ghulam Hussain as chief minister.[12] So at this juncture, Graham concluded he was left with no choice but to ask Sir Ghulam Hussain to form the government, which he did.[13]

Thus, by the time Graham made his choice between leader and party, in his own view he really only had one choice to make, that of leader. His alternative choice of party had been greatly diminished when the SUP offered 'no real programme and old enmities and new jealousies dissolved what unity' the party had.[14] But such circumstantial considerations should not in themselves be accepted as a total explanation of Graham's choice. It should be noted, too, that of the two choices, he likely preferred a leader over a party as the instrument to form a government, and that this preference played some part in his choice of Hidayatullah.[15] Graham has been strongly criticized for his choice of a prominent leader over the dominant party on grounds that his action exposed his insensitivity to democratic principles, and plunged Sindh into a recurrent cycle of political instability.[16] Whatever truth there may be in such criticisms, their weakness lies in apportioning all the blame to Graham and placing none on the shoulders of the Muslim politicians who by their enmity, jealousy and disunity forced Graham to act as he did.

A week before the new government assumed office, its members were made public.[17] In addition to Sir Ghulam Hussain Hidayatullah, the chief minister, there were two other ministers, Mukhi Gobindram and Mir Bandeh Ali Talpur. Gobindram was a forty-year old Hyderabad merchant, and as his title *'Mukhi'* attests, he was head of the Sind Hindu *Panchayats.* Before being elected to the Assembly, he had served for fifteen years on Hyderabad's Municipal Council, and presided over several social welfare organizations that managed schools, dispensaries, and industrial homes for men and women.[18] Mir Bandeh Ali, younger by seven years, was a big *jagirdar* of Hyderabad and Dadu Districts, and a member of the Manikani branch of the Talpur clan, the former rulers of Sindh. Bandeh Ali had been educated at Aligarh and Cambridge, and before his election to the Sindh Assembly, he had represented Hyderabad District in the Bombay Legislative Council.[19] At the time his ministers were named, Hidayatullah claimed that his ministry had the support of twenty-eight members in the Assembly and that they together would constitute the Sind Democratic party.[20]

That Sir Ghulam Hussain was able to increase his support from his post-election total of four to his pre-ministry total of twenty-eight so suddenly points to the intricacies of Sindhi politics in which personalities predominated and party loyalties were virtually absent. Hidayatullah won his largest measure of support by his shrewd choice of ministers. By selecting Gobindram, he brought over to his side the largest bloc of Hindu votes.[21] In picking Mir Bandeh Ali, Hidayatullah won the support of the key Mir-Baluch bloc of ten votes,[22] of which Mir Bandeh Ali was the leader. This group, which had remained mostly independent during the election, with some Hidayatullah leanings, became a crucial swing bloc in the post-election jockeying for power and office. It represented a natural choice for Hidayatullah especially considering the only alternative he had was the SUP with which he had recently quarrelled. Hidayatullah could have made his peace with the SUP and formed the government largely with their support, but he perceived that in order to have a stable government in Sindh, the Hindus would have to be given an active voice.[23] Thus, Hidayatullah's strategy was to rely on the support of two new blocs instead of coming to terms with his rival, the SUP.

It was not just its rival status that led Hidayatullah to ignore the SUP. Another factor, surely, was the SUP's increasingly eroded position since the elections. The defeat of its two leaders in the elections was a demoralizing blow which caused a number of members to leave the party. In the weeks that followed, the party claimed to have eighteen supporters but the real total was closer to twelve, the number that attended the party meeting on 3 April 1937.[24] The party was further weakened by an internal power struggle which surfaced at this meeting.[25] At the 3 April meeting the party officially decided to go into the opposition, a policy it had contemplated as early as 24 March, when it was clear it would not be given a ministership.[26] Also at this meeting, the resignation of Bhutto was accepted and in his place, Haroon was made the officiating leader and Allah Baksh Soomro, the new rising light in the party, was made the Parliamentary leader.[27]

While the SUP leadership had decided to go into the opposition, it viewed the Assembly speaker's election as one last opportunity to challenge Hidayatullah's ministry and possibly force an opening into the government. The candidate the SUP chose to back was Sheikh Abdul Majid. Majid was commonly viewed as a committed political worker as well as an idealistic politician whose political status had been greatly increased by defeating Bhutto. These attributes, the SUP felt, made him someone all the Muslims could agree to support. The choice of Majid was made at a time when the political situation was still fluid; Hidayatullah had made known his choice of ministers but was still undecided about the speakership.[28] The SUP strategy was that Majid would succeed in keeping Sir Ghulam Hussain off balance for a time and possibly force him to concede a larger role to the SUP. When word leaked that Bhojsingh, the Hindu candidate, was also Hidayatullah's, it became clear that the latter's strategy was to rely heavily on Hindu support.[29] The SUP leadership realized, then, that their chances of success were slimmer but they perservered, nonetheless, attempting to bring Hidayatullah down by fermenting discord in the Hindu Sabha and wooing Congress support away from Bhojsingh.[30] However, even before the election for the speaker took place, it was evident that the SUP was waging a losing battle.

Two days before the election the SUP candidate, Majid, announced he was joining Hidayatullah and urged others to do so.[31] On the same day, twenty-four Muslim members of the Assembly signed a pledge supporting Hidayatullah as did twelve members of the Sindh Hindu Sabha. The new chief minister's majority position was clearly demonstrated on 28 April, when his candidate, Bhojsingh, won handily over Majid in the speaker's election by a vote of forty to eighteen.[32] After the large-scale defection to Hidayatullah on 26 April, only a few remained within the folds of the SUP, chiefly Allah Baksh Soomro,[33] Mohammed Hashim Gazdar and G.M. Sayed. With the SUP's support shrunken to a handful, Hidayatullah and his followers emerged as the single largest bloc in the Assembly, but not all political observers were convinced the group's solidarity was as certain as it appeared.[34] The manner in which Hidayatullah came to power clearly demonstrated a triumph of personality over party; with the vagaries of personal ambition as the key determinants of political power, rather than loyalty to party principles, the future of Sindhi Muslim politics seemed destined to follow an unstable course.[35]

Before discussing the fate of Hidayatullah, some mention needs to be made of developments involving the Indian Muslim community at the level of all-India politics. In the results of the 1937 elections, the All-India Muslim League generally fared poorly, winning only 109 of the 482 seats reserved for Muslims.[36] Its worst showing was in the Muslim majority provinces, particularly the Punjab and Sindh.[37] The League's greatest success was in those areas where it had traditionally been strong—the Muslim minority provinces. In the United Provinces, the League fought thirty-five of the sixty-six Muslim seats, winning only twenty-nine.[38] Despite the League's general lack of success, its president, M.A. Jinnah described the election results as 'very hopeful' considering the League was not organized six months before the election.[39] Jinnah's positive reaction to the mediocre League performance was part of his design to create an image of a strong, vibrant League in the eyes of Congress and the British, particularly the former. Jinnah's purpose was to achieve League-Congress cooperation in the formation of government in the provinces where the League had done well. Jinnah was confident the recent changes in the League, particularly its alterations in composition and its adoption of a progressive platform in the elections, would make the Congress receptive to his scheme of cooperation.[40]

The Congress however, viewed the situation rather differently. The leaders in the Congress were not persuaded that the League had really rid itself of its reactionary, aristocratic membership; they considered the League to be primarily a communal party, contributing little to India's progress, a view they felt was vindicated by the League's weak electoral showing.[41] For these reasons the Congress was reluctant to join hands with the League in a coalition government. In the case of the United Provinces, which subsequently became a symbol of Congress' repression for Muslims all over India, the Congress stipulated that unless the Leaguers ceased to function as a separate group, there could be no understanding with them.[42]

The refusal to admit Leaguers into Congress-controlled ministries was not the only Congress policy that aroused the feelings of League-minded Muslims. In the Muslim minority provinces, Congress also initiated a campaign of 'mass contact' designed to bring lower class Muslims and peasants into the Congress fold.[43] Furthermore, Congress instituted a social policy that offended the cultural and religious sensitivities of Muslims.[44]

It was against this background that the Muslim League met in its annual session in Lucknow in October, 1937. The Leaguers gathered in a mixed mood of anxiety and determination. The Raja of Mahmudabad, in his welcoming remarks, described the political situation as 'delicate'[45]. On the one hand the Leaguers felt beset upon by a tyrannical Congress, on the other they were resolved to secure safeguards for the protection of their rights. In confronting these challenges, the League was strengthened by the recent changes that had taken place in its composition. A new League emerged at Lucknow; for the first time, middle and lower class Muslims were allowed to attend a League session.[46] The trend toward broadening the League's class base, begun in April 1936, became institutionalized at the Lucknow session when a minimal two *anna* free for membership was written into the League Constitution.[47] The new membership fee was the first change; the second was equally significant. For the first time, the Muslim majority provinces gave support to the League at the Lucknow session. Sikandar Hayat, the Punjab's premier, and Fazlul Haq, premier of Bengal, who had both shunned the League in the 1937 elections, joined the League and attended the session at Lucknow.[48] Their presence has been described as a 'tonic' which 'invigorated the League'[49]; in Khaliquzzaman's assessment, who was there, 'Sir Sikandar and Fazlul Haq saved Muslim India by throwing their full weight at the crucial hour behind the Muslim cause.'[50]

Strengthened by a new found sense of social depth and geographic breadth, the League at Lucknow took the bold step of altering its constitution and setting for itself a new, more radical goal. In Resolution No. 2, the League declared that its object 'shall be the establishment in India of full independence...'[51] This new step represented a departure from the League's earlier goal of 'complete responsible government' which differed only in degree from British policy, and ironically, the new aim brought the League in line with its opponent Congress, as it (Congress) had the same goal.[52] If noticed, however, this fact went unmentioned at the session. The Leaguers were more mindful of their differences, particularly those highlighted by Congress policy in the Muslim minority provinces, about which there were three strongly worded, anti-Congress resolutions passed at the session.[53]

The success of the Lucknow session was reflected in the rapid organization of the League soon after the session concluded. According to one account, as many as ninety bracnches of the League were established in the United Provinces and forty in the Punjab. Nearly 100,000 new members were enrolled in the United Provinces alone.[54] Branches were opened in remote villages, and workers and speakers travelled about and preached the gospel of Muslim unity.[55]

At the beginning of 1937, the position of the League in Sindh appeared strong in terms of organization. The 1937 list of Council members of the All-India Muslim League shows that Sindh's quota was full.[56] The election results and the formation of Hidayatullah's government, however, considerably weakened the League's position in Sindh. With the formation of the ministry, at least half of the Council men left the League and either joined or supported Sir Ghulam's government.[57] The list for the following year showed only four members from Sindh on the Council of the All-India Muslim League: Kazi Khuda Baksh, Gazdar, Alavi and Sheikh Abdul Majid.[58]

Some Leaguers from Sindh did attend the Lucknow session,[59] but the prominent leaders were not present. Indicating that he was still interested in the League, Majid sent a wire expressing his regret that he could not attend the Lucknow session. He added that 'Sindh Muslims are wholeheartedly with the League, (and that they are) establishing a branch within a fortnight.'[60] Another telegram and a letter from two other leaders indicated the thinking of League-minded Sindhi Muslims around the time of the Lucknow session. The two communications were from the two political foes, H. Alavi and Gazdar. Their correspondence, besides revealing their differing personal political outlooks, demonstrated a consistency with an earlier duality of interest among Sindhi Muslim politicians: a concern for Indian Muslims at the all-India level, on the one hand, and an abiding preoccupation with the welfare of Sindhi Muslims on the other. Alavi represented the first focus of interest; in his wire to Jinnah he addressed his attention primarily to the Muslims at the national level and the League's responsibility for them:

> [The] League's greatest need effectively answers Jawaharlal's criticism that, [the] League has all officers but no soldiers.
> [The] Muslims being educationally, economically [and] politically backward, [the] League must creatively work on all three fronts.[61]

Gazdar's letter, reflective of the common preoccupation of the leadership with provincial concerns, omitted any mention of all-India issues. But in one way, his letter represented a subtle but highly significant shift in the thinking of the League-minded Sindh Muslim leadership. What Gazdar sought to do was lay stress on the political predicament of Sindhi Muslims sufficient to attract the attention and support of the All-India Muslim League. He requested the League secretary Jinnah to place his letter 'before meetings of the Council and the League (session) for their consideration.'[62] In his letter, Gazdar summarized the political situation in Sindh since separation and concluded that the position of Sindh Muslims 'has become rather bad.' He placed all the blame for this state of affairs on the Governor, the ministerial party and the government's mutual pact with the Hindus. He supported his claim by stating that almost all major appointments have gone to Hindus, including the Assembly speakership. As a result of this Hindu-favoured political balance, Gazdar argued, all legislative measures intended for 'the social and economic amelioration of the masses (Muslims) in the Province' had been thwarted. He mentioned the measures the Muslims wanted passed[63] and suggested that the League 'pass a *resolution requesting Sir Ghulam Hussain, our Chief Minister and the Governor* to help us in passing these measures and fixing the ratio of future appointments to public services on the population basis' (emphasis Gazdar's). He ends the letter by saying 'without the League's agitation, I am afraid the pact with the Hindus would stand and ruin Muslims.' The importance of Gazdar's letter was that it represented the first time a Sindhi Muslim leader appealed to the All-India Muslim League to help solve the difficulties that beset the Sindhi Muslim community.

Gazdar was not successful in getting his resolution passed at the Lucknow session, but within a short time he found that the Hidayatuallah government had moved closer to his views and the views of the SUP, with the result that the SUP and the ministerial party entered into an agreement.[64] Actually Hidayatullah's coming to terms with the United Party was part of his carefully orchestrated plan to keep himself in power.[65] Ever since becoming chief minister with a slender majority, Hidayatullah had been forced to walk a very narrow line and be careful that he did not alienate his key blocs of support. He began by courting the Hindus, and winning their support by backing their candidates for the speakership and for Parliamentary secretary[66], and by taking identical stands on certain issues such as favouring joint electorates[67] and the abolition of nominations.[68] But then he began to be too closely identified with the Hindus[69] so he moved closer to the Muslim camp and the Democratic Coalition was the result.

Hidayatullah's strategy worked for him until his Hindu minister was forced to resign for business reasons.[70] Because Gobindram had been the only one who could command the majority of Hindu support, there was no one Hidayatullah could select to maintain the delicate balance the ministry depended upon. In the end, he selected Hemandas Wadhani, a bland forty-two year old physician and lawyer from Jacobabad,[71] because he was favoured by a majority of the Muslim members of the Assembly which was the new bloc of support Hidayatullah hoped would keep him in power.[72] Subsequent developments further alienated the Hindus from the ministry: they felt threatened by the proposed legislation of the Democratic

Coalition party[73] and they were angered by the election of Miran Mohammed Shah, the Coalition candidate, over their own candidate to be the new Speaker.[74]

At the beginning of 1938, Hidayatullah attempted to consolidate his support by having the SUP and his own supporters band together in one party under a new name, the Sindh Democratic Party.[75] With the Hindu Sabha members and the Congress in opposition, the new ruling party contained most of the Muslim groups in the Assembly: Hidayatullah's supporters, the remnants of the SUP, and a few Muslim independents. It was the first time since the elections that the Muslims had united under one banner. But their unity was short-lived.

Early in the March budget sessions, Allah Baksh, G.M. Sayed and their supporters deserted the ranks of the government party and voted with the opposition to defeat and bring down Hidayatullah's ministry.[76] Allah Baksh claimed the decision to defect stemmed from the ministry's failure to carry out the party principles and programme[77], but the Governor suggested that the reasons may have been personal. Graham cited two actions of Hidayatullah's that angered Allah Baksh. First of all, Sir Ghulam Hussain had ordered that no contracts of the Public Works Department (PWD), with which Allah Baksh had close ties, were to be awarded to any member of the Legislative Assembly (MSLA).[78] Secondly, the chief minister failed to approve an exchange of land to which Allah Baksh was entitled.[79] The reasons Sayed gave were similar to Allah Baksh's: the weight of the bureaucracy and officialdom would block any progressive legislation, and furthermore Sir Ghulam was too old and tired to be able to guide and push through such a programme of legislation.[80]

Hidayatullah's ministry resigned on 22 March 1938, and the Governor asked Allah Baksh to form the government. Allah Baksh did so with the support of Nichaldas Vazirani and his group of ten Hindu Independents,[81] seventeen Muslims (including twelve of the SUP, three Europeans and two independents.)[82] This gave the new chief minister a majority without the backing of Congress though he did seek their tacit support.[83]

With the formation of the Allah Baksh ministry, the segment of Sindhi Muslim leadership that had remained loyal to Sir Ghulam Hussain, namely Majid, Gazdar and Khuhro, began to coalesce into an opposition group. They felt compelled to do so for three main reasons; they were bitter that the Allah Baksh forces had fractured the carefully nurtured Muslim unity just to secure office; they viewed as traitorous Allah Baksh's openness with the Hindus and his dependence on them for support; and they were fearful that his Congress-dominated programme would repeat in Sindh the scenario of Congress oppression in the Muslim minority provinces.[84]

Shortly after the ministry took power, Majid, Gazdar and Khuhro called a public meeting of the Muslims of Karachi in an attempt to marshal support to oppose the new government.[85] Majid presided at the meeting which was attended by 3,000 people and introduced a resolution calling upon Sindhi Muslims to accept the leadership of the All-India Muslim League and to begin establishing League branches in the towns of the province.[86] Gazdar also spoke at the meeting and refuted the Congress charge that the Muslim League was a communal organization, and asked how the Congress could claim to be non-communal when it was Hindu-dominated. A resolution was passed at the meeting characterizing Allah Baksh as traitorous and denouncing his ministry for its dependence on Congress and Mahasabha support to the detriment of Sindhi Muslim interests.

The very next day, on 29 March, the Muslim supporters of the ministry called a meeting to explain to the Muslim public the reasons behind their position. This meeting drew an even larger crowd of 4,000 people, but the majority of them opposed the ministry. They kept the ministry spokesmen, Sayed, Ali Mohammed Rashidi and Pir Illahi Bux from speaking, and the meeting ended soon after it began.[87]

While the League did not begin to organize in Sindh immediately after Lucknow, as was the case in other parts of

India, it did begin before the Allah Baksh ministry was formed.[88] Once again it was Majid who took the initiative in organizing the League in Sindh. He called a meeting at his Karachi home in early February to form a provisional committee to establish a Muslim League branch in Sindh. The following office-bearers were elected at the meeting: Majid, president, Sir Abdullah Haroon, vice-president, G. Allana, secretary (to be assisted by Mazhar Alavi) and Hassanali Mohammed Baloch, treasurer. In addition, a twenty member working committee (which included Gazdar and Miran Mohammed Shah) was established. This committee was empowered to convene a provincial conference of the All-India Muslim League during the Easter holidays.[89]

By taking upon himself the responsibility of organizing the League in Sindh, Majid made it clear he was willing to forget or at least ignore the unsuccessful attempt at election time to establish the League in Sindh. But what of Mr Jinnah, did he feel the same way? A factor which prompted Jinnah to direct his attention to Sindh once again was an address presented to him by the Sindh Students' Association at Aligarh a few days after Majid's February provisional meeting. The address claimed that the Muslim League had treated Sindh as a backward area, and as a result the ministry had played into the hands of the Hindus.[90] Jinnah, in his response, denied that the League had neglected Sindh and spoke of his 'peculiar affection for Sind.' He stated that the 'coldness' of Sindh leaders and their internal differences had kept him from doing full justice to the province, and he promised to turn to Sindh and try to lift up the masses and organize the League forces. A month and a half later it was reported in the press that Jinnah would visit Sindh in late April and consolidate the League ranks.[91]

Organizational efforts of the League received a fresh impetus from the formation of Allah Baksh's government. In early April, Majid went to Delhi to confer with Jinnah over what future course to pursue.[92] The League's strategy was revealed in Majid's announcement shortly after his return that a majority of Muslim members in the Assembly had agreed to join the Muslim

League, and that the League would continue to support the present ministry provided its members joined the League.[93]

The League's prospects in Sindh were strengthened in late April by Sir Abdullah Haroon's formal declaration of support.[94] Haroon's endorsement of the League, however, was not unqualified. In his 24 April press statement he stated the 'only purpose' of the Muslim League was to unify the Muslims and 'create a healthy consciousness among the Muslim masses;' he eschewed any League role of seeking office or opposing the ministry.[95] Haroon limited the scope of the League to non-Sindhi affairs and issues because he wanted to reserve the realm of Sindhi politics for the SUP. Evidentally, Haroon still had hope that the SUP would fulfil its role of unifying the Muslims and serving their interests, despite the severe strains put on the party's unity by Allah Baksh's ascension to power.[96]

The month of April 1938 witnessed a flurry of League organizing activity in Sindh. By the third week of April, League branches had been organized in Thar Parkar, Nawabshah, Sukkur, Jacobabad and Larkana.[97] Thus, the League gained an early foothold in upper Sindh, in Larkana district particularly, on account of the energetic efforts of the district League president and general secretary, Khuhro and Kazi Fazlullah.[98] One method used to organize the League branches was to summon former *Khilafat* committees and then instruct those in attendance to strengthen the League. This method was used by Majid and others in Hyderabad and Dadu districts where there was less interest in the League.[99]

Not all the League's efforts at organization met with success, however. Majid's attempt to establish a branch in Dhoro Noro, a town in Thar Parkar, was met by black flags and a *satyagraha* campaign supported by the Muslim inhabitants.[100] But Majid claimed that, despite this temporary setback, the effect of the Dhoro Noro incident was to create even more enthusiasm for the League.[101] Haroon interpreted the opposition to the League in Dhoro Noro as a reaction to an earlier statement by Majid and his supporters condemning the ministry. Haroon informed Jinnah that he was puzzled by his friend, Majid, and his group for denouncing the ministerial party because they were only 'alienating the League further.'[102] Haroon also stated that there was 'a section of Muslims in Sindh favourable to the ministerial party but the League tactics of hostility are causing opinion to coalesce against the League.'[103]

In spite of these behind-the-scenes differences between Haroon and Majid,[104] the work of organizing the League went ahead. By the beginning of June, branches had been opened in Thatta city and Matiari town, adding two more districts (Karachi and Hyderabad respectively) to the five where the League was already established.[105] By the middle of July, forty League branches had been established throughout Sindh. The total enrolled membership was 15,000 and of these 2,000 or roughly twelve per cent were from Karachi.[106] These figures indicated that the League, after six months of organizing, found most of its support in the rural sector, but in the province as a whole, the League had achieved only limited success as its total membership represented barely one percent of Sindh's Muslim population.

Despite their slow progress, League organizing efforts continued, culminating in an important conference at Sultankot, Sukkur district at the end of July. A new name joined the other Leaguers at Sultankot—Sir Ghulam Hussain Hidayatullah had been leaning toward the League for some time[107] but the Sultankot conference represented the first instance of his open support. Other prominent leaders attending included Haroon, Majid and the following MSLA: A.B. Gabol, A.S. Pirzada and Agha Shamshuddin Khan. The latter was an influential Afghan *Zamindar* from nearby Garhi Yasin whose younger relative, Agha Ghulam Nabi Pathan, was chiefly responsible for organizing the conference.

Outside League influence provided some impetus for holding the Sultankot conference,[108] but the Sindhi Leaguers labelled the conference a success primarily because of the support it received from within the province. Over 4000 people from all over Sindh attended the three day conference and gave their strong backing to the numerous resolutions which were passed.[109]

All of the resolutions contained a Sindhi theme, reflecting the continuing preoccupation of the Sindhi Leaguers with provincial concerns. One resolution blamed the government for failing to pass the Land Alienation and Money-lending Bills, followed by another which called for the formation of a Muslim League party in the Assembly to ensure passage of such legislation. A third asked the Muslim ministers to resign and support a no-confidence motion against the ministry. The common anti-ministry theme of these resolutions revealed the League's strategy to marshal support against the Allah Baksh government by depicting it as harmful to Sindhi Muslim interests.

Another resolution at the Sultankot conference charged that the proposed revision of land revenue assessments in the Sukkur Barrage area would be harmful to the province's *zamindars.* The whole issue of enhanced assessment came to a head in early July with the publication by the Sindh Government of the *Gorwalla Report* which set new, higher assessment rates.[110] The revision was undertaken at this time both because the term of the earlier rates had expired, and because enhancement had been decided upon as part of an official scheme, devised at the time of the province's separation, whereby Sindh would pay back its Sukkur Barrage debt.[111] Two positions developed on the assessment issue. The official Sindh view supported immediate implementation of the enhanced rates, after listening to, but not necessarily following the ministers' advice.[112] The second position represented the policy of Sindh's political parties which all, to one degree or another, opposed the enhancement measure.[113.]

Thus, the ministers found themselves caught in the middle of two opposing sides; the officials were counting on the ministers to win the parties over to the government's view, while the parties trusted the ministers to persuade the government to adopt the parties' line. In the end, the ministers supported the government side on the issue which naturally precipitated a crisis in their party support.[114] G.M. Sayed and his followers withdrew their support from Allah Baksh[115] which prompted the chief minister to move closer to Congress, hoping to secure their support.[116]

As Allah Baksh strengthened his ties with Congress, G.M. Sayed gravitated toward the League. Sayed was angry with both Allah Baksh and the Congress for he was convinced that behind their handling of the enhancement issue lay a primary motive to keep themselves in power.[117] Though he was reluctant to do so, he felt he had no choice but to resign from Congress, of which he had been a member since the *Khilafat* days, and join the League. The failure of the SUP indicated to him that a non-communal approach would not work in Sindh to create strong public opinion among Sindhi Muslims, which they needed desperately if their community's interests were to be realized. Thus, he concluded 'the only course that remained to be tried for the improvement of political conditions and the enactment of benevolent measures was an organization of the Sindhi Muslims on communal lines.'[118]

The addition of Sayed to the League ranks brought another influential Muslim leader[119] into the League, which served to broaden the party's political base. Sayed's inclusion in the League occurred soon after another significant development which further brightened the League's prospects. In early July, Haroon and Hidayatullah created an alliance between their two families through the marriage of two of their children.[120] Thus, by the end of July 1938, the League in Sindh, having secured the considerable support of Hidayatullah, Haroon, Majid, Sayed, Khuhro and Gazdar, began to emerge as an important political force on the stage of Sindhi politics.

Conscious of its new-found strength, the League leadership decided to call a province-wide conference to further consolidate the League's position in Sindh as a preliminary step to establishing a full-fledged Muslim League ministry.[121] Jinnah was notified of these plans and invited to preside over the conference.[122] Other prominent leaders of Muslim India were also invited and the dates for the conference were set for October 1938.

The period of Sindh's first two ministries represented a significant phase in the continuing politicization of the Sindhi Muslim elite for it revealed among them the first signs of an emergent political sophistication. The experience of the Hidayatullah and Allah Baksh ministries demonstrated two realities of the politics of Sindh at this time: Sindhi Muslims had lost their favoured post-separation position of political dominance by pursuing their penchant for self-centered, personalized politics, and in their place their rivals, the Sindhi Hindus, had emerged to hold the balance of power in the province's ministerial politics. Weak, divided and riven by factions, the Sindhi Muslims began to search for a way to displace the Hindus from their position of political control and restore to their own majority community their separatist vision of political power. As a consequence, a majority of the Sindhi Muslim leadership found themselves gravitating to the All-India Muslim League. The League had the prestige of an all-India organization, a prestige which the party had enhanced at its recent Lucknow session by remoulding its image and opening its ranks to all classes. The Sindhi Muslims were also attracted to the League because it provided a banner under which they could unite themselves, and thus strengthen their political standing. In addition, their interest in the League reflected a willingness to broaden their political horizons beyond Sindh, thus restoring a measure of equilibrium to province-centre relations.

NOTES

1. *D.G.,* 20 February 1937, p. 7.
2. *D.G.,* 19 February 1937, p. 7.
3. *D.G.,* 26 February 1937, p. 7.
4. In October 1936, Graham had noted that 'Hidayatullah is probably the ablest politician in Sindh, and is determined to be the Chief Minister in the first government.' IOR, Linlithgow Papers, MSS Eur F 125/112, Graham to Linlithgow, No. 1, 16 October 1936, p. 1.
5. Alavi clearly exaggerated the SAP's results by stating that the three candidates the party supported were all successful. He did add, however, that the 'other candidates' would have won had there been more money. Also, Alavi's claim that Majid defeated Haroon in Karachi was a distortion of fact. QAPC, F 209, Mazhar Alavi to Jinnah, 14 March

1937, pp. 1-2. Lack of funds was also a factor which limited the League's success in other provinces, such as the UP. Khaliquzzaman, *Pathway to Pakistan*, p. 152.

6. *D.G.*, 11 April 1937, p. 1. In contesting for the speakership, Majid gave 'no party' as his affiliation. *PSLA*, vol. I, Book 11, 28 April 1937, p. 63.

7. IOR, Linlithgow Papers, MSS Eur F 125/112, Graham to Linlithgow, No. 1, 16 October 1936, p. 1.

8. Graham wrote to Linlithgow 'at first I had great hopes of uniting the Muslims into one party, the Sind United Party but Ghulam Hussain Hidayatullah, the most prominent man in the province, was left out and the two leaders (Bhutto and Haroon) were defeated.' IOR, Linlithgow Papers, MSS Fur F 125/113, Graham to Linlithgow, No. 1, 19 April 1937, p. 2.

9. IOR, Linlithgow Papers, MSS Eur F 125/112, Graham to Linlithgow, No. 6, 18 February 1937, p. 6.

10. IOR, Linlithgow Papers, MSS Eur F 125/112, Graham to Linlithgow, No. 6, 22 March 1937, p. 8.

11. The two parties, along with the independent Baloch faction, agreed to form a new party. Their common agreement recognized Hidayatullah as chief minister and either Bhutto or Allah Baksh as one of the ministers, depending on whether Bhutto was able to secure a seat. They also agreed to rotate the Assembly presidentship among the cooperating parties every two years. The party would be non-communal and would cooperate with the Hindus. *D.G.*, 9 March 1937, p. 7.

12. IOR, Linlithgow Papers, MSS Eur F 125/112, Graham to Linlithgow, No. 9, 22 March 1937, p. 8.

13. Graham describes Hidayatullah as 'easily the most competent man in the province,' and adds that when Hidayatullah came to see him, the chief minister-designate already had his ministry in his pocket. Graham did not like his choices and offered alternatives but in the end acquiesced—'he's a wise old bird and I am afraid he is right.' Ibid.

14. IOR, Linlithgow Papers, MSS Eur F 125/113, Graham to Linlithgow, No. 1, 19 March 1937, pp. 1-2.

15. Zaidi, *'Muslim Politics in Sind,'* pp. 9ff.

16. Sayed writes '...Provincial Autonomy...received a heavy blow even at the moment of its inception when...Graham conveniently cast the fundamental principle of democracy to the winds and summoned Sir Ghulam Hussain to form the Ministry although he commanded the strength of only 3 members.' Sayed, *Struggle for a new Sind*, p. 6. Another historian writes, 'the action of the Governor in passing over the claims of larger parties and entrusting the Government to a small group started an unending round of inter-group intrigues and manoeuvres in which Congress fully exploited its opportunities and

kept the Muslim factions in battle array against each other.' Abdul
Hamid, 'Efforts at the Consolidation of the Muslim Position,' *History
of the Freedom Movement,* Vol. 3, Part 2, (Karachi: Pakistan Historical
Society, (1963), pp. 1909-1936.

17. *D.G.,* 23 March 1937, p. 1.
18. Ibid.
19. Ibid., In a later issue, the *Daily Gazette* noted all three ministers were
from Hyderabad and were popular among their respective communities.
All were well-dressed, cultured and had close friends on the Hyderabad
Municipal Council. *D.G.,* 4 April 1937, p. 7. The emergence of
Hyderabad as a centre of political leadership was a new development;
its new prominence was likely a result of most of the Assembly seats
going to the rural constituencies.
20. Ibid.
21. This was the Hindu Sabha bloc of votes. The Congress was out of
consideration at this point because it was still undecided about office
acceptance. According to Ghulam Hussain, Gobindram was the only
ministerial candidate the Hindus could all agree on. IOR, Linlithgow
Papers, MSS Eur F 125/112, Graham to Linlithgow, No. 1, 19 April
1937, pp. 1-2.
22. This bloc comprised as alliance of prominent Talpurs and the heads of
some of the Baluch tribes in Sindh. G.M. Sayed says they numbered ten
and he names the following as some of them: Mir Bandeh Ali
(Hyderabad, East), Mir Ghulam Ali Khan (Thar Parkar West),
Mir Mohammed Khan Chandio (Larkana West), K.B. Kaiser Khan
Bozdar (Sukkur Northeast) and Mir Zenuldin Sunderani (Upper Sind
Frontier, East). Interviews with G.M. Sayed, Sann, 8 April 1975. His
claims are corroborated by the *D.G.,* 16 February 1937, and *Election
Returns,* pp. 115-117; sources I would use to suggest the three names
Sayed forgot: Allah Baksh Gabol (Karachi, North Urban), Sohrab Khan
Sarki (Upper Sind Frontier, Central) and Jaffer Khan Burdi (Upper
Sind Frontier, West). The parentheses are used for constituencies.
23. The Hindus were assured of at least a seat in the Cabinet according to
the terms of The Government of India Act, 1935. *Government of India
Act, 1935,* Sections 50, 52. For further elaboration on this point see,
Sayed, *Pakistan: The Formative Phase,* p. 84ff; R. Gopal, *India
Muslims,* pp. 253-254.
24. *D.G.,* 4 April 1937, p. 1.
25. Miran Mohammed Shah, who claimed leadership of the Saiyid bloc in
the party (eight members), felt slighted by the party selection of Allah
Baksh Soomro over him for the parliamentary leadership of the party.
Shah had hoped his group would serve as a power broker between the
ministerial party and the opposition. Ibid.
26. Ibid., *D.G.,* 24 March 1937, p. 2.

27. With his resignation, Bhutto retired from political life and joined the Bombay Public Service Commission.

28. *D.G.,* 23 March 1937, p. 1.

29. Graham discloses that Hidayatullah's deal with the Hindu party included not just a Hindu minister but a Hindu speaker as well. IOR, Linlithgow Papers, MSS Eur F 125/113, Graham to Linlithgow, No. 1, 19 April 1937, pp. 1-2.

30. *D.G.,* 11 April 1937. The United Party hoped to create a rift between the *Amils* and *Bhaibunds* in the Sind Hindu Sabha and woo Congress away by reminding them of their plans to wreck the constitution.

31. *D.G.,* 27 April, 1937, p. 1.

32. Bhojsingh, a Sukkur leader, had represented Sind in the Bombay Legislative Council from 1920 to 1930. Majid received only the support of Congress and the remnants of the SUP. Graham explained Majid's defeat by his failure 'to carry weight with the *zamindar* class.' IOR Linlithgow Papers, MSS Eur 125/113, Graham to Linlithgow, No. 13, 13 May 1937, p. 10 *PSLA*, Vol. 1, Book 2, 28 April 1937, p. 63.

33. Hereinafter simply Allah Baksh.

34. Graham predicted 'a great deal of intrigue between now and the budget session in July.' He added, 'my Chief Minister is in the embarrassing position of having little to offer' creating the prospect that he will 'quite likely lose one, maybe two ministers within the year.' IOR Linlithgow Papers, MSS Eur 125/113, Graham to Linlithgow, No. 1, 19 April 1937, p. 1-2.

35. About this time Graham wrote Linlithgow that 'until stable parties are formed with a distinct programme and principles but also commanding personal loyalties, ministries are bound to be short lived. This will go on until I can get Muslims working harmoniously on a single platform. At present they have two platforms which are indistinguishable from each other except by enmity.' IOR Linlithgow Papers, MSS Eur 125/113, Graham to Linlithgow, No. 1, 19 April 1937, p. 1-2.

36. Hardy, *The Muslims of British India,* p. 224; B.N. Pandey, *The Break-up of British India* (New York: St. Martin's Press, 1969), p. 144.

37. The League did somewhat better in Bengal. Ibid. See also R. Gopal, *The Indian Muslims,* p. 247.

38. Khaliquzzaman, *Pathway to Pakistan,* p. 186. Pandey and Gopal, whose figures differ slightly base their accounts on P. Sitaramayya, *The History of the Indian National Congress,* 2 vols. (Bombay: Padma Publications, 1946), 2:161.

39. Jinnah also said that in each province where a League Parliamentary Board was constituted, sixty to seventy percent of the seats contested were won by League candidates. MLA, Annual Session at Lacknow, 1937 (4), Vol. 187, Jinnah's Presidential Address, p. 94. Muslim accounts generally cast the League's election outcome in a favourable

light. See Noman, *Muslim India*, p. 333; Saiyid, *Jinnah*, p. 177; Rajput, *Muslim League*, p. 60.

40. For an elaboration of the alterations in the AIML, see Noman, *Muslim India*, pp. 343ff.

41. Humayun Kabir, *Muslim Politics 1906-47 and other Essays* (Calcutta: Firma K.L. Mukhopadhyay, 1969), p. 27; Pandey, *The Breakup of British India*, pp. 145-46.

42. See Khaliquzzaman, *Pathway to Pakistan*, pp. 173-188 for his view of this controversy in which he played an important part.

43. See Sayed, *Pakistan*, p. 90; Hardy, *Muslims of British India*, pp. 227-228.

44. Examples given were the public singing of *Bande Mataram*, the Congress anthem, forcing cow protection upon Muslims, promoting Hindi at the expense of Urdu, and interfering with Muslim worship. These charges against Congress were later investigated in two Muslim League reports: The Raja of Pirpur, *Report of the Inquiry Committee appointed by the Council of the All-India Muslim League to inquire into Muslim grievances in Congress provinces*, (1938); S.M. Shareef, *Report of the Inquiry Committee appointed by the Working Committee of the Bihar Provincial Muslim League to inquire into some grievances of Muslims in Bihar*, (1939). For critical assessments of these *Reports*, see S. Abid Hussain, *The Destiny of Indian Muslims* (London: Asia Publishing House, 1965), pp. 107ff, also Kabir, *Muslim Politics*, pp. 27-28.

45. Pirzada, *Foundations of Pakistan*, 2:264.

46. Hussein Imam, a prominent Bihar Muslim Leaguer, claims this was the first League session that was open to everyone. Interview with Hussein Imam, Karachi, 12 September 1975.

47. This change occurred in 1937 but it first appears in the 1940 constitution, the next revised constitution after 1937. See Article 5, *The Constitution and Rules of the All-India Muslim League*, (Published by Liaquat Ali Khan, Honorary Secretary, 1940), p. 2. The earlier subscription had been prohibitive for many, it was one *rupee*, eight times the new amount. See Article 5, *The Constitution and Rules of the All-India League, 1937*, (Delhi: National Printing and Publishing House, 1937), p. 4.

48. Both leaders agreed to support the AIML only on all-India policy questions. Imran Ali, *Punjab Politics in the Decade before Partition* (Lahore: University of the Punjab Press, 1975), pp. 17-19, also Gopal, *India Muslims*, p. 246.

49. Sayeed, *Pakistan*, pp. 87-88.

50. Kaliquzzaman, *Pathway to Pakistan*, p. 171.

51. The resolution contained a condition: 'Full independence in the form of a federation of free democratic States in which the rights and interests of the *Musalmans* and other minorities are adequately and effectively safeguarded in the Constitution.' Pirzada, *Foundations of Pakistan*, 2:274.

52. It differed in language and stipulations from the League goal, however. It is interesting that the same sort of changes that were affecting the League in 1937 in Lucknow—goals and organization—took place seventeen years earlier in the Congress, at Nagpur in 1920. See S.C. Bose, 'The League is Un-Socialist' in Sheila McDonough, *Mohammed Ali Jinnah: Maker of Modern Pakistan* (Lexington, Mass.: D.C. Heath and Co., 1970), p. 20.

53. Pirzada, *Foundations of Pakistan*, 2:278-279.

54. R. Coupland, *The Indian Problem*, p. 183.

55. Pandey stresses the main part of the Muslim League strategy was communal propaganda such as the use of such slogans as 'Islam in danger' and 'Hinda *Raj.*' Pandey, *The Break-up of British India*, p. 148.

56. According to the 1932 League Constitution, Council members were elected for three years, nine-tenths by the provincial League and the remaining tenth by the League at its annual session. See *The Constitution and Rules of the All-India Muslim League* (Delhi: Jayyad Electric Press, 1932), pp. 3-4. The Sindhi members of the AIML Council in 1937, all with a Karachi residence, were: Kazi Khuda Baksh, (advocate), M.H. Gazdar, Hatim Alavi, K.S. Haji Fazul Elahi, (Honorary Magistrate), Sheikh Abdul Majid, Maulana Mohammed Siddique, Hakim Fateh Mohammed Sehwani, K.B. Mohammed Ayub Khuhro, Mir Bandeh Ali Talpur, and Syed Miran Mohammed Shah. MLA, *List of Members of the Council of the All-India Muslim League, 1937* (Delhi: National Printing and Publishing House, 1937), p. 12.

57. Mir Bandeh Ali became a minister and Khuhro and Shah both became Parliamentary secretaries. *D.G.*, 22 July 1937, p. 9.

58. MLA, *List of Members of the Council of the All-India Muslim League, 1938* (Delhi: National Printing and Publishing House, 1938), p. 12.

59. Khaliquzzaman mentions that Sindhi leaders were present but he does not give their names. Khaliquzzaman, *Pathway to Pakistan*, p. 170. In the proceedings of the session, no Sindhis are listed in attendance nor do any take part in the debate, Pirzada, *Foundations of Pakistan*, 2:273-281. It is likely Sindhi leaders stayed in Sindh because of a political crisis precipitated by the resignation of the Hindu minister and related matters. *D.G.*, 10 October 1937, p. 9 Ibid. 14 October 1937, p. 1.

60. MLA, Annual Session at Lucknow, 1937, (3), Vol. 179, Majid to secretary, AIML, 16 October 1937, p. 72.

61. Ibid., Alavi to Jinnah, 15 October 1937 pp. 53-4. The reference to Jawaharlal is clearly a reference to Nehru, the Congress president, and his January letter to Jinnah that the League did not really count as a political force in India; that there were only two parties, the British and Congress. See Gopal, *Indian Muslims,* p. 251. Actually Haroon had come out in support of Jinnah over the Nehru statement much before Alavi did. *D.G.,* 21 May 1937, p. 7.

62. MLA, Lucknow Session (1), Vol. 170, Gazdar to AIML Secretary, AIML, 29 September 1937, p. 19.

63. Gazdar listed the proposed legislation as follows: a) Land Alienation Bill, b) Money lending Bill (fixing rates of interest and conciliating agriculturalist debts), c) a Bill to increase rural educational facilities to raise Muslim literacy from four to fifty percent in ten years, and d) a Bill to give a fair share to Muslims in the services. Gazdar stated that 'we opposition members have introduced Bills for a) and b) and tabled a resolution for c).' The Bills were introduced in August. *PSLA,* Vol. 2, Book 16, 20 August 1937, pp. 31-2.

64. On 19 October 1937, it was announced the two parties would form a coalition to be called the Democratic Coalition Party. *D.G.,* 19 October 1937, p. 2. Earlier a memorandum of Allah Baksh, the SUP parliamentary leader, to Hidayatullah, had been published outlining the coalition which was to be basically a cooperative group effort to review needed legislation. *D.G.,* 10 October 1937, p. 2.; also Sayed, *Struggle for a New Sind,* p. 7.

65. Graham, in commenting on Hidayatullah's strategy, pinpointed the reason why he eventually fell from power: 'the weakness of Sir Ghulam is that he had no programme of his own and was prepared to accept anybody else's in receiving promises of support.' *IOR,* Linlithgow Papers, MSS Eur 125/93, Governor of Sind to Governor General, 19 March 1938, p. 36.

66. *D.G.,* 22 July 1937, p. 7.

67. *D.G.,* 24 July 1937, p. 4.

68. *D.G.,* 28 September 1937, p. 2.

69. Sayed claims the reason why Hidayatullah moved away from the Hindus was their increasing demands upon him in exchange for support. Sayed, *Struggle for a New Sind,* p. 7.

70. Mukhi Gobindram lost six to seven *lakhs* rupees (pound sterling 50,000) as a result of the plunge in price of American cotton. *D.G.,* 14, 16 October 1937, p. 1. Coupland, *The Indian Problem* p. 66.

71. *D.G.,* 5 November 1937, p. 1.

72. In choosing Wadhani, Hidayatullah ignored the Hindu Sabha choice, Nichaldas Vazirani, a forty-seven year old lawyer form Karachi. Sayed, *Struggle for a New Sind,* p. 8. *D.G.,* 22 March 1938, p. 1.

73. Sayed, *Struggle for a New Sind,* p. 8. Sayed states the Hindu money-lending and rural landed interests felt threatened by his Debt Conciliation Bill and Gazdar's Land Alienation Bill.
74. Bhojsingh had died in office at sixty-seven. *D.G.,* 17 February 1938, p. 1.
75. *D.G.,* 5 January 1938, p. 1.
76. The ministry was defeated in a routine rupee 1 cut motion on the budget. Hidayatullah told Graham the government lost because some of its supporters were absent for the roll call. *IOR,* Linlithgow Papers, MSS Eur F 125/93, Governor of Sind to the Governor-General, No. 24, 18 March 1938, p. 35. *D.G.,* 19 March 1938, p. 1.
77. Allah Baksh along with G.M. Sayed, M. Usman Soomro, Ghulam Nabi Shah, Rasul Bux Khan, Pir Ilahi Bux, Jaffer Khan Burdi and Khairshah all signed a letter to Mir Bandeh Ali, leader of the Coalition Party in the Sindh Assembly, stating 'We members of the United Party resign from your party as the programme and principles have not been realized.' *IOR,* Linlithgow Papers, MSS Eur F 125/93, Governor of Sindh to the Governor-General, No. 123, 22 March 22 1938, p. 49.
78. According to Graham, Allah Baksh was the son of a mason whose main business was contracting work for the PWD. Allah Baksh inherited the business, maintained good relations with senior PWD officials and then used his contacts to purchase non-barrage land near Shikarpur. IOR, Linlithgow Papers, MSS Eur F 125/93, Governor of Sindh to the Governor-General, No. 130, 25, 26 March 1938, p. 54.
79. Ibid.
80. Sayed also supported the overthrow of Hidayatullah 'due to my over-enthusiasm and eagerness for the speedy realization of my cherished dreams of a reconstructed Sind.' Syed, *Struggle for a New Sind,* pp. 9-10.
81. (The Hindu Sabha members were also known as Hindu independents).
82. IOR, Linlithgow Papers, MSS Eur F 125/93, Governor of Sind to Governor-General, No. 28-C, 19 March 1938, p. 39.
83. In a subsequent telegram Graham stated that 'Allah Baksh does not propose to take Congress in but hopes to have an arrangement with them that they will not join with Sir Ghulam, merely to wreck the new ministry.' Ibid., No. 30-C, p. 41.
84. Sayed, *Struggle for a New Sind,* pp. 12-13. *D.G.,* 22 March 1938, p. 1.
85. *D.G.,* 29 March 1938, p. 1.
86. Majid, ignoring his earlier rift with Jinnah, sent a telegram to the AIML president requesting affiliation for a Sindh League branch even before the Hidayatullah government fell. QAPC, F 516, Majid to Jinnah, 14 March 1938, p. 27.
87. *D.G.,* 30 March 1938, p. 1. Sayed, *Struggle for a New Sind,* p. 13.

88. The League began to organize at this time partly in response to the new Allah Baksh ministry, but chiefly in reaction to a recently initiated Congress 'mass Contact' campaign among the Sindhi peasantry. FR for March 1938 (2), Kilpalani to Thorne, 9 April 1938. *D.G.,* 1 February 1938, p. 9.

89. *D.G.,* 8 February 1938, p. 7. FR for February, 1938 (s), Kirpalani to Thorne, 7 March 1938. This meeting was also taken note of in Kirpalani's report for the second half of February 1938.

90. *D.G.,* 12 February 1938, p. 11.

91. *D.G.,* 2 April 1938, p. 11. The report also mentioned that Jinnah was also coming because he feared important office bearers would go into the Congress ranks with the recent formation of Allah Baksh's ministry.

92. FR for April 1938 (1), Kilpalani to Thorne, 20 April 1938.

93. *D.G.,* 10 April 1938, p. 9.

94. Actually Haroon had joined the League at the Lucknow session along with Sir Sikandar Hayat. Shortly after the session, he issued an appeal to Karachi Muslims to join the League and establish League branches. *D.G.,* 24 October 1937, p. 9.

95. *D.G.,* 24 April 1938, p. 9.

96. Haroon continued to support the SUP as late as June 1938. In a press statement he mentioned his confidence in Allah Baksh and warned that if the United Party was not strengthened, communal parties would develop in Sindh. He added that he supported the Muslim League at the 'Higher (all-India) political level but sees it gaining roots in Sind if the Hindus persist in communal ways and fail to join the United Party.' *D.G.,* 2 June 1938, p. 9.

97. *D.G.,* 22 April 1938, p. 7.

98. These two announced plans to enrol 10,000 members in one month and establish fifty branches of the League in the district. Ibid. p. 3. At the end of April, Khuhro challenged reports that the League had no support in Larkana. He claimed at the 18 April meeting in Rijn Bagh that twenty Municipal Councillors and Local Board members had signed the League pledge, half of whom were British titleholders and respected citizens. He attributed the League's appeal to the need to serve the masses with zeal, discipline and sacrifice and denied any communal inspiration based on such slogans as 'Islam in danger.' *D.G.,* 29 April 1938, p. 9.

99. FR for April 1938 (2), Kirpalani to Thorne, 9 May 1938. *D.G.,* 26 April 1938, p 10.

100. Apparently this anti-League demonstration was inspired by the *Jamiyyat al-ulama-i Hind. Sind Observer,* 4 May 1938, p. 2. The *Daily Gazette* claimed the demonstration was ministry instigated. *D.G.,* 5 May 1938, p. 2.

101. QAPC, F 16 Majid to Jinnah, 17 May 1938, pp. 109-110. In a press statement Majid claimed branches had been established in ten more villages in the area of Dhoro Noro. *D.G.,* 17 May 1938, p. 1.
102. QAPC, F 612, Haroon to Jinnah, 4 May 1938, p. 1.
103. Ibid. Several days later Haroon wrote again to say that he would try to persuade the Muslim groups in the Assembly to join the Muslim League but it 'will take a little time as they are afraid lest the other party may play their tricks and thereby again come into power.' QAPC, F 274, Haroon to Jinnah, 15 May 1938, p. 5. Majid identifies the two principal groups, as the Hidayatullah and Allah Baksh factions. QAPC, F 16, Majid to Jinnah, 17 May 1938, pp. 109-110.
104. The two leaders also differed over how to go about organizing the League in Sindh. Majid's idea to get money and workers for the League was to compile a list of 1,000 sympathizers, each to contribute ten rupees a year. Haroon thought this was 'impractical' and suggested an alternate scheme of writing to friends around the province and requesting their voluntary help. He felt volunteers were more useful than paid workers, at least in getting the League office established and functioning. A second difference, Haroon felt it imperative to establish a Karachi office first and then organize the *mofussil.* Majid had set to work immediately organizing in the rural areas. QAPC, F 274, Haroon to Majid, 18 June 1938, Majid to Jinnah, 17 May 1938, pp. 109-110.
105. This left only Dadu district where the League had no branches. Sindh's Chief Secretary, Bhat, stated that League branches were being formed 'with a view to counteract the Congress propaganda.' FR for May 1938 (2), Bhat to Thorne, 10 June 1938.
106. *D.G.,* 12 July 1938, p. 2.
107. Hidayatullah had sent a telegram wishing success to the 1937 Lucknow session and in June 1938, he signed a pledge with Majid revealing his pro-League stand. In their joint statement, Hidayatullah and Majid pledged, on behalf of their respective backers, their support for Allah Baksh's ministry if, in turn, Allah Baksh and his group promised to support the AIML's programme and form 'one solid and united' Muslim League party in the Sindh Assembly. QAPC, F 16, handwritten and signed pledge, dated 7 June 1938, p. 129.
108. Pathan, a student at Aligarh at the time, attributed his organizational inspiration to Jinnah who stressed in an Aligarh speech the need to establish the League in the Muslim majority provinces. Interview with Agha Ghulam Nabi Pathan, Karachi, 26 February 1976.
109. FR for July 1938 (2), Bhat to Thorne, 4 August 1938.
110. IOR, Linlithgow Papers, MSS Eur F 125/93, Governor of Sind to Governor General, No. 321, 14 July 1938, p. 122. *D.G.,* 7 July 1938, p. 1.

111. The terms were elaborated in the Niemeyer Report. IOR Linlithgow Papers, MSS Eur F 125/93, Linlithgow to Graham, No. 3, 2 February 1938, p. 3.

112. IOR, Linlithgow Papers, MSS Eur F 125/93, Graham to Lord Brabourne, No. 305, 6 July 1938, p. 115.

113. *D.G.*, 14 July 1938, p. 1; 15 July 1938, p. 1; 17 July 1938.

114. IOR, Linlithgow Papers, MSS Eur F 125/93, Governor of Sind to Governor General, No. 321, 14 July 1938, p. 122.

115. Sayed, *Struggle for a New Sind,* p. 17.

116. The Sindh Congress initially favoured an anti-enhancement position contingent upon the approval of the All-India Congress leadership. Instead, the Congress high command forced the Sindh Congress to support enhancement, an outcome which served to strengthen Allah Baksh's political position. *D.G.,* 19 August 1938, p. 1.

117. Sayed, *Struggle for a New Sind,* pp. 22-23.

118. Ibid., p. 23.

119. Following Miran Mohammed Shah's election to the speakership, Sayed became the informal leader of the *Saiyid* bloc in the Assembly which included Khair Shah and Mohammad Ali Shah of Nawabshah district and Ghulam Hyder Shah of Thar Parker. Interview with G.M. Sayed, Sann, 18 February 1976.

120. Graham maintained this alliance was part of Sir Ghulam's plan to get revenge on Allah Baksh. IOR, Linlithgow Papers, Mss Eur F 125/93, Graham to Brabourne, No. 306, 17 July 1938, p. 116a.

121. PDH, Haroon to the Raja of Mahmudabad and Nawab Ismail Khan, 23 August 1938.

122. Haroon was careful to indicate to Jinnah the growing strength of the League in the Assembly as Jinnah had earlier made it known that he would only visit Sindh if the League had secured a large measure of Assembly support. QAPC, F 1098, Haroon to Jinnah, 2 August 1938, p. 57; Ibid. F 1129, Haroon to Jinnah, 25 August 1938 p. 186; Ibid., Haroon to Jinnah, 29 August 1938, p. 197.

5

THE SINDH PROVINCIAL MUSLIM LEAGUE CONFERENCE, 1938

The pro-League leadership in Sindh looked forward to the October Muslim League conference in Karachi with great anticipation. They were confident that the conference, blessed with the presence of the all-India Muslim leaders, would be able to break Allah Baksh's stranglehold on power and they, in return for their support for and allegiance to the League, would be rewarded the political prizes of power and office.

In preparation for the Karachi conference, the focus of League organizing and canvassing shifted from the rural areas to the urban centres, particularly Karachi. During the month of September, 1938, a number of meetings were held in various parts of Karachi to enlist Muslim support for the League. On 1 September, a meeting was held in Saddar, the central market and business area, and 2,000 Muslims attended.[1] Abdullah Haroon spoke, encouraging the Muslims to attend, mentioning the up coming conference, and warning them they may have to practice *satyagraha* to get their grievances redressed. Pir Ali Mohammed Rashidi, a recent addition to the League forces,[2] also spoke, discussing the Land Alienation and Debt Conciliation Bills and charged that the ministry had done nothing to implement these measures to benefit the Muslim masses. Majid also gave a speech denouncing the exploitative and divisive tactics the Congress and Hindu parties used against the Muslims. Before the meeting ended, a branch was formed and office-bearers were elected.

Other meetings were subsequently held in other parts of Karachi. On 8 September, a large meeting was held at Nawabad, presided over by Abdullah Haroon and the same day 2,500 Muslims attended a meeting at Jhuna Market where Majid presided and Rashidi and Yusuf Haroon, Sir Abdullah's eldest son, spoke.[3] The largest gathering of these various meetings was held four days later in Karachi when 3,000 met to hear Yusuf Haroon and Rashidi issue attacks on the Congress and the Sindh ministry.[4] At a meeting on the 14th, Yusuf Haroon distorted history in order to enhance the League's appeal; he claimed the Muslim League had conceived of Sindh's separation long before Sindhis thought of the idea and it was solely through the League's efforts that separation was achieved.[5] His father also spoke and, in alluding to the Land Alienation and Debt Conciliation Bills, called on the Sindh ministry to pass such bills as passed by Congress ministries.[6]

These series of meetings held as part of the League's new urban-oriented strategy, broadened the scope of the League's organizational focus and encompassed new forces which brought pressure to bear on its president, Sheikh Abdul Majid. Earlier, Majid, on his own initiative, had begun to organize the League, devoting his energies to establishing as many branches as possible in the rural sector. In his view, the League could only become a force in Sindhi politics if it developed a strong rural mass base. Majid's success was limited, however; by late August he had managed to establish only fifty branches though he remained optimistic that the figure could reach 100 in a month's time. But he conceded in a letter to Jinnah 'progress is slow (owing) to a lack of funds and a dearth of workers.'[7] Later, in the same letter, Majid made clear his realization that his own leadership role was in eclipse and that Abdullah Haroon, a man more in tune with recent developments, would soon take over the League leadership.[8] It was likely Haroon actively sought the League presidency[9] but even had he not, it would have come to him in natural course. Haroon was favoured to become League president by several factors including the recent emphasis on League urban organization, the selection of Karachi as a site for the conference, and the planned attendance of the leading lights of Muslim India, including Jinnah. As a resident of Karachi, and particularly as a *Memon* businessman, Haroon was in a position to undertake the League's organization and to re-establish the Leagues's ties with its former supporters in the Muslim trading castes, the *Bohras, Memons* and *Khojas*.[10] As a wealthy sugar merchant, his contributions would help ensure the success of the coming conference, and as a member of the Central Legislative Assembly in Delhi, and of the recently formed working committee of the All-India Muslim League[11], he knew many of the leading Muslims of India on a personal basis and would have no trouble in inviting them. The clearest sign that Haroon was to become the new League president in Sindh was his selection as chairman of the Reception committee established to welcome the delegates to the conference.[12]

The conference, which was to last four days, opened in Karachi on 8 October amidst 'scenes of great enthusiasm.'[13] Jinnah, the star attraction of the conference, had arrived in Karachi by special train the previous day, accompanied by Mir Ghulam Ali Khan Talpur, a scion of the former ruling family of Sindh, the Talpurs.[14] The League president was greeted at the Karachi railway station by Abdullah Haroon, Chairman of the Reception Committee, in a manner 'befitting a king.[15] Mr Jinnah was driven through the streets from the station in an open conveyance, in a three mile long procession behind a contingent of volunteer National Guards, to the accompaniment of bands playing rousing welcome music.[16]

Other distinguished leaders of Muslim India who attended the conference included Mr Fazlul Haq, premier of Bengal, Sir Sikandar Hayat, premier of the Punjab, and the venerable old *Khilafat* leader, *Maulana* Shaukat Ali. The *Raja* of Mahmudabad, an important financial backer of the League, *Nawabzada* Liaquat Ali Khan, one of the League's chief organizers, Sir Currimbhoy Ibrahim and *Maulana* Hamid Badayum also graced the conference with their presence.[17]

The conference began on a high note and the excitement did not subside for the session's full duration. The meetings, which began at eight o'clock in the evening often continued until two o'clock in the morning, and in the estimation of the League's

General Secretary, A.M. Rashidi, over 20,000 delegates attended the conference.[18] Rashidi has also stated that this conference 'for its grandeur, majesty and attendance was never equalled in the history of the Muslim League movement.'[19]

Sir Abdullah Haroon, opening the conference with his welcome address, began his speech with a reference to the all-India issue of finding an amicable Hindu-Muslim political settlement. He stated that the efforts over the past fifteen years by prominent Muslim leaders to achieve a settlement had been constantly frustrated by the failure of the Hindus to grant adequate safeguards and protection for minority interests. He referred to the anti-Muslim policies of Congress governments, and warned that we 'have nearly arrived at the parting of the ways' and that if no agreement is reached soon 'it will be impossible to save India from being divided into Hindu-India and Muslim-India both placed under separate federations.'[20]

Haroon continued his theme of Congress oppression and exploitation of Muslims, but in the second and longer part of his speech he switched his focus to the Sindh political situation. He charged that the Congress party had connived with the Hindu Mahasabha to deprive Sindhi Muslims of a ministry in which the majority Sindhi community could place its confidence.[21] Haroon's harsh words indicated he felt it was becoming necessary for the Muslim leadership to adopt a more militant posture with regard to an agreement between the Hindu and Muslim communities, an attitude that foreshadowed the conference's most significant resolution. The thrust of Haroon's speech was that Indian Muslims must set for themselves a new policy and a new goal. The old policy of pursuing safeguards and seeking accommodation with the Hindus was bankrupt; Muslims must boldly break away on their own and discover their own destiny.

In his presidential address, Jinnah ignored the challenge implicit in Haroon's remarks and stuck to the milder and safer themes he had voiced again and again since Lucknow—Muslim unity and Congress oppression.[22] He praised the recently divided Sindhi Muslims for the 'wonderful public spirit, solidarity and unity' they were demonstrating at the conference and predicted 'with proper organization if you mobilize and harness your powers there is nothing to prevent the Muslim League of your province from assuming the reins of Government.'[23] But Jinnah warned the Sindhi Muslims that, in addition to their responsibility for the welfare and progress of Sindh, they faced a 'far graver task: to guard yourself in the All-India Muslim struggle against the various forces which are out to destroy and divide *Mussalmans* by means of corruption and dishonest propaganda.'[24] Finally, Jinnah appealed to them to stand solid behind the All-India Muslim League...'the only authoritative organization of the *Mussalmans* of India.'[25] For the remainder of his speech, Jinnah reverted to the all-India level of politics, and focused his remarks on the attitudes and behaviour of Congress which he attacked for its 'arrogance, opportunism and oppression.'

Following his speech, Jinnah invited the Bengal and Punjab premiers to speak. Fazlul Haq, a rousing orator, spoke first, and strongly admonished the Muslims to unite under the League banner and form the first League ministry in India.[26] Sir Sikandar Hayat followed Haq, and spoke in the same vein as Jinnah, and denounced Congress policy. Most of the outside speakers echoed Jinnah's sentiments in their remarks, while the Sindhi speakers spoke mainly about the Sindh political situation and attacked the ministry in strong terms.[27]

During the last three night sessions, the conference adopted a series of resolutions which addressed all-India as well as Sindhi issues.[28] Several of the more important all-India resolutions focused on such issues as: the cancellation of the mandate and full independence for Palestine, efforts to organize the League nation-wide, socio-economic means to uplift the Muslim community, and greater facilities for Muslims on pilgrimage.[29]

Of all the resolutions of an all-India nature, however, the one of greatest significance—a veritable landmark resolution—was Resolution No. 5 which was entitled 'Communal Settlement.'[30] This was a lengthy resolution which began by reiterating the familiar litany of Muslim woes: Congress tyranny in Muslim minority provinces. But the resolution added an important new note; a paragraph was included which enlarged the scope of Congress misrule to take in the Muslim majority provinces as well. Thus, significantly, Congress became a common symbol of oppression for Muslims in both minority and majority provinces and, furthermore, Congress as the object of their combined opposition, played the ironic role of bringing the two blocs of Muslim provinces together on one platform.[31]

Inspired by a new sense of common purpose and unity within the Indian Muslim community, the resolution's authors decided to issue a bold claim that India in reality was not one nation but two, one Hindu and one Muslim. This assertion was included in the resolution to strengthen the demand that the League devise a new constitution for India. The last part of the resolution read:

> This Conferences considers it absolutely essential in the interests of an abiding peace of the vast Indian subcontinent and in the interests of unhampered cultural development, the economic and social betterment, and political self-determination of the two nations known as Hindus and Muslims to recommend to the All-India Muslim League to review and revise the entire question of what should be the suitable constitution for India.'[32]

The historical significance of this resolution was that it represented the first time a Muslim organization had supported a resolution that viewed India as two, separate, Hindu and Muslim nations.[33] Though the language was impressive, this resolution was clearly a precursor to the historic Lahore Resolution of 1940 which firmly established Pakistan as the League's ultimate goal.

Resolution No. 5 was significant in another way for it provided further evidence of an increasingly sophisticated political outlook on the part of the League-minded Sindhi leadership among whom were the resolution's primary authors.[34] The political astuteness of the authors was revealed in their intention that the resolution serve a dual purpose of satisfying the All-India League's need for a new national goal, and the

Sindhi Leaguer's interest in replacing the Allah Baksh ministry.[35] Thus, by integrating in one resolution issues of national as well as provincial concerns, the Sindhi supporters of the resolution demonstrated their growing political maturity. In addition, their sponsorship of the resolution reflected a shift in their thinking from a sole preoccupation with Sindhi affairs to a broader view that incorporated considerations of all-India importance as well.

That the impetus for this resolution came from the League's provincial leaders—non-Sindhi[36] as well as Sindhi—was clear; it was certainly not, as one scholar has claimed 'almost surely the brainchild of Mr Jinnah.'[37] An early indication of Jinnah's reaction to Resolution No. 5 was provided in his presidential address in which he deliberately avoided any mention of the separate, religious-based Indian federations cited by the more radically-inclined Haroon. Initially, Jinnah stood opposed to the passage of the resolution, but after considerable discussion, he was persuaded to allow it to pass.[38] The League president changed his mind largely because he realized the resolution's potential to serve as a trial balloon to measure Indian public opinion. If the Hindus remained intransigent, however, and the Muslims embraced the two-nation theory, then, Jinnah reasoned, the solution should be embodied in League policy but, for the time being, he decided to withhold his support.[39]

Resolution No. 5 overshadowed the other resolutions at the conference and obscured momentarily the other significant resolutions among them.[40] In keeping with the purpose of the conference and reflecting its venue, numerous resolutions were passed on pertinent Sindhi issues, and of these the two most important ones were passed during the last night of the conference.[41] The first resolution criticized the Sindh Governor's refusal to convene a special session of the Assembly, and the second expressed the conference's no-confidence in the ministry as it was maintained contrary to the wishes of the overwhelming majority of Muslim members in the Assembly.[42]

These two strongly worded resolutions came at one stage in a negotiation process begun at the beginning of the conference to establish a Muslim League ministry in Sindh. Toward this end,

Jinnah held a meeting on 9 October with all of the important Sindhi Muslim leaders, including the premier, Allah Baksh, at which it was decided to form a Muslim League party in the Assembly as a preliminary step. It was also announced at the meeting that 'in order to facilitate the formation of a new ministry, the present Muslim ministers have agreed to tender their resignations (which) would be submitted to the Governor simultaneously with the proposal of the leaders of the Muslim League party to constitute a new ministry.'[43] The decisions of this meeting were written down and the document was signed by the following leaders: Hidayatullah, G.M. Sayed, Mir Bandeh Ali, Allah Baksh, Pir Illahi Baksh and Sheikh Abdul Majid.

In the end, a Muslim League Assembly party was formed but the hopes of the League leaders in forming a League ministry in Sindh did not come to fruition.[44] Allah Baksh ended those hopes when he and his backers withdrew their support for the 9 October agreement. In a 14 October press statement, Jinnah accused Allah Baksh of betraying the agreement and charged that he had done so, firstly, because the premier had been informed that Congress was willing to reconsider the possibility of supporting his ministry[45] and, secondly, because Allah Baksh had insisted on continuing as prime minister if a League cabinet was formed.

In replying to Jinnah's charges, Allah Baksh denied that either forthcoming Congress support or his continuation as premier had influenced his action. He based his explanation for ending the 9 October agreement on his party's two-fold policy of giving support to the AIML on matters of all-India importance, but maintaining freedom from League control in provincial affairs which, Allah Baksh asserted, precluded membership in a Muslim League Assembly party.[46]

The premier's denials, however, were mostly mere face-saving tactics.[47] Even if he did believe sincerely in a posture of provincial independence with regard to the League, Jinnah posed no threat to Allah Baksh's realization of such a policy.[48] Commenting later on why he had refused to join the League, Allah Baksh gave additional reasons. On two different occasions[49] he stressed his antipathy for communal organizations such as the League, and at a third time he pointed to the probable impermanence of a League ministry resulting from the League's predilection for factionalism.[50] But a reason which the premier failed to give which was most likely the key reason—one cited by Jinnah—was that Allah Baksh spurned the League in order to stay in office. In addition to Jinnah, several of the Sindhi Leaguers believed Allah Baksh's rejection of the League was based on his hunger for power, but more significantly this was also the conclusion of the impartial Judge Weston in 1940.[51]

Allah Baksh's frustration of the League goal of establishing its own ministry in Sindh left Jinnah a disappointed man. His high hopes so clearly expressed in his presidential address had not become a reality. To Jinnah's mind, it was the old problem of an absence of unity and discipline among the Muslim leaders in Sindh, particularly the Muslims in the Assembly. If they had all stood together, united beneath the League banner, Allah Baksh would not have been able to survive as premier and in his place a Muslim League ministry could have been ushered in.

By the end of the conference, Jinnah realized it had been premature to try and set up a League ministry in Sindh. The ground had not been prepared and the conditions were not right; Sindhi Muslims were not ready for the sudden appearance of an outside party demanding their immediate allegiance. It would now be necessary, Jinnah reasoned, to build up the League gradually in Sindh through the network of a party organization. Once a firmly rooted, tightly-knit organization had been implanted in Sindh, then it would be possible to establish an effective, stable League ministry. Jinnah voiced this change in strategy from ministry formation to party organization in his concluding speech:

> I attach more importance to outside work than inside legislatures. The foundation of solid work is outside legislatures. The making and breaking of ministries is not the issue before us...We have

yet to organize ourselves. I am confident that within four years
there will be no organization more powerful among the Muslims.[52]

In order to capitalize on the momentum generated by the
Karachi conference, Jinnah wasted no time in appointing a
League organizing committee to spearhead efforts to spread a
League network throughout Sindh. Within a week of the
conference's conclusion he had appointed Abdullah Haroon,
chairman, and Abdul Majid, General Secretary of this
committee.[53] One of Haroon's first steps was to try and establish
immediately a close working relationship between the League
Assembly party and the League party organization. In a
confidential letter to the leader of the League Assembly party,
Hidayatullah,[54] Haroon outlined ways in which the two arms of
the League could cement their partnership.[55] It may appear
surprising that Haroon should go back so soon on Jinnah's clear
admonishments to shirk Assembly politics and concentrate on
building up the League organization.[56] But Haroon was simply
acting in accord with the realities of Sindhi Muslim politics: all
of the Muslims with power and influence (excluding himself)
were in the Sindh Assembly; therefore, the only way for the
League to become a force in Sindh was for the League
organization to come to terms with the MSLA. Haroon realized
the typical MSLA member cared little for the party organization,
but he hoped the MSLA could be kept responsible to the League
organization through popular pressure on a League-inspired
legislative programme.[57]

After the conference's conclusion, Jinnah undertook a tour
into Sindh's interior to establish League branches and popularize
the League cause among the rural masses. Upon returning to
Karachi, Jinnah stated he was pleased with his tour and that
Sindhi Muslims were now 'awakened.'[58] Furthermore, he warned
the League's opponents that they 'will come to regret it because
soon the League will be well organized.' He reiterated once
again that ministry formation was not 'an acid test in our
struggle' and declared that his main purpose 'to organize
Muslims under the League banner throughout Sindh' had been

accomplished. 'My mission has succeeded beyond expectations and I see a bright future for Sindh.'

Subsequent developments, however, were to prove Jinnah's optimism premature. No sooner had Jinnah left Sindh than signs of trouble began to appear within the League organization. In the absence of Jinnah's disciplining presence, personal ambitions as well as petty jealousies began to emerge again, and splits and factions began to appear. For example, in Larkana, where Jinnah visited on his tour, those within the League fold began to squabble among themselves. Mohammed Ayub Khuhro and Ali Gohar Lahori sided with each other against their League colleague, Nabi Baksh Bhutto. They criticized Bhutto at a local League meeting for voting to allow Pir Illahi Baksh, the Revenue Minister, known for his 'mean and malicious attacks on Mr Jinnah' to present an address in Larkana.[59] The real intent of Khuhro and Lahori was quite different. They viewed Bhutto's family, long the most powerful in the district, as a threat to their political ambitions and they sought by their efforts to reduce the Bhuttos' influence.[60]

Another incident which clearly reflected the struggles for personal power within the Sindh League leadership was the formal election for party office-bearers, in particular the contest for president.[61] The two candidates were Majid and Haroon. Hidayatullah and his supporters sided with Majid, seeing him as malleable and fearing Haroon's securing a potential rival power base.[62] Leading the Haroon faction was Khuhro, who supported Haroon for reasons of his money and respect but more importantly because he viewed Haroon's election as favourable to his own political aspirations.[63] According to one account, the vote was taken and Majid won by a margin of one vote.[64] A commotion ensued amidst demands for a recount. Khuhro, who occupied the chair, and who had earlier ruled out secret balloting procedures,[65] granted a second vote. In the meantime, a new Haroon voter was brought in to make the second vote a tie, which was then broken by Khuhro's casting the deciding vote in Haroon's favour.[66] Thus, the first election for the Sindh League president was conducted in an atmosphere of intrigue[67] and factional strife with a patent disregard for democratic practices. The rapid substitution by Sindh Muslim leaders of their own brand of self-serving, power-seeking politics for Jinnah's version of principled and constrained politics bode ill for the future prospects of a strong, united and flourishing Muslim League organization in Sindh. These prospects became increasingly remote in the days and weeks ahead as support for the League began to weaken even further. This tendency was shown first by the League MSLA, who began to feel the League was no longer an important political force when it failed to secure a League ministry. Also, some of them had developed, in response to sentiments of Sindhi patriotism, some respect for Allah Baksh for his defiant stance in confronting an all-India leader of the stature of Jinnah.[68]

The downturn in League fortunes caused by its unsuccessful efforts to form a ministry affected even Haroon, the confident and outspoken party leader. The contradictions in his post-conference statements suggested Haroon's uncertainty about League policy[69] but such restraints did nothing to dampen his spirit of enthusiasm for the League. Haroon viewed the failed ministry effort merely as a temporary setback for the League that would soon be obscured by the imminent emergence of the Party as a dominant and formidable political force in Sindh as well as in India. In late October, Haroon issued a statement proclaiming that within a fortnight the 'League will be strong enough to bury all competing organizations.'[70] The following month he announced he was giving practical shape to the bold ideas he had enunciated at the Karachi conference, and that soon details of his two-federation scheme for India would be released to the press.[71] Haroon's absorption with the national affairs of the League were a result of his own elevation to the top leadership of the League, and his confidence in the League's ability to carry out the best interests of the Indian Muslim community.

Haroon's involvement with the League's all-India matters did not preclude his taking an interest in developments in his own province. In fact, in December 1938, he allowed local considerations to take precedence over national concerns. He wrote to Jinnah that he was cancelling plans to attend the League meetings in Patna in order to stay in Sindh and await the outcome of the most recent 'Ministerial tangle.'[72] He mentioned the Assembly was scheduled to meet in early January and 'there is every likelihood of the Ministry crumbling.' He said he would notify Jinnah at the appropriate time and Jinnah 'could come down to Sindh to settle up the details for the formation of a new ministry.'

League optimism once again proved premature. The League forces planned to introduce a no-confidence motion in the Assembly in the hope that they could force Allah Baksh's government out of office. The Leaguers were aware their strength was waning, including rumours that Hidayatullah intended to resign from the League, but they chose to ignore these warning signals.[73] In reality, there was substantial truth to the rumours about Hidayatullah. Governor Graham, whose December return from home leave facilitated the early calling of the January session, noted in letters to Linlithgow that Allah Baksh and Hidayatullah were carrying on negotiations with the purpose of bringing the latter into the ministry.[74] Hidayatullah's resignation did finally come in the form of a letter to the Sindh League secretary.[75]

Hidayatullah's defection was a severe blow to the political fortunes of the League. His departure removed not only his support but also that of his eleven supporters, reducing the League's once sizable numbers to a small group of seven.[76] Thus, the outcome of the no-confidence motion in the Assembly was determined even before it was moved on 12 January; Allah Baksh's government survived it easily and his ministry continued in power.[77] The Muslim League, weakened by defections and humiliated in its latest confrontation with Allah Baksh's ministry, retreated into the opposition to concentrate on supporting agrarian reform measures in the Assembly and strengthening its grass roots organization.[78] It would bide its time until conditions were once again ripe to mount a challenge to Allah Baksh's government.

The Sindh Provincial Muslim League Conference held in Karachi in October 1938, signified, briefly, a high point in the political evolution as well as the political destiny of the League-minded Sindhi Muslim leadership. During the resolutions phase of the conference, they were successful in achieving a wide measure of unity, particularly in support of Resolution No. 5, the conference's most important resolution. Their role in the drafting and passage of this key resolution indicated a broadening of their political outlook to encompass compelling provincial as well as national issues which, in turn, represented a restoration of some balance to province-centre relations.

The Sindh Leaguers maintained their solidarity following the conference and were almost successful in their efforts with Jinnah to bring Allah Baksh into the League fold and establish a full-fledged League ministry. But the talks ended in failure as a result of partly ideological, but largely personal considerations among the Sindhi Muslim leadership. Following the departure of Jinnah's disciplining presence, the unity and solidarity the Sindh Leaguers had achieved at the conference began to dissolve and they reverted to their old ways as reflected in the election for a Sindh League president. Though Sindh's Muslim League leaders were unable at this stage to dislodge the premier from power, they did not dismiss the unseating of Allah Baksh from their list of primary objectives. They simply looked for another opportunity to try again.

NOTES

1. *D.G.,* 2 September 1938, p. 2.
2. Rashidi had defected from Allah Baksh's side with G.M. Sayed. Interview with Rashidi, Islamabad, 3 June 1975; also Shafi, *Haji Sir Abdoola Haroon,* p. 138.
3. Jhuna Market is the jewellery bazaar in Karachi where most of the shopkeepers are *Bohras* or one of the other Muslim trading castes.
4. *D.G.,* 13 September 1938, p. 7.
5. *D.G.,* 17 September 1938, p. 7.
6. Ibid.

7. QAPC, F 1095, Majid to Jinnah, 23 August 1938, p. 514.
8. Ibid., Majid felt a tinge of pride and resentment at the prospect of Haroon's leadership: '(I am) prepared to make room for him even at the cost of the movement.' Majid did add however, that Haroon's money would benefit the League. But, most of the workers opposed his leaving the movement so he decided to 'work as an ordinary member.'
9. An indication was a movement away from all-India issues in his statements, to strictly Sindhi issues in an effort to align himself more closely with the increasing League-minded public opinion in Sindh. *D.G.*, 21 May 1938, p. 7. *D.G.*, 2 September 1938, p. 2.
10. Merchants from these communities were important financial contributors to the League; they numbered half of the forty-two large contributors (Rupees 50-Rupees 500) to the Karachi conference. Pir Ali Mohammed Rashidi, *Report of the General Secretary of the First Sind Provincial Muslim League Conference, 8 to 12 October 1938*, pp. 21-22. MLA, Sind Provincial League Conference, 1938, Vol. 242, p. 9. (Hereinafter Rashidi's *Report* cited as *SPML Conference Report*).
11. See Khaliquzzaman, *Pathway to Pakistan*, p. 192. Majid was the other member from Sindh; there were twenty-two in all.
12. *D.G.*, 3 September 1938, p. 9.
13. FR for October 1938 (1), Bhat to Thorne, 18 October 1938.
14. *D.G.*, 8 October 1938, p. 1.
15. MLA, *SPML Conference Report*, Vol. 242, Pir Ali Mohammed Rashidi, *Report of the General Secretary of the First Sind Provincial Muslim League Conference, 1928*, p. 9.
16. *D.G.*, 8 October 1928, p. 1. Even the anti-League newspaper, the *Sind Observor* described the reception as one 'a prince might well envy,' quoted in Sayed, *Struggle for a New Sind*, p. 24.
17. Nripendra Nath Mitra, ed., *The Indian Annual Register, 1938*, 2 vols. (Calcutta: The Annual Register Office, 1939), 2:352.
18. *SPML Conference Report*, p. 22. The *Daily Gazette's* estimate of those in attendance was more conservative—10,000. *D.G.*, 19 October 1938, p. 1.
19. Interview with Pir Ali Mohammad Rashidi, Islamabad, 3 June 1975.
20. Mitra, *Indian Annual Register 1938*, 2:352.
21. Ibid.
22. FR for October 1938 (1), Bhat to Thorne, 18 October 1938, Mitra, *Indian Annual Register 1938*, 2:353-34, *D.G.*, 9 October 1938, p. 3.
23. Ibid.
24. Ibid.
25. Ibid. Jinnah defended the League as a national and progressive body and blamed the Congress press for falsely propagating the image of a reactionary League.
26. *D.G.*, 9 October 1938, p. 2. Haq exhorted them to put away selfishness; they could not all be leaders, they should choose one and unite behind

him. He contrasted Orissa with Sindh where the government was functioning smoothly. Only in Sindh, Haq claimed, did Muslims 'bicker and get nowhere.'

27. FR for October 1938 (1), Bhat to Thorne, 18 October 1938.

28. The conference passed twenty-one resolutions in all; ten with an all-India theme and eleven with a Sindhi theme. *SPML Conference Report,* p. 22ff. As Rashidi's *Report* represented the official version of the Conference proceedings, his account is accepted as authentic. Other sources, however, give different resolution totals. The *Daily Gazette* reported seventeen resolutions in all and, later, the Sindh League's secretary listed only twelve. *D.G.,* 11 October 1939, p. 2. Ibid., 12 October 1939, p. 2, Ibid., 13 October 1939, p. 2, MLA, SPML Conference 1938, Vol. 242, Khalique to Liaquat Ali Khan, 4 March 1939, p. 10.

29. Ibid.

30. For the full text of the resolution as it was passed in its final form see Ahmad, *Historic Documents,* pp. 255-58.

31. Interview with Rashidi, Islamabad, 11 September 1975.

32. Ahmad, *Historic Documents,* pp. 255-258. Early in the conference a more radical version of this final part of the resolution was introduced but it was overruled as too extreme in its language. See the *Statesman* and *The Star of India* for 11 October 1938, also, S.R. Mehrotra, 'The Congress and the Partition of India,' and Z.H. Zaidi, 'Aspects of the Development of Muslim League Policy, 1937-1947,' In C.H. Philips and M. Wainwright, eds., *The Partition of India, Policies and Perspectives, 1935-1947* (London: George Allen and Unwin, 1970), pp. 206-261.

33. This idea had been broached before, most notably by Sir Muhammad Iqbal in his 1930 League presidential address but this was the first time an official meeting of Indian Muslims had endorsed the concept of a two-nation India. See Pirzada, *Foundations of Pakistan,* 2:153.

34. Majid and Ali Mohammed Rashidi wrote the resolution but Haroon had a close hand in its drafting as well. Interview with M.A. Khuhro, Islamabad, 24 December 1976.

35. For support for this view, see V.V. Nagarhar, *Genesis of Pakistan* (Delhi: Allied Publishers, 1975), p. 283.

36. Of the five instrumental in the resolution's passage, three came from provinces other than Sindh (one each from the Punjab, the United Provinces and the Central Provinces). *SPML Conference Report,* p. 14.

37. Mary Louise Decker, 'The All-India Muslim League, 1906-1047' (Ph.D. Dissertation, Harvard University, 1957), p. 307.

38. Interview with Pir Hissamuddin Rashidi, Karachi, 30 September 1975. Pir Hissamuddin is Ali Mohammed Rashidi's brother and attended the Karachi conference. Jinnah's reservations stemmed from his fear that the resolution's implicit divisiveness would destroy any remaining prospects for the Hindu-Muslim settlement he still hoped for. Interview with

Khuhro, Karachi, 23 January 1976. See also, Saiyid, *Jinnah,* p. 216. Jinnah also decided to allow the resolution's passage because he viewed the Karachi conference as only a provincial conference, and thus its resolutions were not tantament to establishing League policy as were the resolutions passed at League Annual Sessions. Interview with Yusuf Haroon, New York City, 26 May 1976. Yusuf is Abdullah Haroon's eldest son and was in attendance at the Karachi conference.

39. Interview with Khuhro, Karachi, 23 January 1976.

40. In an interview with Rashidi, Haroon referred to the Hindu Press in Punjab criticizing the Karachi resolution and labelling it a demand for Pakistan. He used this as an ironic example of how the Hindu press, in the absence of a Muslim press, would popularize Muslim goals and thus accomplish the Muslim's task for them. Shafi, *Haji Sir Abdoola Haroon,* p. 135.

41. Other resolutions on Sindh dealt with the liquidation of the Sukkur Barrage debt, more holdiays to mark Muslim festivities, Muslim control of the Sukkur *Manzilgah* mosque, agrarian reform bills to protect Muslims, and repeal of the oppressive Sindh Frontier Regulation. *SPML Conference Report,* pp. 14ff.

42. Mitra, *Indian Annual Register 1938,* 2:357. Hidayatullah and Gazdar had both taken the initiative before the conference convened to try and get a special Assembly convened. In their correspondence with the Governor, the reason they gave was that prolonged intervals between sessions violated the spirit of the 1935 reforms but the real reason was that the Muslim forces hoped to bring Allah Baksh's government down by means of a no-confidence vote. *D.G.,* 24 September 1938, p. 9. Ibid., 1 October 1938, p. 9. IOR, Linlithgow Papers, MSS Eur F 125/94, Garrett to Brabourne, No. 392, 19 September 1938, p. 11. Garrett was acting Sindh Governor and Brabourne was acting Viceroy while Graham and Linlithgow were on leave.

43. QAPC, F 134. Jinnah's notes of the 9 October meeting pp. 35-41. Other decisions taken at the meeting included turning over the still unsettled assessment question to Sir Sikandar for his 'final' proposal, and selecting a party leader and new ministers by a unanimous party vote, failing which Jinnah's nominations would be accepted as final. The terms of the 9 October agreement also appeared in the *Daily Gazette, D.G.,* 14 October 1938, p. 2.

44. On 12 October, Jinnah announced that twenty-seven members of the Assembly had signed the League pledge and accepted its programme and policy. The seven who refused to join were Allah Baksh and his supporters. *D.G.,* 13 October 1938, p. 2, Mitra *India Annual Register,* 1938, 2:357.

45. *D.G.,* 14 October 1938, p. 2. Jinnah was informed of the Congress development by Hatim Alavi who in turn heard of it from the C.I.D.

(Criminal Investigation Department). QAPC, F 599, Alavi to Jinnah, 12 October 1938, p. 1.
46. *D.G.*, 14 October 1938, p. 2.
47. Garrett, the acting Sindh Governor, informed Brabourne of Allah Baksh's interest in Congress support. IOR, Linlithgow Papers, MSS Eur F 125/94 Garrett to Brabourne, No. 11, 12 October 1938, p. 18.
48. In an interview with Garrett, the AIML president stated 'that the Muslim League did not seek to follow the Congress method of controlling a ministry from outside by a Higher Command. Each Muslim League ministry would be autonomous and in the event of violation of Muslim League principles, the only action to be taken would be expulsion from the League.' Ibid., Garrett to Brabourne, No. 12, 17 October 1938, p. 19.
49. The first occasion was a speech shortly after the conference and the second was his testimony before a 1940 court of inquiry. Mitra, *Indian Annual Register, 1938,* 2:358, n.a. *Causes of Sukkur Disturbances: Important Findings of the Court of Inquiry into the Sukkur Riots of November, 1939* (Karachi: Sindh Provincial Muslim League, 1940), p. 41.
50. From an Assembly speech by the premier, *PSLA,* Vol. 6, Book 7, 12 January 1939, p. 73.
51. On 15 October, Haroon, Mir Bandeh Ali and G.M. Sayed had issued a joint statement which supported Jinnah's charges against Allah Baksh. *D.G.,* 15 October 1938, p. 2. In his concluding remarks written for his 1940 Report, Weston stated, 'In evidence Allah Baksh has expressed his personal indifference to office but it is plain he has made every effort to remain in office.' E. Weston, *Report of the Inquiry appointed under section 3 of the Sind Public Inquiries Act to inquire into the Riots which occurred at Sukkur in 1939* (Karachi: At The Government Press, 1940), p. 17.
52. Mitra, *Indian Annual Register,* 1938, 2:358.
53. *D.G.,* 22 October, 1938, p. 2. Factors that influenced Jinnah in making Haroon rather than Majid chairman were the former's considerable wealth and prestige as well as his urban political base. Shafi, *Haji Sir Abdoola Haroon,* p. 135.
54. The party had met on the 14th at Haroon's residence to elect office-bearers. In addition to Hidayatullah's election as leader, Mir Bandehali was elected deputy leader, Gazdar, Mir Ghulamali and Nur Mohammed Shah as assistant whips and Khuhro, general secretary. *D.G.,* 15 October 1938, p. 18.
55. Haroon notified Hidayatullah that he had provided at the League's Karachi headquarters a chair and table for the Assembly party secretary whose 'coming there would mean coordination of all League activities and would be conducive to the efficiency of the organization.' Haroon listed some possible functions for the secretary such as replying to anti-League propaganda in the press, drafting bills based on the League programme

and preparing questions and resolutions based on complaints submitted to the provincial office. But the secretary's most important function would be 'to carry on publicity to popularize the Legislative programme of the party so as the party wins the confidence of the people its members will be under popular pressure to continue in the party.' This last point was an encapsulation of Haroon's theory of how the League could operate as a popular, effective and responsible political party. PDH, Haroon to leader, Sindh Muslim League Assembly Party, 22 October 1938.

56. Jinnah reiterated these instructions upon concluding a tour of Sindh. *D.G.*, 21 October 1938, p. 2.

57. See n. 55.

58. *D.G.*, 21 October 1938, p. 7.

59. Karachi, The Pakistan Movement Foundation, I.I. Chundrigar Road, *Papers of M.H. Sayyid and Rizwan Ahmed,* Ali Gauhar Lahori to Mr Jinnah, 20 November 1938 (Hereinafter PSA). QAPC, F 1094, Khuhro to A. Haroon, 16 November 1938, p. 176. QAPC, F 365, Khuhro to Mr Nabi Baksh Bhutto, 13 November 1938, p. 1.

60. Interviews with Rashidi and Khalid Baksh, 3 June 1975.

61. At this Karachi meeting only thirty attended and of them only five were MSLAs, far short of the twenty-seven the League claimed in its ranks. This was another indication that the solidarity Jinnah had achieved was already beginning to erode. *D.G.*, 29 November 1938, p. 1.

62. Despite the recent marriage between their two families, Hidayatullah still viewed Haroon as a possible political threat to him. He instructed G.M. Bhurgari to vote against Haroon at the meeting because he wished to end Haroon's potential rivalry. Interview with G.M. Bhurgari, Karachi, 28 September 1975.

63. Khuhro had started out as a political understudy of Hidayatullah but now he was pursuing his own course which at such times brought him into direct conflict with his former mentor. Khuhro shrewdly viewed the League as a channel to political prominence and from this time on he became one of the League's most steadfast supporters. Interview with G.M. Sayed, Sann, 8 April 1975.

64. Interview with Bhurgari, Karachi, 28 September 1975. The *Daily Gazette* account did not report this first vote but mentioned simply a tie vote and Khuhro's breaking it. On essential points the two accounts corroborate each other. *D.G.*, 29 November 1938, p. 1.

65. Gabol proposed the secret ballot at the meeting and attempted to have the meeting endorse this procedure but Khuhro objected, saying there was no sanction for a ballot as the provincial League's rules and regulations had not yet been framed. Ibid.

66. The voter, Sheikh Noor Ahmed, a friend of Bhurgari's was not entitled to vote, not being elected to the Council of the League. Interview with Bhurgari, Karachi, 28 September 1975.

67. Pir Ali Mohammed Rashidi, who earned a reputation as a behind-the-scenes manipulator, confessed, 'I must admit that while organizing these elections I had made it a point to see that Sir Abdullah became the first president.' Quoted in Shafi, *Haji Sir Abdoola Haroon*, p. 134.

68. *D.G.*, 29 October 1938, p. 9. Coupland, *The Indian Problem*, p. 67.

69. In one statement Haroon lashed out at Congress; in another he invited Hindu and Muslim leaders to sit down and pursue an agreement. *D.G.*, 22 October 1938, p. 2. Ibid., October 29 1938, p. 9.

70. *D.G.*, 22 October, 1938, p. 2.

71. The following March, at a working committee meeting of the AIML, Haroon was appointed to a committee to examine and report on various federation schemes. See *Resolutions of the All-India Muslim League from March 1939 to March 1940* (Delhi: All-India Muslim League, n.d.), pp. 1-2. For a discussion of Haroon's scheme and others see Sayeed, *Pakistan: The Formative Phase*, pp. 108ff. Also, A. Haroon, Foreword to *The Muslim Problem in India together with an alternate Constitution for India*, by Syed Abdul Latif (Bombay: Times of India Bombay Press, 1939), pp. v-vii.

72. PSA, Haroon to Jinnah, 20 December 1938.

73. Rashidi issued a press statement denying rumours that any of the twenty-seven League MSLAs had resigned or that Hidayatullah intended to join the ministerial party. He also predicted the defeat of the ministry in the Assembly. *D.G.*, 28 December 1938, p. 9.

74. IOR, Linlithgow Papers, MSS Eur F 125/95, Graham to Linlithgow, No. 2, 4 January 1939, p. 1. Ibid., No. 4, January 9 1939, p.2.

75. Hidayatullah's letter, published in the *Daily Gazette,* stated his reasons for resigning were intrigue within the party, the defection of others from the party and other reasons he declined to disclose. *D.G.*, 10 January 1939, p. 1. It is probable the reasons he did not wish to reveal involved his rivalry with Haroon noted above.

76. The League stalwarts in the Assembly were Majid, Sayed, Khuhro, Khairshah, Gazdar, Isran and Nur Mohammed Shah. The latter two were large rural landlords from Dadu and Hyderabad districts, respectively. *Papers of G.M. Sayed* (Hereinafter cited as PGMS), File 2 (unpaginated) Minutes of League Assembly Party meeting, 25 January 1939.

77. The vote was thirty-two to seven. Those who opposed the motion included the supporters of Allah Baksh and Hidayatullah (the latter did not vote), members of the Hindu Independent Party and the European members. The League supported the motion and the Congress remained neutral. See Division of the Assembly, PSLA, 12 January 1939, Volume 6, Book 7, pp. 85-86.

78. Interview with Agha Ghulam Nabi Pathan, Karachi, 26 February 1976.

6

THE *MANZILGAH* AFFAIR

The opportunity the League needed to challenge the Allah Baksh government came in 1939 during an agitation resulting from the disputed status of a domed building in the northern Sindh town of Sukkur.[1] This site, *Manzilgah* by name (meaning a place of rest), was in the government's hands but the Sukkur Muslims claimed the building was really a mosque and should be restored to the Muslim community.[2] The dispute was essentially a matter between the government and the Muslim community, but the issue assumed a communal aspect when the Hindus became concerned with its settlement.[3] The Muslim demand for the *Manzilgah* attracted Hindu interest not simply because of its religious nature but also because the claim bore some relation to the widely disparate socio-economic levels of the two communities in Sukkur.[4] The feelings of fear and insecurity aroused during the separation movement days had never entirely left Sindhi Hindus and they viewed the Muslim claim to the *Manzilgah* as a threat to their position of dominance and control. Thus, they opposed the claim and declared that the building should remain under government control.[5]

Earlier deputations and appeals to the government by Sukkur Muslims to grant their claim had failed[6] but they were encouraged to issue their demand again in May 1939. Their renewed hope stemmed from the government's successful settlement of the *Om Mandli* and *Hanuman Mandir* affairs, two issues which in recent months had created strife and dissension in the Hindu community.[7] Anticipating the determined opposition of the Sukkur Hindus, the Muslims in Sukkur realized that in order to be successful this time they would need outside help. So they approached the Sindh

Muslim League, the major Muslim political organization in Sindh[8] and asked them to give their support for the restoration of the *Manzilgah* mosque.[9] Haroon then went to Sukkur to assess Muslim sentiment on the question of the Sindh League's active support for the *Manzilgah's* restoration. Finding a universal positive response from the town's various Muslim *anjumans,* Haroon publicly declared League support at a meeting in Sukkur on 19 May 1939.[10]

A few weeks later Haroon and Khuhro, the League Assembly party leader, met with the chief minister, Allah Baksh, to place before him the League demand for restoration.[11] At the meeting, Allah Baksh stated the government could not take immediate action on the issue but he assured the League the matter would be settled soon after the current Assembly session. Subsequent appeals by Khuhro soon after the meeting failed to elicit any government response.[12]

The government's failure to undertake immediate steps for the *Manzilgah's* restoration prompted the League to appoint a restoration committee to bring still greater pressure on the government. The first meeting of the committee was held on 22 and 23 July, and was presided over by Khuhro in the absence of the committee chairman, Haroon.[13] The first resolution called upon the Muslim members of the Assembly to withdraw their support for the Allah Baksh government and form an alternate government should their combined force fail to secure the restoration. A second resolution set 18 August as '*Manzilgah* Day' throughout the province, on which day meetings and demonstrations would be held in towns and villages all over Sindh to popularize the demand and bring pressure to bear on the government. Finally, the meeting resolved to meet again on 27 August to seek the sanction of the All-India Muslim League for starting a movement of civil disobedience or *satyagraha,* set tentatively for 1 October in anticipation of the centre League's approval.

The primary significance of these resolutions[14] can be seen in two ways. First, these resolutions made it clear that by this time the League leadership had perceived in the *Manzilgah* question, not simply a campaign to restore a mosque to Muslims, but a much larger, more volatile issue which, if exploited, could bring Allah Baksh's government down. Thus, the leadership was confronted with the opportunity it had long awaited and it seized upon its chance without delay. Secondly, these resolutions reveal, by their language and content, the emergence of two competing groups within the League organization. The two groups differed primarily over tactics;[15] one group, headed by Haroon and Khuhro, sought to use moderate tactics such as petitions, appeals and press statements to pressure the government into conceding the restoration demand. The other group, led by Majid and comprised of the Sukkur Muslims, favoured more radical tactics such as popular agitation to force the government into granting the Muslim wish.

In subsequent weeks the League leadership continued its efforts through interviews, petitions and appeals to come to terms with the government over the *Manzilgah*.[16] But the government failed to grant the Muslim demand; it adopted a policy of avoiding the issue and postponing its settlement. Allah Baksh felt unable to take a stand on the *Manzilgah* issue because in his cabinet his Hindu ministers opposed the restoration while his Muslim ministers supported it.[17] But Allah Baksh's pre-eminent goal was to stay in office;[18] he realized if he granted the Muslims their demand, he would lose his Hindu supporters and fall from power.

The inability of the moderates, Haroon and Khuhro, to persuade the government to grant the *Manzilgah* demand, gave ascendency to the radical wing in the League. In order to retain their leadership in the League, Haroon and Khuhro were compelled to support the radical method of *satyagraha* though they hoped to obscure their action by maintaining a public front of issuing appeals and letter writing.[19] The emergence of the radical wing as the dominant group in the party was clearly reflected in the resolution passed at the next meeting of the restoration committee on 29 September 1939. The resolution called for the commencement of *satyagraha* within three days unless a settlement was reached.[20]

Haroon and Khuhro invited Allah Baksh to Sukkur in a final effort to persuade the government to concede the Muslims' demand. The chief minister arrived on 1 October, the day *satyagraha* was scheduled to begin, and held talks with the League leaders. But once again, no agreement was reached and as a result *satyagraha* was begun.[21]

Satyagrahis and volunteers had been streaming into Sukkur over the past several days at the urging of Wajid Ali, a local League leader and a barrister from nearby Shikarpur, who was given the title of 'Dictator.'[22] By the second day of *satyagraha* about two thousand people had gathered, and on the morning of the third day, a group of them pushed past the police and occupied the building.[23] Thus, for the time being, restoration of the *Manzilgah* was achieved.

The government reaction[24] to the taking of the *Manzilgah* was one of shock and embarrassment but Allah Baksh, undaunted, adopted an unusual tactic which he hoped would return the situation to normal. On the day following the occupation, Allah Baksh gave orders through the Sukkur District Magistrate that all Muslim *satyagrahis* were to be released and all police withdrawn.[25] He said he had taken this decision because the jails were full and there was no more food to feed the prisoners, but his real intent was quite different. He hoped to defuse the situation, reasoning the *satyagrahis* would lose their cause and disperse if the government demonstrated leniency.[26] But subsequent events proved Allah Baksh had misjudged the situation. The *Satyagrahis* did not leave, thinking the government had capitulated to their demand. Their jubilation turned to bitterness when they realized the government had no intention of giving up the mosque. This experience made the Muslims even more determined to keep the mosque until the government officially conceded their claim.

The League gave proof of its firm resolve about a week later by deciding to initiate *satyagraha* in Karachi in the form of picketing the ministers' homes. When the Governor received word of the League's plans, he promulgated an Ordinance on 14 October, giving power to local authorities to make arrests without a warrant. The Governor, in a letter to the Viceroy, explained his action by saying that none of the Defence of India Rules was adequate to deal with the situation and that he hoped 'to nip the movement in the bud' before it was allowed to create a major law and order situation involving bloodshed.[27] The Muslims were outraged by the Ordinance, seeing it mainly as a measure passed for the benefit of Allah Baksh to help him recoup his position following his initial mistake in withdrawing the police. They also viewed it as a design to placate the Hindus on the one hand, and intimidate the League leadership into capitulation on the other.[28]

At the time the Ordinance was announced in Sindh, Haroon was busy in Delhi conferring with Jinnah. Haroon had two purposes in mind when he went to Delhi: to restore the Sindh League's ties with the All India League[29] and to establish jointly a future course of action for the *Manzilgah* issue. He decided the best way to achieve his two aims was through a resolution passed before the All-India League working committee. A resolution was passed which echoed the Sindh League's position on the *Manzilgah* issue.[30] It called for the return of the *Manzilgah* to the Muslim community and denounced the Sindh government's policy of postponement and repression. In this resolution, the AIML working committee was to investigate the issue but in the end this step was never undertaken.[31] Jinnah refused an inquiry on behalf of the All-India League though he was not against a private inquiry being undertaken by prominent Leaguers. Jinnah opposed the inquiry because '*Satyagraha,* which had caused such a disaster, was not sanctioned by the parent body.'[32] Thus, Haroon returned to Sindh not completely empty-handed; he had managed to gain the support of the All-India League for the Sindh League's struggle over the *Manzilgah,* but he had failed to extend that support into an official inquiry into the matter.

When he returned from Delhi, Haroon also brought with him a formula, fashioned by Jinnah and designed to seek a way out of the *impasse* into which negotiations between the government and the League had fallen. Jinnah's formula was essentially a modification of the government's offer made on 24 October. The government's terms were that the Ordinance would be withdrawn if the League called off *satyagraha* and evacuated the buildings. The government also promised to make a decision about the future status of the *Manzilgah* within six weeks.[33] The two alterations Jinnah made were that the government take 'a favourable view of the situation' in exchange for the League's evacuation of the *Manzilgah*.[34] Jinnah second condition was that a four week time period be set for a decision rather than six. The negotiations involving these formulas and others similar to them achieved no breakthrough.

On 15 November, the revived Sindh League restoration committee met in Sukkur and passed resolutions which the government interpreted to mean a rejection of the government's offer.[35] In fact, the restoration committee at this late stage had been unable to evolve a clear position enjoying wide support because of a revival of the moderate-radical struggle within the League party[36]. This lack of a definite direction from the League side gave the government the impression that the League's uncertain position was a deliberate tactic to forestall the negotiations. The ministry concluded that no agreement was going to be reached so they broke off negotiations and began to make plans to retake the *Manzilgah*.[37] On the morning of the 19th of November, G.M. Sayed and the other leaders of the restoration committee were arrested in Sukkur, and at noon the police took possession of the *Manzilgah,* expelling the *satyagrahis* with tear gas.[38] After forty-eight days of Muslim occupation, the *Manzilgah* was once again in government hands.

The expulsion of the Muslims from the *Manzilgah* and its reoccupation by the government was followed by a wave of communal disturbance and rioting that began in Sukkur and spread into the surrounding district. Apparently the rioting was started by Hindus who jeered at the returning *satyagrahis* that 'they had gotten what they deserved.'[39] This provoked the Muslims, who felt that the government had been forced to retake the mosque because of Hindu pressure. Rioting ensued for several days and reached such proportions that it was necessary to send a military force numbering about 1,000 to Sukkur to reinforce the police and quell the disturbances.

Both communities suffered comparative losses in the riots in terms of property, injuries and loss of life in Sukkur town, but the Hindus suffered most dramatically in Sukkur District as more of them were killed than were Muslims.[40] The trauma of the *Manzilgah* disturbances for the Hindus led them eventually to withdraw their support from the Allah Baksh government. The breakdown in law and order demonstrated clearly to them the inability of the government to safeguard their property, interests and lives. Consequently, they joined with the Muslims in the next session of the Assembly to bring the Allah Baksh government down. Thus, the long awaited League goal of defeating Allah Baksh and removing him from power was finally achieved;[41] the irony was that the goal was accomplished not by their efforts alone but also with the help of the Hindus, with whom they were most often in opposition.

The failure of post conference negotiations to bring Allah Baksh into the League camp and form a new League ministry served to raise doubts in the minds of the Sindh Leaguers as to the efficacy of all-India efforts to order provincial affairs. So, in searching for a way to defeat Allah Baksh's ministry, the Sindh Leaguers decided to exploit the communally explosive *Manzilgah* mosque issue which they hoped would expose the premier's strong reliance on Hindu backing and marshal broad Muslim support to pressure and topple the Allah Baksh ministry. The choice of *Manzilgah,* a strictly provincial issue, marked a return to a strong preoccupation with Sindhi concerns in terms of province-centre relations; a trend which was further reflected in the Sindh Leaguers pursuit of *satyagraha* without the approval of the central League.

In their campaign to restore the *Manzilgah* mosque, the Sindhi Leaguers were aware of the issue's potential to engender communal tension and strife, but they were divided by what tactics they should use and how far they should go in their prosecution of the issue. Thus, the emergence of moderate and

extreme factions within the League leadership provided a further
example of their increasing political sophistication. But their
failure to exercise restraint and evolve a united course of action
produced an outcome of dubious success. The Sindh Leaguers
achieved their primary goal of bringing Allah Baksh down, but
at great cost to both the League's image and Sindh's communal
peace; results that posed serious questions about the Leaguers
ability to govern should they now come to power.

NOTES

1. Actually there were two buildings on the site, one adjacent to the other,
   but the status of only one was in question. The following year an inquiry
   was undertaken to determine the true status of this building. E Weston,
   *Report of the Inquiry appointed under section 3 of the Sind Public
   Inquiries Act to enquire into the nature of the Manzilgah Buildings at
   Sukkur.* (Karachi: Government Press, 1941), 36pp.
2. This was not a new claim. Sukkur Muslims, beginning in 1920 had sent
   numerous petitions and appeals to the government to have the *Manzilgah*
   recognized as a mosque and the site turned over to Muslims. They claimed
   the building had been designated a mosque by its seventeenth century
   builder, Mir Masum, a prominent *Saiyid* of Sukkur. During the British
   period the site had been used only for non-religious activity but the
   government could not disprove the Muslim claim so the issue continued
   unresolved. A further elaboration on the various appeals and evidence is
   given in Weston's Report cited above. See also n.a. *Causes of Sukkur
   Disturbances: Important Findings of the Court of Inquiry into Sukkur
   riots of November 1939, Presided over by Judge Weston* (Karachi: Sind
   Provincial Muslim League, 1940), pp. 7ff. (Hereinafter cited as *Causes
   of Sukkur Disturbances*).
3. Sukkur, unlike most other towns and regions in Sindh, had a history of
   communalism. The first major communal riot in Sindh took place in
   nearby Larkana in 1927 and three years later a major riot broke out in
   Sukkur. See *Causes of Sukkur Disturbances,* Appendix B, pp. 46ff.; also
   Flynn '*The Communalization of Politics*,' p. 73. Elements that fostered a
   communal atmosphere in Sukkur included the presence of numerous old
   religious shrines, both Hindu and Muslim, and more recently the influx
   of settlers from the Punjab. For shrines see J.W. Smyth, *Gazetteer of
   Sind, Sukkur District,* B Series, Volume III (Bombay, 1928), pp. 48-50;
   Dayaram Gidumal, *Something about Sindh* (Hyderabad: Blavatsky Press,

1882), pp. 58-60; for influx, FR for March 1940 (2), Taunton to Conrad-Smith, 4 April 1940.

4. A British observor at the time wrote, 'The Muslims in Sukkur are a poor community of little influence and have for long been smarting under the oppressive behaviour of more wealthy and influential Hindus who control the Municipality and can easily obtain the ear of the Ministers.' He mentioned a recent 'severe boycott of Muslim cartmen, shopmen and labourers' and inferred a connection: 'the demand for restoration of the *Manzilgah* is therefore an expression of desire among Muslims to assert themselves,' IOR, L/P&J/7/2892 File 4447 of 1939 entitled the *Manzilgah* Occupation. P&J 4889 'Note on the Honourable Home Minister's Tour' by R.M. Maxwell, I.C.S., n.p.

5. The Hindu position on the *Manzilgah* was a) it was not a mosque initially and b) it's recognition as a mosque would jeopardize Hindu use of *Sadh Belo,* a monastery and shrine in the middle of the Indus river, which faced *Manzilgah.* IOR, Linlithgow Papers, MSS Eur F 125/96, Graham to Linlithgow, No. 1, 4 January 1940, p. 1.

6. See p. 185, n. 2.

7. The Om Mandli was a social reform society started for Hindu women in Hyderabad which became suspected of immoral activities. The Hindu community became divided over the issue but it was settled by the appointment of a tribunal and the eventual abolition of the Association. IOR, Linlithgow Papers, MSS Eur F 125/95, Graham to Linlithgow, No. 89, 16 May 1939, p. 64; also FR for March 1939 (2), Tarenton to Puckle, April 1939. The *Hanuman Mandir* affair involved a Hindu temple built on government owned land in Karachi. The government claimed the temple construction was an illegal encroachment and took over the land but returned the property to the Hindu community following protests. Sayed, *Struggle for a New Sind,* p. 31.

8. There were only two other Muslim organizations in Sindh of note at this time: the Sindh branch of the *Majiyyat al-Ulema-i-Hind,* an urban-based Urdu speaking party of *maulvis* with little rural following in Sindh and the Sind Ahrar Conference, a pro-Congress group which formed in Sindh in June 1939 but had a small following, a fifth to a tenth of the size of the League's. Interview with Maulvi Mohammed Ismail Hafiz, Karachi, 25 October 1975, and FR for May 1939 (2), Taunton to Conrad-Smith, 6 June 1939.

9. Hakim Tajuddin, president of *Itihad-i-Millat,* on behalf of the other Sukkur Muslim leaders wrote a letter dated 5 May, 1939, to Sindh League president Haroon requesting the League's support for the *Manzilgah* claim. From testimony in E. Weston, *Report of the Court of Inquiry appointed under Section 3 of the Sind Public Inquiries Act to inquire into the Riots which occurred at Sukkur in 1939* (Karachi: At the Government Press, 1940), p. 8. (Hereinafter cited as *Weston Report*).

10. *Weston Report,* p. 8.
11. The League leaders were acting under the authority of a Sindh League resolution passed on 4 June 1939. Ibid., p. 26.
12. Ibid., It was clear from Governor Graham's correspondence for this period that Allah Baksh and the government did not deem the *Manzilgah* issue to be important. Indeed there is no mention of *Manzilgah* in Graham's letters until the middle of August when it was described as 'a possible source of trouble.' IOR, Linlithgow Papers. MSS Eur F 125/95, Graham to Linlithgow, No. 228, 17 August 1939, p. 107.
13. *Weston Report,* pp. 27ff. The Sindh League's working committee also met in Karachi in July under the chairmanship of Sheikh Abdul Majid (Haroon and Khuhro were absent) and passed a resolution demanding restoration, and outlining a plan for province-wide agitation to achieve that end. For the purpose, Rs. 50,000 was to be raised and 10,000 volunteers recruited. Interview with Hafiz Khair Mohammed Ohidi, Sukkur, 18 December 1975. (Rs—short for rupees)
14. Including the working committee resolution, see n. 13.
15. In terms of goals both groups sought the replacement of Allah Baksh's government but the more extreme group wished, too, to make the restoration a symbol of League power and success in order to attract the Muslim masses to the League banner. Interview with Agha Ghulam Nabi Pathan, 26 February 1976.
16. Haroon's chief interest during these months was Pakistan and he devoted most of his energy to that cause. *Manzilgah* was only of secondary interest to him.
17. IOR, Linlithgow Papers, MSS Eur F 125/95, Graham to Linlithgow, No. 273, October 15 1939, p. 117.
18. *Weston Report,* p. 17.
19. Graham provided evidence that Haroon and Khuhro did actually support *satyagraha,* IOR, Linlithgow Papers, MSS Eur F 125/95, Graham to Linlithgow No. 83, 11 October 1939, p. 114. Also QAPC, F 460, G.M. Sayed to Jinnah, pp. 1-3; *Weston Report,* pp. 2829.
20. Haroon had second thoughts about adopting a course of *satyagraha* and in a letter to Jinnah later he tried to disassociate himself from that policy. He wrote, 'I have tried to dissuade Muslims from strong action but now they have declared *satyagraha* and are intent on throwing Allah Baksh out. 'QAPC, F 274, Haroon to Jinnah, 10 October 1939, p. 34.
21. Allah Baksh, accompanied by a Hindu minister and a Hindu MSLA toured the *Manzilgah* site but he was unable to persuade the Hindus to accept the Muslim claim. Not wishing to decide against Hindu wishes, Allah Baksh once again postponed a decision. *Weston Report,* p. 30.
22. At the 29 September meeting the restoration committee and the war council (a body created on 16 September) were abolished and in their

place a 'Dictator' was set up. This was an effort on the part of the prominent Leaguers such as Haroon and Khuhro to avoid the responsibility for *satyagraha*. Ibid., p. 28.

23. The police at the *Manzilgah* were given orders by Allah Baksh through the district Magistrate in Sukkur to behave nonviolently in the event of trouble. Ibid., p. 34. It is not known for certain who gave the order to take the mosque but it was likely Wajid Ali and the other local Muslims who were caught up in the excitement of the moment. Ibid.

24. The reaction among Hindus was one of alarm. They were especially angry with the government's failure to prevent the occupation of the *Manzilgah* and fearful that their access to the *Sadh Belo* would be jeopardized. IOR, Linlithgow Papers, MSS Eur F 125/96, Graham to Linlithgow, No. 1 4 January 1940, p. 1.

25. 500 arrests had been made on the 2nd, 300 on the 3rd. Ibid.

26. *Weston Report,* p. 39, Syed, *Struggle for a New Sind,* p. 34.

27. IOR, Linlithgow Papers, MSS Eur F 125/95, Graham to Linlithgow, No. 273, 15 October 1939, p. 117.

28. Syed, *Struggle for a New Sind,* p. 37; QAPC, F 274, Haroon to Linlithgow, 5 December 1939, pp. 64ff.

29. Haroon felt that the relationship between the two Leagues had been damaged as a result of the Sindh League's *Satyagraha* and possession of the mosque without the parent League's approval. The Sindh League had sought sanction on two instances but approval had not been forthcoming. See p. 137, for the first, the second was a resolution at a meeting on 2 October, 1939. MLA, Working Committee Meetings of 1939, Vol. 128, 'Resolutions passed at Working Committee Meeting,' 22 October 1939, p. 23.

30. In its resolution the working committee gave its approval for the way *satyagraha* was carried out, 'in a most peaceful and non-violent manner' but avoided endorsing the principle of *satyagraha* itself and instead laid stress on the view that the *Manzilgah* buildings 'constitute Muslim property of great religious and historical importance with which no other community or party had anything to do.' Ibid.

31. Haroon likely wanted an All-India League inquiry into the *Manzilgah* because the Congress had undertaken one, and he wanted to neutralize its influence on the Sindh government.

32. From a CID report of a League meeting at Haroon's residence in Karachi on 20 December 1939, at which Haroon discussed his meeting with Jinnah. Enclosed with one of Graham's letters to the Viceroy. IOR, Linlithgow Papers, MSS Eur F 125/95, Graham to Linlithgow, No. 126 23 December 1939, p. 168.

33. These terms were outlined in a telegram from Graham to Linlithgow. IOR, Linlithgow Papers, MSS Eur F 125/95, Graham to Linlithgow, No. 302, 30 October 1939, p. 128. With the Ordinance and the restitution

of Section 144, Criminal Procedure Code, arrests of agitating Muslims had resumed in Sukkur.

34. Graham interpreted Jinnah's offer to mean government capitulation followed by League withdrawal from the buildings. He described Jinnah's offer as 'about the most impudent and irresponsible production that was ever issued by one who claims to head an important party in India.' Ibid.

35. The restoration committee had been resurrected following the *Manzilgah's* occupation. *IOR*, Linlithgow Papers, MSS Eur F 125/96, Graham to Linlithgow, No. 3, 9 January 1940, p. 18.

36. Haroon and Khuhro, since the occupation, had reverted to their moderate position. At this latest stage in the negotiations they were ready to come to terms with the government but their efforts were frustrated by the radicals, now led by G.M. Sayed, who were adamantly opposed to the government unless the government capitulated to the restoration demand. FR for October 1939 92), Taunton to Conrad-Smith, 22 November 1939. Sayed who had initially opposed the League's support for the *Manzilgah* restoration, was converted to the cause when the government passed its Ordinance. He was later elected secretary of the restoration committee. FR for November 1939 (2), Taunton to Conrad-Smith, 12 December 1939.

37. The government by this time was impatient to have the issue settled and in Weston's judgment they acted too hastily, ending negotiations before they had been allowed to run their course. *Weston Report*, p. 43. Factors that compelled the government to act included the ministry's prolonged embarrassment over the Muslim occupation of the *Manzilgah* and the strain that fact placed upon Hindu support for the ministry. In addition, two recent events had raised the communal temperature in Sukkur, and two weeks later a Sindh Hindu Sabha meeting presided over by Dr Moonje, the All-India Mahasabha leader, passed resolutions condemning the government, and demanding the resignation of Hindu ministers unless the Muslims were immediately evicted from the *Manzilgah,* and the site returned to the government. IOR, Linlithgow Papers, MSS Eur F 125/95, Graham to Linlithgow, No. 124, 22 December 1939, p. 163.

38. Ibid.

39. Ibid.

40. In Sukkur town the figures of casualties in both communities was comparable: in two days of rioting fifteen Muslims were killed and four were injured; the corresponding figures for Hindus were nineteen and six. But in Sukkur district the Hindus clearly suffered more: fifty-seven Hindus were killed and nine injured as against only one Muslim killed and one injured. Ibid.

41. The Muslims were also awarded their claim to the *Manzilgah* during the successor government to Allah Baksh. See Chapter 7, p. 233, n. 4.

7

THE LEAGUE EXPERIMENTS
WITH POWER

The outcome of the *Manzilgah* affair produced mixed results
from the Muslim League in Sindh. Aside from the defeat of the
Allah Baksh ministry, the chief advantage the League gained
form *Manzilgah* was the popularization of its name throughout
the province, particularly among the communally-minded rural
Muslim peasantry, who, in considerable numbers, enrolled
themselves as new League members.[1] But while *Manzilgah*
helped the League to strengthen its grass-roots support, it placed
a heavy strain on the loyalty of the League leaders in Sindh to
the extent that some tried to down-play their association with
the League. Haroon, Khuhro and Rashidi, for instance, attempted
to obscure their part in the whole affair when violence had
appeared imminent. Others tried to exonerate the League of
blame and pointed the finger of responsibility at the government
and the Hindus instead[2], though privately they realized the
League could not be absolved of all guilt as it had openly
championed the *Manzilgah* cause. In the period following
Manzilgah, the general tendency among the Sindh Leaguers was
to turn away from the League and its all-India concerns, and
concentrate instead on the political situation in their own
province and on ways to heal the communal relations so severely
disrupted by *Manzilgah*. Writing in his historical account of the
period, G.M. Sayed captured well the post-*Manzilgah* mood of
the provincial leadership of both communities:

...the tragic event of Sukkur did not fail to touch our (Muslim) sense of responsibility as well as (generate) a genuine sympathy for the Hindu masses...We were in a mood to extend our hand of cooperation and friendship to them, as we found that there were many amongst them who were now prepared to take a long-range view of things and work hand in hand with the Muslims for the good of the Province as a whole.[3]

At the beginning of 1940 the Allah Baksh government was still in power. It was commonly felt, however, that the Assembly session which commenced toward the end of January, as the first since the *Manzilgah* affair, would expose the serious erosion of support for the government on account of its weak handling of the affair, particularly its failure to avert the riots. Given these circumstances, the government was not expected to survive much longer.[4] Indeed, even before the Assembly met, the government received a serious setback when the two Hindu ministers, under pressure from the Hindu *Mukhis,* resigned.[5] However, despite this loss of support, Allah Baksh decided to try to continue without Hindu support, and took to himself the portfolios of his departed ministers. He managed to stay on in office but before the Assembly was three weeks old, his government suffered a defeat during a vote on an amendment to a minor bill. Allah Baksh, frustrated and embittered by his loss of support, gave notice to the Governor that he was resigning.[6]

Though he resigned, Allah Baksh did not leave office as the Governor refused to accept his resignation until a suitable government could be formed. This state of affairs encouraged political intrigue in the Assembly as groups and parties jockeyed to gain control of the new government. Khuhro, as leader of the Muslim League Assembly party, led his party into the fray in an effort to capture ministerial office. Haroon, the Sindh League president, sent instructions by telegram from Delhi that the Leaguers should resist entering into an alternate coalition ministry as such an outcome would 'jeopardise Muslim interests.'[7]

Khuhro, disagreeing with this course of action, telephoned Haroon to try and persuade him that the League should seize the opportunity to assume power and office, especially since Allah Baksh, the League's arch enemy, was now out of the way. In the end, Khuhro was able to persuade both Haroon and Jinnah to support League efforts to come to terms with the Hindu Independent party, short of forming a coalition with them or any other party which favoured the retention of either Allah Baksh or Ghulam Hussain Hidayatullah in the ministry.[8] Khuhro argued that the restoration of harmonious communal relations in Sindh was a matter of the highest priority which would be facilitated by the Muslim League taking a pro-coalition stance. Notwithstanding the force of Khuhro's position, Jinnah himself was more amenable to the principle of coalition government, having since relaxed the harsh anti-Assembly, anti-ministry posture he had adopted in Karachi in 1938.[9] Thus, Jinnah gave the League's blessing to the idea of a coalition government in Sindh, reflected in Haroon's 20 February press statement which concluded: 'If the Muslim League Assembly Party can be a party to the formation of a coalition ministry in Sindh, I do not understand what there is to prevent the consummation of such a development, especially as this is bound to bring good relations and brotherliness between the two communities in Sindh.'[10]

The political situation in Sindh remained fluid for several weeks, with Allah Baksh trying to keep his crippled ministry afloat, while behind the scenes various parties and groups continued to negotiate and vie for power. Finally, in the middle of March, a new party called the Nationalist party began to take shape based on a twenty-one point agreement reached between the Muslim League Assembly Party and the Hindu Independent Party.[11] But the Nationalist party was basically a party in name only; it was a politically expedient union of two Assembly parties which, before this time, were radically opposed to one another, chiefly on communal grounds. But this political alliance had considerable backing in the Assembly, which the party managed to convert into majority support by winning over Mir Bandeh Ali and his bloc of eight Assemblymen with the promise that the Mir could head the new party and become the next chief minister.[12] So the Governor, having finally found a majority party in the Assembly, asked Mir to form the new government on 18 March.

The new cabinet consisted of six ministers in all, four Muslim and two Hindu. The two Hindus were Nichaldas Vazirani and Rai Sahib Gokaldas Mewaldas, both Hindu Independents. The former had been in the previous ministry and Gokaldas, the landlord and merchant from Larkana, was selected to represent the *Bhaibund* interests of the party which had suffered during the *Manzilgah* agitation.[13] Except for Mir, the Muslim ministers—K. B. Khuhro, G.M. Sayed and Sheikh Abdul Majid—were members of the League, but upon assumption of power they relinquished their Assembly party affiliation as did the Hindu members in accordance with their joint agreement.[14] This action by the League ministers was tantamount to the dissolution of the League Assembly party as they had comprised its leadership[15], but despite this apparent setback to the League's interests, Haroon stuck to his previous pro-coalition stance. A few days after the new government took office, the Sindh, League president signified his approval in a press statement by extending his congratulations to the new ministry.[16]

At the outset, the new ministry undertook the challenge of healing the province's communal wounds in a spirit of sobriety and conciliation. The chief minister, at an evening reception on the day the Assembly opened, alluded to the need for communal harmony and stated that the formation of the Nationalist party in the Assembly was 'an outward manifestation of the inborn desire for communal accord and mutual goodwill.'[17] Earlier in the day, he based his opening speech in the Assembly on the same theme; he appealed for a stable ministry 'in which the minority communities share willingly the burden of joint responsibility.[18]

But despite the ministry's outward show of sincerity and commitment in confronting the difficult task of restoring communal peace, few had much hope that it would survive very long. The *Daily Gazette* in an editorial, expressed its 'serious doubts' whether the ministry 'will be more than a nine day wonder.'[19] It stated further that 'people in Sindh look upon the ascension of the ministry as it appears a patchwork affair simply to gain office.'[20] Graham, the Governor, was hardly more optimistic. Even before Mir had taken power, he informed the Viceroy: 'I have no confidence that the Mir ministry will be lasting...'[21] Sometime later, Graham explained why: 'Mir is the plaything alike of his three Muslim League colleagues and Nichaldas, the clever, pushing Hindu. There is no sort of unity or teamwork about my Council of Ministers, and the lack is due to my chief minister's weak leadership...'[22] The Governor's view was echoed by one of his ministers, G.M. Sayed. In his book *Struggle for a New Sind,* Sayed states that Mir Bandeh Ali 'is a gentlemen, honest and harmless but what made us hesitate to accept him as Prime Minister was his lack of qualities of leadership.'[23] Thus, the outlook for the Mir ministry was an uncertain one; it lacked the requisite characteristics of dynamism, imagination and direction if it was going to achieve the difficult goal of restoring communal harmony in Sindh.

In addition to the factors of weak leadership, a patchwork cabinet and strained communal relations, another issue surfaced immediately to further cloud the ministry's political future. In his opening Assembly speech, Mir Bandeh Ali, while outlining in broad, general terms the policy and programme his government would follow, stated that his government would sponsor a bill in the Assembly to introduce the principle of joint electorates in borough and municipal elections in Sindh.[24] This bill, initially introduced by the Allah Baksh government, was one of the points of agreement reached between the League and the Hindu Independents prior to forming the government.[25] Mir voiced his government's intention to pursue the bill as a deliberate demonstration of the ministry's commitment to its goal of repairing communal relations. The government acted quickly and introduced the Joint Electorates Bill as the first major order of business. In a rare display of unity, cutting across party lines, the measure was passed and become law on 1 April 1940.[26] It was clear from the passage of this bill that the desire for better communal relations extended beyond the leadership of the various Assembly parties to the Assemblymen themselves.

The government's commitment to joint electorates as well as its speed in taking action surprised Haroon and the League organization, and placed them in a difficult if not embarrassing situation. The government to which he had pledged the League's backing had now pushed through the passage of a bill which, in principle, directly contravened one of the All-India Muslim League's longest standing and most sacrosanct precepts: separate electorates. Yet, Haroon had no one but himself to blame for this new and sudden development which threatened the League's interests and prestige. He had been absent from Sindh for most of the month of March, and had allowed other concerns to take precedence over political developments in Sindh[27]

The passage of the Joint Electorate Bill exposed the weakened state of the League's leadership and organization at this stage; Haroon's absence created a vacuum in the League party which might have been filled by such leaders as Sheikh Abdul Majid, Khuhro and Sayed except that all three were now members of the government, and accordingly, supported the government's rather than the League's line on the issue of electorates. Thus, the electorate issue created a split in the ranks of the Sindh League which divided along lines of all-India interests versus provincial concerns. Haroon, whose outlook was all-India in scope, sought the preservation of separate electorates in keeping with the all-India League's policy, while Syed and the others, motivated by provincial considerations of communal peace, supported joint electorates.[28] This represented a new example in which considerations of principle supplanted factors of personal interest as the cause of disunity in the League ranks. As such, it reflected a growing degree of maturity in the behaviour of the Sindh League leadership.

Inspired by the League session at Lahore, at which he had played a significant role in establishing the League's new goal of Pakistan,[29] Haroon returned to Sindh in April with a mind to bring the members of the Sindh League in line with his views on the electorate issue. At a series of meetings of the Sindh Provincial Muslim League and its working committee in Karachi on 19, 20 and 21 April, the League took a hard line position which clearly reflected the influence of Haroon. These meetings reaffirmed the Pakistan Resolution of the recent Lahore session and then, adopting a more militant tone, the Sindh League party denounced the concept of joint electorates, and attacked the Mir ministry for yielding to Hindu demands on electorates and other issues.[30] Then, in an effort to bring the League ministers under the control and discipline of the League organization, the meeting urged that in matters of policy, the ministers abide by the decisions of the provisional League Parliamentary committee and further, that they should deposit their resignations with the committee which would then tender them when the ministers took a decision detrimental to the interests of the League and the Muslim community.[31]

However, the Council of the Sindh Muslim League, a larger body with greater constitutional authority, met the next day, and passed a lengthy resolution that reflected a retreat to a more moderate and conciliatory position. For instance, the end of the resolution, instead of containing criticism of the ministry, read:

The Council is confident that the Sind Assembly Nationalist Party will run the administration of the Province in such a manner that the legitimate and fundamental rights of all the communities in the Province are fully protected and every section of the population enjoys the fullest measure of the sense of security.[32]

Thus, it was clear that the ministers who were both on the Council and present at this meeting had more influence on the Council than Haroon did, as this resolution reflects their thinking much more than Haroon's.[33] But the resolution did not represent a pro-ministry position entirely. One significant portion of the resolution was included as a concession to Haroon's point of view, which read:

(The Council) is also of the view that 4 out of the 21 conditions, on the basis *of which the new government has been created, are such that unless some suitable modifications are made in them,* there will be difficulties in the achievement in the fullest measure of the purposes of re-establishment of intercommunal peace and harmony, which, the Council understands, is the real object behind the new arrangement.[34]

The Council did not pass this resolution easily. It was debated for six hours and each minister had to present his case but, in the end, the resolution was passed unanimously.[35] This outcome suggests that in this first confrontation between the ministers and Haroon, the former emerged in the stronger position. Haroon continued to wield some influence,[36] but it became clear in the days ahead that his own political position as well as the League organization's was declining rather than improving. The League party's weak position was reflected in mid-April in the Muslim League candidates' 'conspicuous lack of success' in the Karachi Municipal Corporation elections.[37] Also, the Muslim League came under increasing attack in the press[38] and in late April, the League suffered a further eclipse in its prestige when news reached Sindh of Allah Baksh's triumphant presidentship of the nationalist Muslims' conference in Delhi.[39]

In subsequent weeks, the League organization maintained a low profile but when it did surface to take a stand, its position usually reflected a lack of clarity or consistency. For instance in late May, the League announced that it continued to have faith in the present ministry but at the same time expressed dissatisfaction that the ministry was not doing enough to finally resolve the *Manzilgah* issue.[40] The Sindh League had become displeased earlier with the Mir ministry's approach to the *Manzilgah* issue, particularly its consent to an inquiry to determine the true nature of the *Manzilgah* building. The League had opposed the appointment of an inquiry for fear no proof could be found that the *Manzilgah* was a mosque. The League ministers, however, had been compelled to accept the inquiry as it was part of the agreement reached with the Hindus, but according to Graham, the ministers hoped to pre-empt the inquiry by announcing the *Manzilgah's* restoration to the Muslims before the inquiry could present its findings.[41]

During May and June, Haroon, troubled by the League's weak position, continued to look for ways to revive the party's influence, particularly over its ministers in the cabinet. With Judge Weston's inquiry on the *Manzilgah* taking place at this time,[42] and the press carrying lengthy accounts of the investigation, Haroon saw an opportunity to exploit the *Manzilgah* issue once again for the benefit of the League, by using it to bring pressure on the League ministers to conform to the League's policy and discipline.[43] He wrote a letter to the ministers calling on them to resign, giving as reasons their support of joint electorates and their failure to give adequate relief to the Muslims arrested in Sukkur.[44] The ministers chose to ignore the letter,[45] but both sides were called upon to test their strength at a meeting of the Sindh League council in early July.

At the meeting, Haroon introduced a motion that the League ministers should resign as they had betrayed the party. This motion was defeated, however, in favour of a motion expressing confidence in the ministers.[46] Thus, the ministers again emerged victorious in the second confrontation with Haroon. The outcome suggests that the majority sentiment in the League was still on the side of the ministers and that Haroon, who was trying to keep the provincial League in line with the policy of the All-India Muslim League, now found himself politically isolated within his own party. Thus, the League in Sindh had become more responsive to the political currents and issues in the province than to the dictates of the parent League and All-India considerations.

Haroon, defeated and bereft of political support, had little choice but to defer to the position of the ministers and allow them to pursue their own course. He turned his energies instead to the task of extending the League's organizational network throughout the province in the weeks and months ahead. During July and August, Haroon called meetings of the League at which appeals were issued to the League branches throughout the province to spread the League's message of Pakistan among Sindh's rural masses, and plans were undertaken to establish the Muslim National Guard, the militant, service-oriented youth wing of the League, in various parts of Sindh.[47]

While Haroon directed his attention to organizing the League, the League ministers exulted over their victory in their intra-party struggle.[48] The success of the ministers was, however, of little benefit on the wider stage of ministerial politics in Sindh. In fact, ironically, the outcome of the confrontation between Haroon and the ministers placed the ministers in a weaker position because by prolonging their quarrel with Haroon, they sacrificed any formal League support which could have served to strengthen their hand in the ministry.

The tenuous nature of the League ministers' support worked to compound rather than alleviate the ministry's increasing inability to provide efficient, dynamic and stable government. Other factors that subverted the orderly and effective functioning of the ministry, aside from the Mir's weak and indecisive leadership, were the absence of a clear and definite government programme and the lack of any cooperative or cohesive spirit among the ministers.[49] Furthermore, new initiatives that were undertaken, such as the establishment of a Board of Industries and a university for Sindh, were not sustained because the cabinet failed to meet on a frequent and regular basis to deliberate and continue support for these schemes.[50] Also individual members, aside from having difficulties grasping the details of their portfolios, would often become preoccupied with numerous routine matters which then obscured from their vision more important long-range goals.[51] Thus, the ministers, especially the League ministers, exposed their lack of experience and knowledge in running a government which threatened to doom any present or future League ministry.

Nonetheless, the primary goal of the ministry remained the restoration of communal peace and harmony in the province. But even before the ministry was able to accomplish much toward reaching its objective, complaints, protests and angry mumblings began to issue from both the Hindu and the Muslim camps. When the ministry tried to initiate a legislative programme of agrarian reform, entrenched landed interests, largely Hindu, protested the legislation was designed to benefit the rural masses at their expense.[52] Nor did the Muslims remain silent and refrain from criticizing the ministry. As Sayed explained:

> The Muslims felt resentful firstly as a result of the misery consequent upon the Sukkur riots, which though we (the League ministers) did our best to mitigate, could not be sufficiently relieved by us and secondly, because of the mass persecution launched by certain officers under Chapter VIII of the criminal code.[53]

This opposition and criticism from both communities served only to weaken the ministry further, and it found itself unable to end the continuing sense of fear and insecurity in the province, especially among the Hindus of the Upper Sindh Frontier district. In that region, an occasional robbery or assault or murder would take place with the victim invariably a Hindu. These crimes reached a climax in July with the murder of Pamnani, a Congress Hindu Assemblyman and communal tension rose considerably, particularly after it was suspected that the son of Pir Bharchundi, a fanatical Muslim spiritual leader, was involved in the murder.[54] Thus, with a weak ministry, the prospect of continued communal trouble persisted, and in the Governor's view communal peace would not be restored in Sindh until the government's final judgment on the *Manzilgah* mosque was revealed.[55]

By the end of the summer of 1940, the Mir ministry was in anything but a strong and secure position. It continued to drift along, without purpose or direction, and its failure to solve the communal problem, as well as its growing unpopularity among Hindu and Muslim political circles, began to bring into question its continued existence. As doubts about the ministry proliferated, politicians began to agitate and scheme for a change in the ministry, and once again politics in Sindh entered upon a stage of instability and uncertainty.

One of the earliest signals for change came from within the ministry itself. Sayed, Minister of Education, made it known to his colleagues as early as August that he felt 'a strong urge to resign rather than take upon my shoulders the odium of the existing state of affairs.'[56] As he contemplated resigning, Sayed considered ways in which he could resign and yet at the same time strengthen the prospects for a more progressive Sindh. He approached Allah Baksh with an offer of two Cabinet seats (his own and Sheikh Abdul Majid's), with a mind to persuade the former chief minister to join hands with the Leaguers as a preliminary step to forming a united front of Muslims in the Assembly. Sayed was convinced that once the Muslims in Sindh formed a solid and united bloc, the power and influence of the few vested interests could be broken, and concrete steps could be taken for the uplift and betterment of the poor, mostly Muslim masses. Sayed's hopes were not to be advanced at this time, however, for Allah Baksh turned down his offer saying he would not consent to be merely a minister, and added the only condition under which he would join was if 'Mir Bandeh Ali retired in his favour and his old enemy, K.B. Khuhro resigned from the ministry altogether.'[57]

In addition to Sayed's initiative for change, the Hindu Independent Party began to give indications that it regretted ever having entered into a government coalition with the Muslim League. The Hindu Independents were particularly indignant with the League's effort to secure legal protection for Pir Bharchundi whom they regarded as a major threat to their security in the Sukkur region.[58] A further cause for disenchantment among the Hindus was the change of portfolios in the Mir ministry, resulting in less partronage for Hindus.[59]

The Muslim League, for its part, was equally displeased with its inclusion in the government; at a meeting of the working committee of the Sindh Provincial Muslim League held at Nawabshah on 4 October, the League attacked 'the obstructive policies of the Hindu parties which have made it impossible for any ministry to function to aid the oppressed Muslim masses'[60]

The political situation in Sindh continued unstable throughout the month of October with relations between the two communities marked more by deterioration than any real improvement. Responding to this negative trend, appeals from various quarters issued, calling for a climate conducive to communal peace. One of those appeals came from the great Congress leader, Mahatma Gandhi, who addressed a message to Haroon and offered his help and cooperation in fostering an atmosphere of communal harmony in Sindh.[61]

Gandhi's communication to Haroon indicated that the course of Sindh politics was being closely watched in high Congress circles and as further evidence, the Congress president, *Maulana* Azad, visited Sindh in November, principally to evaluate Sindh's preparedness for *satyagraha* but also to see if something could be done to bring stability to the ministry.[62] Azad arrived in Sindh in the midst of ongoing discussions between the various political parties and factions in search of a more suitable ministerial arrangement. Much of the focus of these efforts centered on Allah Baksh, partly because of his past experience, but mostly because of his new political stature gained as president of the recent Azad conference in Delhi.[63] Sayed, for instance, made one more appeal to Allah Baksh to join the League group but finally gave up, concluding that Allah Baksh counted his ties with the Hindu Independents and the Congress as more important than any support the Muslims might give him.[64]

Soon after *Maulana* Azad arrived, he held talks with the leaders of Congress and the Hindu Independents who told him that in their view, the main obstacle obstructing political stability and communal harmony in Sindh was Muslim disunity.[65] Azad then approached the Muslim leaders to determine their views of the situation and as a result a meeting was arranged at the chief minister's house. Finding a consensus at the meeting that Muslim disunity was indeed the chief stumbling block, Azad then suggested ways to achieve a lasting solidarity among the Muslim leaders and legislators. He proposed that Allah Baksh be made to come into the ministry and his group be given two seats in the cabinet. This proposal was found agreeable by all those in attendance and it was accepted. The Congress, hearing about this outcome later, became perturbed for they feared the emergence of a dominant, united Muslim party. So they put pressure on Allah Baksh not to join unless he was made the chief minister. When the Muslims received word of the Congress design, they expressed strong objections and threatened to break the solidarity that had been so carefully nurtured. Azad was finally able to persuade all sides to accept a compromise settlement that one, the Allah Baksh group would be given two cabinet seats and two, the question of the prime ministership would be decided by a majority decision of the Muslim members themselves.[66]

The acceptance of this settlement by all the parties did not end the intrigue, however. Allah Baksh, who was less than happy with the outcome, announced he would send Hidayatullah into the cabinet immediately in his place, and that he would follow after Mir resigned. But Sayed, fearing that Allah Baksh, with his close Congress ties, was remaining out to wait for the ministry to fall so he could then be installed as prime minister, was anxious that Allah Baksh be brought in immediately. So he joined hands with Nichaldas to bring pressure on Allah Baksh to enter the cabinet, with the plea that this was the only course for keeping Muslim solidarity intact. Allah Baksh finally yielded to the urgings of Sayed and Nichaldas and agreed to join the cabinet without delay. The terms of the agreement were drafted and to give it legitimacy, it was signed by Sayed, Khuhro, Allah Baksh and Nichaldas.[67]

On the day the agreement was drafted, Haroon returned from Delhi. Hearing of it and seeking an opportunity to bolster the League's sagging public image, Haroon issued a statement the next day stating that the League had authorized no one to participate in the current negotiations and that barring a decision of the Sindh Provincial Muslim League Council, the League would have nothing to do with the agreement.[68] The Sindh League president also sent a letter the same day to the three League ministers and admonished them not to resign, as no change in the League's support for the ministry could take place without the prior approval of the All-India Muslim League.[69] In contrast to his earlier vacillation, Haroon now took a forthright stance in defence of the ministry because he feared that Congress' reordering of the ministry would reflect poorly on the League's all-India prestige. In addition, he was concerned that the League ministers refrain from acting on their own but that, in accordance with proper League procedure, they seek the League's confidence and sanction before pursuing a course of action.[70]

In his 21 November letter to the ministers, Haroon also requested them to come to see him the following day to discuss the Azad talks, but the ministers failed to attend the meeting. The Governor interpreted this as a further example of the League ministers' disregard for Haroon and the League,[71] but Sayed gave an alternate explanation. He claimed he tried to reach Haroon to explain to him the terms of the agreement but was unable to for lack of time.[72] Thus, Sayed found himself confronted with the conflicting choice of honouring his end of the Azad pact and resigning or following Haroon's direction and staying in the ministry. He chose the former option both because he had committed his personal honour to it and, more importantly, because he felt he had Jinnah's sanction for his choice.[73] Sayed's resignation and Allah Baksh's ascension once again to the ministry were greeted with approval by the Congress and some of the Hindu Independents, but those in the provincial League were disgusted and felt betrayed.[74] Their old foe from the *Manzilgah* days and before was once again in the cabinet, but this consideration mattered less to Haroon than the new loss in prestige the League suffered on account of Sayed's resignation.[75] Haroon viewed Sayed's resignation as the last in a series of serious rebuffs dealt by the League ministers to the League's authority, and he decided to initiate action and have them face the League's discipline. In a long letter to Jinnah in November, Haroon presented a summary of political developments in Sindh since the League's inception, and then went on to cite particular instances where the ministers had acted on their own authority or failed to adhere to the League's declared policy.[76] At the end of the letter he listed charges against the three ministers and called for an investigation of their conduct by the All-India Muslim League Council and Working Committee.[77]

It is noteworthy that Haroon and Sayed continued to occupy opposite political positions though each had altered his initial stance drastically. The situation was even ironical for, in the end, each adopted a position that was similar to the former position of the other. Thus, Sayed, who previously participated in the ministry was now out while Haroon, who, formerly opposed the ministry, now supported it. Why, then, did these leaders continue to oppose one another throughout the changing pattern of ministerial politics in Sindh? The answer lies in their fundamentally different outlooks: Sayed was primarily concerned with provincial issues such as the progress and welfare of Sindh and Haroon was guided by all-India considerations such as the reputation and prestige of the All-India Muslim League. Thus, the differences between Haroon and Sayed serve as another instance of division among the Sindh League leadership along lines of principle rather than personal interest or whim and beyond that, further evidence of their growing political maturity.

Sayed's resignation and Haroon's long letter castigating the League ministers were both clear indications to Jinnah that the League was in serious trouble in Sindh, and that his presence was needed. The League had recently adopted as its goal the establishment of the state of Pakistan, and hence Jinnah felt it was imperative for the League to demonstrate its strength in the Muslim majority provinces such as Sindh but recent events in Sindh were doing more to undermine that goal than promote it.[78] Jinnah decided to visit Sindh, in mid-December and see what he could do to restore the prestige of the League.

Upon arriving in Sindh, Jinnah quickly perceived that the chief causes of the League's travails in Sindh were the 'thoroughly unsatisfactory' conduct of the League ministers and the absence of a League voice in the settlement of government policy.[79] As the best remedy for this situation, Jinnah proposed new Assembly elections but Graham declined, arguing there was not enough time to complete elections before the budget session opened. So Jinnah was left with no choice but to accept the status quo, though the opportunity remained to somehow influence the present situation to the League's advantage. Under the circumstances Jinnah and the provincial League[80] shared some common ground in that they both supported the ministry. Their differences, however, lay in the purposes they hoped to achieve by ministry advocacy. Jinnah viewed support for the ministry as a way of building the League's strength and thus advancing the cause of Pakistan. The provincial Leaguers backed the ministry partly to maintain an appearance of commitment to communal harmony but also to enjoy privately the patronage, power and influence of office.[81] Once again, differences within the League divided along lines of all-India versus provincial considerations.

During the next several weeks Jinnah initiated a campaign of quiet diplomacy with the ultimate objective to bring the Sindh League ministers under the firm discipline and direction of the All-India Muslim League. If this could be accomplished, Jinnah reasoned, the Sindh League would become a united entity and a considerable force in reinforcing and promoting the League's goal of Pakistan.

Thus, while in Karachi, Jinnah adopted the policy position that the League would continue to participate in the ministry but in order to ensure the League's effective voice, all the Muslim ministers must be made responsible to the League. If this were not possible, the League ministers should resign and the League should go into opposition.[82] In an attempt to give effect to this policy, Jinnah held talks with Allah Baksh and his group but as with the discussions following the 1938 conference, the talks failed to produce any agreement. It appeared Jinnah would have to call upon the League ministers to resign and enter the opposition. But at this juncture, a development occurred which transformed the situation and altered considerably the subsequent course of events: in late December, Mir Bandeh Ali decided to rejoin the League party.[83]

Mir Bandeh Ali's action was prompted largely by two considerations. First of all, it allowed him to retain his personal hold on power because his decision met Jinnah's stipulation that the League would continue support for the ministry if the chief minister alone came under the League's control.[84] Secondly, Mir could satisfy his desire to be in power when the government finally turned over the *Manzilgah* to the Muslim community.[85] Mir's decision, however, also raised questions as he had given an understanding during the negotiations with Azad that he would resign on or before February 15.[86] Mir's response to these queries was that his re-entry into the League fold had altered the situation considerably to the extent he could no longer be held accountable to the Azad agreement.[87] Thus, Mir's action had the effect of upsetting the delicate balance of forces on Sindh's political stage. It signified a victory for the League and a setback for the Congress, but these were only interim adjustments because the real, long-range implications of Mir's decision was to prolong rather than resolve the thickening tangle enveloping Sindh politics at this time.

Predictably, the Sindh Congress was the first to react to the realignment of political power precipitated by Mir's action. The Congress, suffering from a loss of prestige and fearful of the League's new ascendency, took steps to recoup its position. Reasoning that Allah Baksh's ambition would render him displeased with the new situation, the Congress approached him, offering their support to make him prime minister if he agreed to leave the Mir ministry.

Sayed, hearing of this Congress move and concerned for Muslim solidarity, decided to try and forestall the Congress plan by reaching Allah Baksh first and offering him the premiership on behalf of the League.[88] It was clear Sayed was still acting with the interests of Sindh and the Sindhi Muslim community uppermost in his mind, despite his pledge earlier to turn his attention to organizing the League in Sindh. Haroon wrote to him and urged him to desist from his plan and again, revealing his all-India outlook, appealed to him to uphold Jinnah's League policy of supporting the Mir ministry.[89] Thus, the two opposing viewpoints of Haroon and Sayed clashed once again, but this time Haroon emerged the victor, though not without Jinnah's assistance. Jinnah brought pressure to bear on Sayed in the form of a stern letter, questioning his word and sense of honour in reconciling his scheming with his declared devotion to the League.[90] Sayed, realizing his hopes of winning Allah Baksh over to the League were in vain, yielded to Jinnah's pressure and reaffirmed his commitment to the League organization.[91] Sayed's submission to the will of Jinnah was an important step in the long-term establishment of the League in Sindh for Sayed, though not a large landlord, had a status akin to a *pir's* and hence was very effective later in attracting many from the Sindhi Muslim rural classes, *zamindars* and *haris* alike, to the League's fold.[92]

The addition of Sayed's energies and talents to the League's organizational work served to greatly reinforce the position of Haroon and Jinnah in their attempt to give the League a solid base in Sindh. There still remained, however, the League ministers and the question of how faithful they would be to the League's policy and programme. In subsequent weeks, Haroon and Jinnah turned their attention to these individuals in an effort to secure their firm commitment to the authority and discipline of the League.

Two issues re-emerged at this time to illustrate that the task confronting the two League leaders was not as easy as they might have thought. The first issue was the continuing one of electorates. Earlier in the year, the provincial League had refrained from taking a strong stand favouring separate electorates because of the government's contrary position but in December, encouraged by Jinnah's presence and charging the Hindus with violation of their mutual agreement, the League saw its way free to take a firm position advocating separate electorates, which it did at its Council meeting on 22 December 1940.[93] Thereafter, the League, under Haroon's direction, took steps to ensure the League ministers and the Muslim MSLA men supported separate electorates by issuing instructions not to enforce the law effecting joint electorates in Borough Municipalities, and not to pass the bill extending joint electorates to Local Bodies.[94] However, this attempt by the provincial League to bring the Mir ministers under the League's discipline on the electorate issue, received a rebuff when Mir later wrote to the Sindh League president, ignoring the latter's instructions and appealing to him to lend the League's support to the joint electorate legislation which the League had helped pass earlier.[95] Haroon then informed Jinnah of this development and requested the all-India League's backing for the Sindh League's stand on separate electorates.[96] Jinnah, in reply, promised the All-India League's support to the Sindh League which reiterated its position at its Council meeting in Sukkur on 26 January 1941.[97] The Sindh League continued to exert pressure, and in the end its efforts were rewarded: the League led a successful campaign to boycott the Thar Parkar District Local Board elections and partly as a result of this, the second Joint Electorate Bill was allowed to lapse.[98] Thus, on the first issue, the League was successful in bringing the League ministers under its authority and discipline.

The issue of electorates, however, was a mere policy position and hence, of considerably less importance than the second issue, the Azad pact. The pact, an agreement to legitimatize a new power balance in the ministry, posed a real test of strength for the League leadership of Haroon and Jinnah. Earlier, Mir Bandeh Ali had tried to deal a death blow to the Azad pact by rejoining the League, but the Congress resurrected it as an issue in early February in an attempt to undermine the authority of the Mir ministry.[99] The Congress initiative confronted the League ministers, particularly Mir, with a dilemma. The pact called upon Mir to resign on or before 15 February, but if he did so, he would disobey the League's and Jinnah's instructions to continue the ministry. But on the other hand, if Mir stayed on in power, he ran the risk of losing the support of the Allah Baksh group which could bring his ministry down. Two of the League ministers, Mir and Khuhro, both personally enamoured of office, decided to try and satisfy simultaneously the conflicting wishes of the League and the Congress in order to stay in power.[100]

Word of the Congress move to discredit the Mir ministry and the ensuing intrigue reached Jinnah in Bombay in early February.[101] He reacted by writing a letter to Haroon on 2 February, issuing instructions to the League ministers and a few days later, he issued a press statement, intended to give moral support to the threatened Mir ministry.[102] In his letter, Jinnah dismissed the validity of the Azad pact and stressed that the proper course was for the ministry to continue without change.[103] However, he did not discount the possible determination of the Congress and the Hindu Independents to break the ministry and in that event, the only honourable course was for the League ministers to resign and go into opposition. Jinnah added that if any one of the ministers, simply for the sake of keeping his cabinet seat 'tries to come to some other arrangement, then the Sindh League should publicly disavow his action and discipline him.[104]

In the meantime, Khuhro, the most resourceful if not the most scrupulous League minister, had been busy building his own power base so he could manipulate Congress and League pressure to strengthen his hold on office. He cleverly took over the resuscitated Muslim League Assembly party[105] in order to confer League legitimacy on his political initiatives, though his actions were not necessarily consistent with the League's policy. Thus, Khuhro wrote in a 8 February letter to Jinnah 'that the unity of the various Muslim groups in the Assembly was essential', indicating that he was placing Sindhi Muslim political solidarity above any commitment to the League's policy and programme.[106] This was precisely the same as Sayed's position before his recommitment to the League and it suggested that Khuhro, aside from acting in his own personal interests, was also in favour of giving precedence to Sindh's ministerial politics over and against the League's all-India concerns. A few days later, Khuhro gave concrete expression to his view by securing approval at a Muslim League Assembly party meeting for a compromise reached with the non-League Muslims, bringing Hidayatullah into the ministry and producing a cabinet, on the Muslim side, of two Leaguers and two non-Leaguers.[107]

Despite Jinnah's express prohibition of just such a compromise in his 2 February letter, Khuhro went to Delhi to try and persuade Jinnah to give his support to the measure. Haroon was already in Delhi and Jinnah hoped that Mir would

accompany Khuhro so that he could hold talks with all three
leaders together, and elicit from them a strong commitment to
uphold the League's policy. Mir was unable to come as the
Sindh governor was away but Jinnah was able to persuade
Khuhro in Delhi to abandon his compromise proposal and
endorse instead the League's position.[108] Thus, Jinnah had
gradually succeeded over a period of weeks in bringing Sayed,
Sheikh Abdul Majid and Khuhro together onto the League's
platform, but it still remained to secure Mir's firm commitment.
The Sindh premier, in a recent letter to Jinnah,[109] had expressed
support for Khuhro's compromise proposal but Jinnah was now
hopeful that as Khuhro had yielded, Mir would follow suit.
Jinnah sent a strong reply to the Sindh premier, rebuking the
compromise position and appealing to Mir to join with his other
colleagues in standing firm on the League policy of continuing
the present ministry.[110]

Several days later, however, it appeared that the newly achieved
solidarity among the Sindh League leaders might be more illusion
than fact. Upon returning to Karachi, Khuhro wrote to the League
president informing him of a new formula for ministry formation
proposed by Allah Baksh. He expressed his hope that Jinnah
would view this new proposal as 'advantageous to us and not to
the other side.'[111] Jinnah, losing patience with the ceaseless pattern
of intrigue in Sindh politics, which he saw as merely a cover for
Hindu exploitation of the divided Muslim leadership, fired back a
telegram to Khuhro demanding that he adhere to the League's
discipline and support the status quo in Sindh.[112]

Jinnah decided to make one last effort to secure solidarity
among the Leaguers in Sindh. He wired Sayed in his village of
Sann and instructed him to go to Karachi and help form a solid
front with the other League leaders.[113] In a following letter,[114]
Jinnah made it clear to the Sindh League leadership that he was
issuing his 'definite and final advice.' The League president
offered no new position in this letter; he simply reiterated the
League policy previously laid down but the message to the
Sindhis was loud and clear: obey Jinnah's advice or else face

his wrath and judgment which would mean almost certain expulsion from the League.[115]

Jinnah's letter had the desired effect, and the Sindh Leaguers banded together and submitted to the League's authority. The real and final test of their commitment to the League came several weeks later when Allah Baksh and the Hindu Independents, realizing that the Leaguers were no longer interested in scheming to alter the ministry, withdrew support and precipitated the resignations of Allah Baksh and the Hindu ministers.[116] Their resignations left the League ministers without a majority to carry on the government but instead of seeking desperately to hold on to office, as they would have done in the past, the League ministers dutifully and in obedience to Jinnah's directions, resigned their seats.[117] Thus, the Sindh League ministers entered into the opposition, and a new ministry was formed once again under Allah Baksh.[118]

The sight of the Sindh League leaders standing united in deference to Jinnah's and the League's authority, at considerable cost to their immediate political interests, was an unprecedented development of major significance in the Muslim politics of Sindh of this period. This event marked the beginning of a new stage in the political consciousness and behaviour of the Sindh League leadership. The reasons that compelled the Sindh Leaguers to accept the League's discipline at this time were the wish to avoid incurring the wrath and displeasure of Jinnah and the prospect of League money and prestige in future elections.[119] But more important than these two considerations, was the Sindh Leaguer's own realization of the validity of a conclusion they had reached earlier. That conclusion, which they now realized with renewed force, was that without the discipline of an outside body such as the All-India League, Sindhi Muslims would continue to remain divided, and remain easy victims of the Sindhi Hindus exploitative designs.[120]

The Sindh Leaguers had reached this conclusion as early as the beginning of 1938, and it had served as their rationale in inviting the League to come and establish itself in Sindh. But now there was a crucial difference. Whereas formerly the

Leaguers had failed to fulfill their promise of commitment to the League; now they did, by forsaking power, resigning and entering the opposition so they could devote their efforts full time to strengthening and organizing the League party in Sindh. Further, the acceptance by the League ministers of Jinnah's demands should not be viewed as a total capitulation to the League president's position. A measure of accommodation was also present, for the League ministers would still be able to pursue their traditional interests, though now that pursuit would have to take place within the framework of the League's authority. The change in the outlook of the Sindhi Leaguers was indicative that a greater measure of political sophistication had come to characterize their political behaviour: they were now more willing to allow issues and principles to take precedence over selfish personal interests as the primary determinants governing their political activity.

During their period of opposition which followed the demise of the Mir ministry, the Sindh Muslim Leaguers remained united and gradually consolidated a position of considerable political strength. The Sindh Leaguers remained in the opposition until October 1942, when, following the Governor's dismissal of the Allah Baksh government, the League once again took hold of the reins of government, and this time formed a full-fledged Muslim League ministry. This ascension to power marked the emergence of the League as the dominant political force in Sindh, a position it did not relinquish for the remainder of the period of provincial autonomy until Pakistan was born in 1947.

The outcome of the *Manzilgah* affair had produced mixed results for the Sindh League leadership. The Sindh Leaguers had achieved a victory by defeating the Allah Baksh ministry but at the same time, they suffered a sharp loss of prestige for having initiated a campaign that precipitated serious communal violence. The opportunity of holding power as well as concern for restoring Sindh's communal harmony prompted several of the Sindh Leaguers to join the new Nationalist government, but they soon found that the policies of the Mir ministry brought them into conflict with the programme and policies of the All-India Muslim League. Thus, disunity continued to characterize the League leadership in Sindh but by this time their division, consistent with their growing political maturity, resulted from differences over principles of policy which assumed an institutionalized form in the shape of the competing League Assembly party and the League party organization.

The repeated success of the League ministers in their struggle with the party organization might have resulted in their eventual supremacy had the position of the Mir cabinet been strong, but the Nationalist ministry's incapacity to provide effective government led to a political crisis that eventually involved the outside leadership of the Congress and the League. Jinnah realized that in order for the League forces in Sindh to provide their full support to the Pakistan cause, the Leaguers must end their discord and stand united even at the cost of losing office. The Sindh Leaguers responded to Jinnah's firm command by forging a new position of solidarity and commitment to the policies and goals of the All-India Muslim League. By achieving unity in their ranks and equilibrium in province-centre relations, the Leaguers provided a secure basis for the League's establishment in Sindh and ensured the League's emergence as the province's primary political force, a position it maintained until Sindh acceded to Pakistan in 1947.

NOTES

1. This was particularly true in the Upper Sindh Frontier district, especially Sukkur and its environs. Interview with Agha Ghulam Nabi Pathan, Karachi, 26 February 1976. The League won new members also by establishing a Sukkur Relief Fund to aid Muslims who had suffered in the riots and in subsequent litigation. PGMS, file 2, item 6, 'Contributions to Sukkur Relief Fund 4 January 1940, to 25 November 1951.' Also PDH, Haroon to K.B. Makhdum Hussain, 5 April 1941.

2. In a letter to Jinnah, Sayed wrote: 'I know the world is being fooled to believe that the League is responsible for the horrible tragedies (of *Manzilgah*)...It will not take long for truth to shine out. K.B. Allah

Baksh and his government whom I hold directly responsible for these atrocities have started tasting the fruits of their devilish deeds.' PSA, Sayed to Jinnah, 1 February 1940.

3. Sayed, *Struggle for a New Sind,* p. 44.

4. Graham writes to Linlithgow that he will be surprised if the ministry survives the next session. He remarks, too, that Allah Baksh is not as confident as he was a month ago. IOR, Linlithgow Papers, MSS Eur F 125/6, Graham to Linlithgow, No. 12, 16 January 1940, p. 34.

5. Their charge against the government was that it had favoured Muslim interests at the expense of the Hindus during the *Manzilgah* disturbance and its aftermath. IOR, Linlithgow Papers, Graham to Linlithgow, Vol. 96, Letter No. 47, 26 January 1940, p. 46.

6. IOR, Linlithgow Papers, MSS Eur F 125/96, Governor of Sind to Governor-General, No. 54-C, 14 February 1940, p. 54.

7. Haroon counselled remaining 'aloof no matter what happens' and stated this was Jinnah's advice as well. IOR, Linlithgow Papers, MSS Eur F 125/96, Graham to Linlithgow, No. 91, 16 February 1940, p. 57.

8. Ibid.

9. In November 1939, Jinnah announced a five point scheme as a basis for arriving at an interim settlement with Congress for the duration of World War II. The first point was the 'establishment of coalition ministries in the provinces.' Sayeed, *Pakistan: The Formative Phase,* p. 102. See also V. P. Menon, *The Transfer of Power in India* (Princeton, N.J.: Princeton University Press, 1957), p. 72.

10. *D.G.,* 20 February 1940, p. 9.

11. These twenty-one points were originally demands formulated by the Hindus designed to restore a sense of security among the Hindu community in Sindh, particularly in the Upper Sindh Frontier. The Weston inquiry proceeded from one of these demands. *D.G.,* 16 January, 1940, p. 1. Also Sayed, *Struggle for a New Sind,* pp. 46-49.

12. *D.G.,* 18 March 1940, p. 5.

13. The majority of the Hindu MSLAs were of the *Bahibund* merchant caste but the Hindu cabinet seats had always been held by *Amils.* Sayed, *Struggle for a New Sind, p. 51:* Sorley, *The Former Province of Sind,* p. 255.

14. IOR, Linlithgow Papers, MSS Eur F 125/96, Graham's commentary on Sindh's Fortnightly Report for the second half of March 1940, 9 April 1940, p. 90.

15. The League ministers, however, remained members of the League organization and were listed as Council members in April. QAPC, 580, 'Minutes of the Sindh Provincial Muslim League Council Meeting, 20 April 1940,' pp. 32-34. In fact, the Muslim League Assembly party was disbanded according to the terms of the agreement and in its place, the Sindh League's working committee was to serve as a provisional

parliamentary committee. GPMS, F 2, 'Resolution #6 of SPML Council Meeting, April 1940.

16. *D.G.,* 22 March 1940, p. 7.
17. *D.G.,* 17 March 1940, p. 7.
18. Ibid.
19. *D.G.,* 19 March 1940, p. 5.
20. Ibid. In an editorial two days previously entitled 'tactics unworthy of a Talpur,' the *Gazette* castigated Mir for his 'dishonourable' behaviour in departing from Allah Baksh's government. *D.G.,* March 17 1940, p. 5.
21. IOR, Linlithgow Papers, Mss Eur F 125/96, Graham to Linlithgow, No. 70, 1 July 1940, p. 118.
22. IOR, Linlithgow Papers, MSS eur F 125/96, Governor of Sind to Secretary of the Viceroy, No. 70-c, 15 March 1940, p. 83.
23. Sayed explains further that Sheikh Abdul Majid was the first choice to be prime minister but Congress reservations and Mir's stipulation that he would only join the government if he was made chief minister, left no alternate choice. Sayed, *Struggle for a New Sind,* p 53.
24. *D.G.,* 27 March 1940, p. 7.
25. According to Sayed the Hindus were split into two groups; one composed of extremist, non-cooperative Hindus, mostly recent settlers from the Punjab and second, *asal* (long-time) Sindhi Hindus who chose to come to terms with the League. Sayed, *Struggle for a New Sind,* p. 48.
26. Mitra, *Indian Annual Register, 1940,* 1:201. The jurisdiction of this Bill was limited to Sukkur district, the scene of the most recent communal violence.
27. Part of the time Haroon had been in Delhi to occupy his seat in the Central Assembly and attend to his business affairs. During the third week of March, Haroon was in Lahore for the League's historic twenty-seventh annual session where he was active in framing and supporting the famous Pakistan Resolution. See Syed Sharifuddin Pirzada, *Foundations of Pakistan* (Lahore: All Pakistan Legal Decisions Press, 1963), p. 152; also G. Allana, *Pakistan Movement Historic Documents* (Karachi: Paradise Subscription Agency, 1967), pp. 172-173.
28. The division in the Sindh League extended to the issue of Pakistan itself. Graham writes to Linlithgow in April after the historic League session in Lahore, '(I) do not find among my ministers any keenness for Jinnah's partition scheme (though) one of my strongest supporters of that scheme is Sir Abdoola Haroon.' IOR, Linlithgow Papers, MSS Eur F 125/96, Governor's commentary on *Fortnightly Report* for the second half of March 1940, 9 April 1940, p. 90.
29. See page 211, n. 1.
30. Mitra, *Indian Annual Register 1940,* 1:63.

31. FR for April 1940 (2), Taunton to Conrad-Smith, 6 May 1940. Also Sayed Ali Abbas and M. Rafique Mughal, A *Chronology of Muslim India, 1932-1947,* 2 vols. (Lahore: Punjab University Press, 1963), 2:28.

32. QAPC, F 580, Resolutions of the Council Meeting of the Sind Provincial Muslim League, 22 April 1940, pp. 32-34.

33. The greater influence of the ministers was also reflected in the sequence of meetings. The last meeting of the working committee was adjourned on the 21st and merged into the Council meeting of the 22nd. Ibid., p. 31.

34. Ibid. The underlining was done apparently by Jinnah's hand after he received a copy of the minutes.

35. Ibid.

36. Garham noted that Haroon and the League ministers had reached a *modus vivendi* but he does not describe its terms. IOR, Linlithgow Papers, MSS Eur F 125/96, Graham's commentary on the F R for the second half of April 1940, No. 59, 10 May 1940, p. 99.

37. Ibid.

38. F R for May 1940 (1), Taunton to Conrad-Smith, May 16 1940. Taunton mentions that the majority of the newspapers in Sindh were speaking out against the League and instead were praising the Delhi Azad conference and Allah Baksh's role in it. This was true of the non-Hindu as well as the Hindu press. For instance, the *Karachi Daily* labelled the Muslim League as 'unpatriotic', and the *Sind Observor* criticized Jinnah's leadership as 'tired'. Only one paper, the *Hayat,* dismissed the conference as organized 'by the Congress henchmen who are Muslim only in name.'

39. In his conference speech Allah Baksh denounced the League's Pakistan platform as 'wholly impracticable' and the 'main obstacle in the way of India's progress as a whole.' *Presidential Address of K.B. Allah Baksh to the All India Independent Muslim Conference, 27 April 1940,* (Delhi: National Journals Press, 1940), pp. 12, 13. For a discussion of the Muslim Nationalists position, see W.C. Smith, *Modern Islam in India,* pp. 278ff., and Kabir, *Muslim Politics,* pp. 42ff.

40. F R for May 1940 (2), Taunton to Conrad-Smith, 6 June 1940.

41. IOR, Linlithgow Papers, MSS Eur F 125/96, Graham to Linlithgow, No. 54, 23 March 1940, p. 87.

42. Judge Weston directed two inquiries related to the *Manzilgah.* The first pertaining to the causes of the riots following the *Manzilgah* agitation was completed in September 1940, while the second, investigating the true nature of the building, was finished in February 1941. See Chapter Six, p. 133, n 1, p. 134, n 9.

43. Haroon may well have taken his cue from the Muslim newspaper, *Islah,* which called upon the three League ministers to resign and stand trial

for their responsibility in the Sukkur tragedy. Cited in F R for May 1940 (2), Taunton to Conrad-Smith, 6 June 1940.

44. F R for June 1940 (2), Clee to Conrad-Smith, 10 July 1940.
45. IOR, Linlithgow Papers, MSS Eur F 125/97, Graham's commentary on the second half of June 1940, No. 73, 13 July 1940, p. 124b.
46. IOR, P&J/5, F 256, Graham's commentary on F R for first half of July 1940, 25 July 1940, pp. 85-89.
47. F R for July 1940 (2), Clee to Conrad-Smith, 5 August 1940, F R for August 1940 (2), Clee to Conrad-Smith, 3 September 1940.
48. In writing to the Viceroy, Graham mentioned, 'My Muslim League ministers claim to have had a great triumph over Sir Abdoola Haroon at the Muslim League meeting.' IOR, P&J/5, F 156, Graham's commentary on the F R for the first half of July 1940, 25 July 1940, pp. 85-89.
49. Graham reported friction between his ministers, especially Nichaldas and Khuhro. The latter, whom the Governor describes as a 'corrupt, dishonest man', had charge of a portfolio formerly in Vazirani's hands and was busy overturning his predecessor's policy of appointing Hindus by filling posts with Muslims. IOR, Linlithgow Papers, MSS Eur F 125/97, Graham to Linlithgow, No. 77a, 29 July 1940, p. 138.
50. Sayed, *Struggle for a New Sind*, pp. 58, 59.
51. Ibid.
52. Ibid.
53. Ibid. p. 55. Graham, in referring to this campaign of repression admits the administration had exceeded its authority but rationalized 'a little summary treatment will do the *badmashes* (bad characters) of Sukkur district no harm and Hindus are more cheerful than they were.' IOR, Linlithgow Papers, MSS Eur F 125/97, Linlithgow to Graham, No. 58, 29 October 1940, p. 54.
54. IOR, Linlithgow Papers, MSS Eur F 125/97, Graham to Linlithgow, No. 75, 27 July 1940, p. 129.
55. IOR, P&J/5, F. 256, Graham's commentary on *Fortnightly Report* the first half of July 1940, 25 July 1940, p. 85.
56. Sayed, *Struggle for a New Sind*, p. 60.
57. IOR, P&J/5, F 256, Graham's commentary of F R for the second half of August, 1940, 6 September 1940, p. 60. Also, Sayed, *Struggle for a New Sind*, p. 61.
58. IOR, P&J/F 256, Graham's commentary on F R for the second half of October 1940, 11 November 1940, p. 25.
59. This was cited in an *Alwahid* editorial in 1941. *Alwahid*, 22 February 1941, p. 8.
60. F R for October 1940 (1), Clee to R. Tottenham, 19 October 1940.
61. QAPC, F 274, Gandhi to Haroon, 12 October 1940, p. 122, also, Mitra, *Indian Annual Register 1940*, 2:35.

62. The policy of Congress in Sindh was to continue to cooperate with the government despite the resignation of Congress governments elsewhere. The Congress gave the Mir ministry conditional support as it had the preceding ministry but at this time it was considering launching civil disobedience at the direction of the Congress high command. Coupland, *The Indian Problem*, p. 71. See also Sitaramayya, *Congress History*, 2:217ff, and R.C. Majumdar, *History of the Freedom Movement*, 3 vols. (Calcutta: Firma K.L. Mukhopadhyay, 1962-63), 3:607-608.

63. IOR, P&J/5 F 256, Graham's commentary on the F R for the first half of September, 25 September 1940, pp. 52054.

64. Sayed, *Struggle for a New Sind*, p. 67.

65. This account is based largely on Sayed's *Struggle for a New Sind*, pp. 67-69.

66. Sayed implies that it was also decided at this time when these changes in the cabinet would take place: the first, immediately with either Sheikh Abdul Majid or himself resigning and the second, when Mir Bandeh Ali resigned. Sayed, *Struggle for a New Sind*, pp. 68-70.

67. This agreement became known as the Azad Pact and its terms, gleaned from several sources, were: 1. One of the League ministers, Majid or Sayed, would resign immediately and Allah Baksh would occupy the vacant seat; 2. On or before 15 February Mir would resign, Hidayatullah would enter the cabinet and then a majority of the Muslim Assemblymen would decide on the next chief minister; 3. If Mir chose not to resign, one of the remaining League ministers would make room for him. Ibid., p. 71. PDH, Haroon to Jinnah, 23 November 1940; Ibid., Sayed to Khuhro, 12 January 1941; Ibid., Sayed to Haroon, 17 January 1941.

68. PDH, 'Press Statement of Sir Abdullah Haroon,' 21 November 1940; Shafi, *Haji Sir Abdoola Haroon*, pp. 173-174.

69. Ibid., Haroon to Sayed, Khuhro and Majid, 21 November 1940.

70. Haroon stresses this last point in two different letters to Sayed. PDH, Haroon to Sayed, 15 January 1941; Ibid., 18 January 1941.

71. IOR, Linlithgow Papers, MSS Eur F 125/97, Graham to Linlithgow, No. 102, 22 November 1940, p. 186.

72. Sayed stated that the agreement had to be acted on that day and if it was not, Azad and Allah Baksh would both back out. Sayed, *Struggle for a New Sind*, pp. 69-70.

73. Sayed is referring to a meeting he had had with Jinnah at the end of August at which the League president had endorsed Sayed's plan to resign from the ministry and devote his time to creating Muslim solidarity in the Assembly and organizing the League among the masses in the countryside. Ibid., p. 61-62.

74. F R for November 1940 (2), Clee to Conrad-Smith, 5 December 1940. Sayed says his action created much misunderstanding in the League

camp because it appeared he was simply doing Azad's bidding. He protests, however, that such was not the case; that negotiations had been going on with a view to change the ministry before Azad ever came to Sindh but that coming when he did, he was able to take credit for ending the political stalemate. Sayed, *Struggle for a New Sind,* p. 70. Sayed's view is supported by Graham, IOR P&J/5, F 256, Graham to Linlithgow, 26 November 1940, pp. 18-20; Ibid., 12 December 1940, pp. 9-10.

75. IOR P&J/5, F 256, Graham to Linlithgow, 26 November 1940, pp. 18-20.

76. During his summary, Haroon casts new light on the formation of the Nationalist government by indicating the Sindh League at first opposed inclusion of its ministers in the government but then gave *de facto* approval to their presence in the ministry in the manner of taking 'a lenient view of the conduct of the Ministers' at an April 1940 meeting of the Sindh Provincial Muslim League. PDH, Haroon to Jinnah, 23 November 1940, p. 3 of Letter.

77. Haroon based his charges on Resolution No. 1 of the All-India Muslim League Working Committee meeting of 3 July 1939, which he himself had drafted and introduced. MLA, Working Committee Meetings of 1939, Vol. 128, p. 48.

78. This thinking of Jinnah's helps to explain his advice to Sayed to devote his energy to organizing Sindh's rural masses behind the League. F R for December 1939 (2), Clee to Conrad-Smith, 4 January 1941.

79. From Jinnah's interview with the Sindh Governor in IOR, P&J/5, F 256, Graham letter to Linlithgow, 18 December 1940, p. 13.

80. The rift in the provincial League discussed above continued at this time. The reference here is to the majority group in the League who were close supporters of the ministers. IOR, P&J/5, F 257, Graham's commentary on F R for the second half of December 1940, n.p.

81. Interview with G.M. Sayed, Sann, 8 April 1975.

82. Sayed, *Struggle for a New Sind,* p. 73.

83. F R for December 1940 (2), Clee to Conrad-Smith, 4 January 1941.

84. Sayed, *Struggle for a New Sind,* p. 75.

85. PSAMS, Mir Bandeh Ali to Sheikh Abdul Majid, n.d., n.p. The Weston Inquiry had determined by the end of January that the *Manzilgah* was a Muslim building and negotiations were taking place to transfer it to the Muslim community. IOR, P&J/5, F 30 January 1941, n.p.; *D.G.,* 6 February 1941.

86. Graham claims Mir informed him that he had given Azad an unconditional undertaking that he would vacate the office of prime minister before 15 February. IOR, P&J/5, F. 257, Governor's commentary on F R for the first half of February 1940, 26 February

1941, n.p. Mir's own claim that during the Azad visit 'I declined (to resign immediately) but mentioned that I might resign at some future date' conveys the strong impression he planned to resign and let this be known. QAPC, F 218, Mir to Jinnah, 3 February 1941, pp. 2-4.

87. IOR, P&J/5, F 257, Graham's commentary on F R for the first half of January, 30 January 1941, n. p.

88. Sayed explained his views in a long letter to Khuhro and sent a copy to Jinnah. His reasoning was that the League ministers would offer Allah Baksh the chief ministership and in accepting it, he would then become beholden to them and in time would convert to the League's view. PDH, Sayed to Khuhro, 12 January 1941, QAPC, F 460, Sayed to Jinnah, 12 January 1941, p. 17.

89. QAPC, F 274, Haroon to Sayed, 15 January 1941, p. 176, same letter in PDH.

90. QAPC, F 460, Jinnah to Sayed, 15 January 1941, p. 20.

91. QAPC, F 460, Sayed to Jinnah, 24 January 1941, p. 32.

92. Sayed became the Sindh League's president following Haroon's death in May 1942 and built the league into a mass organization. Under Sayed's leadership, the League could boast of 441 primary branches and a total membership of 156,097 by the beginning of 1943. The size of the League party organization continued to grow from this time on. MLA, Committee of Action (Inspection Reports) 1944-45, Vol. 200, 'quarterly Report (Confidential),' p. 1 (of report), p. 37 (of volume), also Karachi, North Nazimabad, papers of Syed Shamsul Hasan, Sind, Vol. 2 [same report], n.p.

93. QAPC, F 274, Resolutions of the Sindh Provincial Muslim League Council meeting, 22 December 1940, p. 166. The Hindu Independents had withdrawn ministry support temporarily both because of frustration with the government's inability to ensure the security of the Hindu community as well as the transfer of portfolios. The League charged the withdrawal of Hindu support violated their mutual agreement. *Alwahid*, 22 February 1941, p. 8; also Mitra, *Indian Annual Register, 1940*, 1:4; Ibid., *Indian Annual Register, 1939*, 2:xxvii.

94. Local bodies included District Local Boards and Sanitary Committees. QAPC, F 274, Haroon to Jinnah, 6 January 1941, p. 148.

95. Ibid., Mir to Haroon, 16 January 1941, pp. 182-3.

96. Ibid., Haroon to Jinnah, 16 January 1941, p. 80.

97. PDH, Jinnah to Haroon, 20 January 1941. Jinnah also wrote to Sheikh Abdul Majid and Mir requesting them to stand by the Sindh League, warning their failure to do so could have 'adverse repercussions for the all-India cause of *Mussalmans*.' QAPC F 385, Jinnah to Sheikh Abdul Majid, 20 January 1941, p. 1; Ibid., F 461, Jinnah to Mir, 20 January 1941, p. 1.

98. The Sindh League had decided to make the Local Bodies election in Thar Parkar a test case for its opposition to the second Joint Electorates Bill, and it chose the method of boycott to demonstrate public support for the League's stand. Ibid., F 274, Haroon to Jinnah, 28 January 1941, p. 188. See also Coupland, *The Indian Problem,* p. 71 and Mitra, *Indian Annual Register 1941,* 1:269.

99. Sayed, *Struggle for a New Sind,* p. 74.

100. Mir's desertion of the former Allah Baksh government and his more recent decision to join the League were ample indications of his personal desire for power and office. In Khuhro's case there was evidence he used his office to increase the water supply to his own lands at the expense of his enemies, principally Allah Baksh, IOR, Linlithgow Papers, MSS Eur F 125/97, Graham to Linlithgow, No. 77a, 29 July 1940, p. 138. Unlike the other two, Sheikh Abdul Majid was indifferent to office and was intent on upholding the League's prestige. QAPC, F 454, Sheikh Abdul Majid to Jinnah, 8 February 1941, p. 5.

101. About this time Haroon wrote to Jinnah and referred indirectly to Mir and Khuhro by saying 'Some of them have got their own ambition and choices which they cannot overlook at any cost.' PDH, Haroon to Jinnah, n.d.

102. In his lengthy statement, Jinnah surveyed political developments in Sindh since the inception of the Nationalist government and blamed Congress and Hindu Independent 'machinations' for rendering the ministry impotent and unstable. *Civil and Military Gazette,* 8 February 1941, p. 5. Also, PSA, 'Associated Press of India statement for 8 February 1941.'

103. Jinnah dismissed the pact chiefly on the grounds that the League, was not officially a party to the agreement. PDH, Jinnah to Haroon, 2 February 1941. Also Shafi, *Haji Sir Abdoola Haroon,* p. 174.

104. Ibid.

105. This party was reconstituted shortly after Jinnah's December visit and Khuhro became its chairman. QAPC, F 460, Sayed to Jinnah, 1 January 1941, pp. 14-15.

106. QAPC, F 356, Khuhro to Jinnah, 8 February 1941, p. 6.

107. PDH, 'Minutes of the Muslim League Assembly party meeting, 2 February 1941,' enclosure in letter from Khuhro to Haroon, 14 February 1941.

108. QAPC, F 1060, 'Jinnah's notes of 18 February 1941, meeting in Delhi,' pp. 1-3.

109. QAPC, F 218, Mir to Jinnah, 15 February, 1941, p. 9.

110. QAPC, F 218, Jinnah to Mir, 19 February 1941, p. 13. In a clever tactic designed to bind the Sindh leaders even closer together, Jinnah issued a press statement on the 19th, stating that all the Sindh Leaguers have

promised to stand together and back the League's policy and programme. QAPC, F. 460, Jinnah to Sayed, 29 February 1941, p. 65.

111. QAPC, F 356, Letter of Khuhro to Jinnah, 23 February 1941, p. 6.
112. QAPC, F 356, Jinnah of Khuhro, 25 February 1941, p. 14.
113. QAPC, F 460, Jinnah to Syed, 27 February 1941, p. 62.
114. Ibid., pp. 63ff.
115. Jinnah had acquired enormous prestige by this time and was commonly being addressed as the *Quaid-i-Azam*. A few months later he dramatically demonstrated his authority by forcing the League premiers of Bengal, Punjab and Assam to resign from the National Defence Council. See Sayeed, *Pakistan: The Formative Phase,* pp. 198-9.
116. F R for March 1941 (1), Clee to Conrad-Smith, 21 March 1941.
117. Khuhro informed Jinnah by wire, curtly: 'With your advice, left office.' QAPC, F 356, Khuhro to Jinnah., 19 March 1941, p. 15; Ibid., F 460, Sayed to Jinnah, 20 March 1941, p. 69.
118. IOR, P&J/5 F 257, Governor's commentary for second half of February, 1941, 12 March 1941.
119. This idea was expressed by Haroon in a letter to a Sindhi *zamindar.* PDH, Haroon to Wali Mohammed Gohar, 6 March 1941.
120. Jinnah, aware of the grip this view had on the minds of the Sindh Leaguers, expressed it in his letter of final advice. QAPC, F 460, Jinnah to Sayed, 27 February 1941, p. 62.

CONCLUSION

In evaluating the origins and development of the Muslim League in Sindh during the late 1930s and the early 1940s, the main factors that inhibited the League's early establishment of a strong, well-organized party base in the province were disunity and difficult province-centre relations. These two themes represented the principal forces that worked to preclude the League's early establishment, and postpone the day of the League's eventual succession to full ministerial power in Sindh.

Disunity and province-centre relations were already dominant features of Muslim politics in Sindh before the province entered the post-1935 period of provincial autonomy. Division within the Sindhi Muslim political elite was reflected in the formation of two separate political organizations: the Sind Muhammadan Association, which was comprised mainly of the Sindhi Muslim landed aristocracy, and the Sindh Muslim League which was made up mostly of middle class professionals and merchants. A further difference between the Association and the League related to the second theme of province-centre relations. The SMA, though a Sindh branch of an all-India organization, was primarily concerned with Sindhi issues, while the early Sindh Leaguers were almost exclusively interested in all-India concerns. Both of these Muslim organizations were eclipsed, however, as Sindhi politics became dominated by the issue of Sindh's political and administrative separation from the Bombay Presidency during the middle and late 1920s.

The prospects of a separated Sindh with its obvious benefits for the Muslim community, captured the imagination of the Sindhi Muslim leadership and generated a political movement which had, as its goals, the achievement of separation, and the establishment of Sindh as an independent and autonomous province. In terms of the themes of disunity and province-centre relations, the separation movement, because of its unanimous community support, served to unite all of the Sindhi Muslim leaders under the single banner of the Sind Azad Conference. Furthermore, because of the provincial nature of the separation issue, it created among the elite an almost complete preoccupation with Sindhi issues to the virtual exclusion of interest in all-India affairs. The emergence of a dominant Sindhi outlook among the Muslim leadership at this time was due also in part to the failure of the weak central League to provide substantive leadership for the Sindhi Muslims on the separation issue, a fact which was further reflected in the demise of the nascent Sindh League.

The significance of the separation movement can be seen in the fact that its impact was not limited to the period of the movement itself, but also extended into the early period of provincial autonomy when it played a significant role in giving shape to the formation of political parties in Sindh. The influence of the separatist movement was revealed most clearly in the adoption by the two major Muslim Parties, the Sind United Party and the Sind Muslim party, of a strong, pro-Sindhi platform and in the case of the SUP, the deliberate rejection of the overtures of the All-India League. Only the fringe Sind Azad Party sought to develop all-India ties, but even its resolve was only partial on account of its desire to maintain an independent posture, which, too, was attributable to the lingering legacy of the separation movement. Thus, in terms of the theme of province-centre relations, there was a continuity between the time of the separation movement and the period of political party formation, but the same cannot be said for the second theme of disunity. Instead of institutionalizing in one political party the spirit of unity achieved during the separation movement, the Sindhi Muslim leadership fractured their solidarity by forming several political parties, based largely on personalities rather than principles. This was clearly evident in the case of Hidayatullah, who defected from the SUP to begin his own party in order to outflank Bhutto and Haroon in their common struggle for personal political supremacy and influence.

The incidence of division and factionalism among the leaders of the Sindhi Muslim community was precipitated chiefly by the elections of 1937, because the outcome of the poll determined who the new power holders would be, specifically who would be included in Sindh's first cabinet ministry. The election results did not produce any fundamental alterations in the distribution of political power in Sindh; in fact, the new power holders in Sindh were to be none other than the traditional elite—the large landholders, the religious leaders and the tribal chieftains. As this elite's mode of politics was marked by intrigue and internecine conflict, the outcome of the 1937 poll gave added impetus to the forces of disunity among the Muslim leadership, which became manifest during the subsequent period of ministerial government. With regard to province-centre relations, the weak showing of the SAP, the only party with an all-India outlook, did little to stabilize the lopsided balance heavily weighted in favour of local Sindhi concerns since the end of the separation movement.

The Sind United Party emerged as the dominant party by winning the largest bloc of Assembly seats, but its pre-eminence was vitiated by the defeat of its two top leaders, Bhutto and Haroon. In addition, the party's late start, its non-existent organizational base, and its borrowed platform belied its strength as a political party. The weaknesses of the SUP were further revealed when the Governor, in choosing the leader for Sindh's first cabinet, passed over what SUP leaders remained and chose as prime minister, the leader of the much smaller rival party. Hidayatullah's selection as premier precipitated the large-scale defection of groups and factions from the SUP, who flocked to support the new ministry in the hope of obtaining governmental favours.

The period of Sindh's first two governments provided the first real opportunity for a glimpse into the inner workings of Sindhi politics. As the incident of choosing a premier made plain, the SUP was not really a political party but a collection of factions which banded together to increase each group's chances of securing some measure of political power. Writing later in the period, a noted Sindhi scholar and political observer, I.I. Kazi, provided some insight into the nature of faction formation in Sindh. Kazi states that Sindh's experience with elective government 'proved that the only *Asbiyyat* obtainable was the caste *Asbiyyat*. Sayeds, Talpurs, Soomros and so many other castes are forming political cliques, finding no better and broader *Asbiyyat* than that which would be practical, workable and dependable.'[1] Thus, the role one's clan[2] or caste played as the source of one's political identity as well as the object of one's political loyalty does much to explain the phenomenon of disunity which reached a peak during the period marked by the first ministries of Hidayatullah and Allah Baksh.

At the beginning of the period of provincial autonomy the Sindhi Muslim leadership had formed a solid bloc, strong and united, but before two years had transpired their position had become divided and weak, with a number of them members of an enfeebled opposition remote from the province's centres of power. Even the Muslims who held power—the chief ministers and the coterie of followers that surrounded them—held only limited power for they chose to rely on Hindu support which was more certain, and less prone to division and defection than that of their fellow Muslims. Thus, the small group of Sindhi Hindu leaders emerged in the enviable position of holding the balance of power in Sindhi politics in this early period. This fact was not lost on those Sindhi Muslims who were out of power but ironically, instead of viewing the Hindu position as a reason for ending their factional discord and closing their ranks, the Muslims made the Hindus a scapegoat, and blamed them for the disunity and political impotence plaguing the Muslim leadership. So, out of a growing sense of resentment, frustration and helplessness, some Sindhi Muslims felt compelled to look outside Sindh, seeking the help of the All-India Muslim League to assist them in wresting the province's political control from the hands of the Hindus and restoring it to their own. Sindh's first two years of cabinet government was a period which witnessed Sindhi Muslims at their lowest, weakest and most divided state, but it also revealed that their political outlook was undergoing significant change, for by seeking the outside help of the League they were, in effect, attempting to re-establish an equilibrium in province-centre relations.

The following period, dominated by the first League conference in Sindh and initial efforts to form a League ministry, yielded several important indications of the increasing political sophistication of the Sindhi Muslim leadership. Resolution No. 5, the conference's principal resolution, was a clever scheme designed to integrate in one statement, the local political objectives of the League-minded Sindhi Muslim leaders with the national goals of the All-India League leadership. The resolution, insofar as it was an attempt to throw Allah Baksh off balance, set the stage for the post-conference efforts by the League to persuade Allah Baksh to join the League pursuant to forming a League ministry. The negotiations between the two parties failed, however, partly on ideological grounds but chiefly on personal grounds. Personal considerations also formed the basis of differences that hampered attempts to establish a League organization in Sindh following the conference. The chronic cause of disunity— personal struggles over power—served to undermine the League's initial attempts at establishing branch organizations. Personal competition for power also played a part in the election of the Sindh League's first president, and in the defection of Hidayatullah. Nonetheless, despite the failure to form a League ministry and the limited success in organizing League branches, the period did reflect a growing political maturity, in both behaviour and outlook, among the Sindhi Muslim political elite, particularly the Sindh Leaguers. Personal differences were still responsible for much of the disunity within the pro-League Muslim leadership, but increasingly, considerations of tactics and principles were becoming an important part of their political outlook. In terms of province-centre relations, as symbolized by Resolution No. 5, the Muslim leaders had altered their strong pro-Sindhi perspective to adopt a more balanced view that accommodated local as well as national interests and considerations.

In spite of the otherwise modest achievements of the Sindh Leaguers in establishing a nascent League organization and popularizing the League throughout the province, the event in 1938 which had the greatest impact on subsequent political developments was the League's failure to form a ministry by imposing its will on Allah Baksh. The premier emerged from the talks in a stronger position than before which in turn strengthened the resolve of the Sindh Leaguers to bring him down. The outcome of the League negotiations with Allah Baksh had, to the minds of the local Leaguers, exposed the inability of the All-India League leadership to meet a pressing local demand and so, as an alternative approach, the League leaders in Sindh decided to exploit a provincial issue in a final campaign to defeat Allah Baksh. The communal demand for the *Manzilgah* mosque's restoration was deliberately chosen to consolidate Muslim support and lay bare Allah Baksh's crucial reliance on the Hindus to stay in power. The *Manzilgah* campaign engendered disunity within the Sindh League camp, but in keeping with their new level of sophistication, their differences resulted more from disagreements over points of tactics and strategy and less from questions of personal political power. By nature a provincial issue, the *Manzilgah* restoration also represented a tilting of the balance in province-centre relations once again toward the Sindhi side.

This emphasis on Sindhi rather than all-India concerns was reinforced by the tragic outcome of the *Manzilgah* agitation. The campaign achieved the Sindh Leaguers' goal of bringing Allah Baksh down but only at great cost to communal harmony and peace and, ultimately, to the welfare of the province. Therefore, in the aftermath of the *Manzilgah* trouble, a group within the Sindh League leadership, namely Majid, Khuhro and G.M. Sayed, found themselves in a dilemma over loyalty: should they devote their efforts to repairing the communal relations of the province or should they stand by the League which bore the onus for the *Manzilgah*-incited violence? They decided to opt for provincial loyalty, which they demonstrated by diminishing their ties with the League and embracing the conciliatory platform of the new Nationalist government. Thus, the Sindhi emphasis in province-centre relations, re-established at the time of the *Manzilgah* affair, continued into the period of the Mir ministry.

The pro-government group of Sindh Leaguers did not constitute the entire League leadership in Sindh, though in early 1940 they certainly represented the dominant element. There were also those, notably Haroon, who remained loyal to the League and opposed the group who joined the government, particularly over the League ministers' support for joint electorates, which directly contravened the All-India League's longstanding policy of separate electorates. Accordingly, disunity continued in the circle of the League leadership, but as evidence of their growing political development and maturity, their division had assumed an institutionalized character in the form of the League Assembly party, which was dominated by the League ministerial group, and the League party organization which was headed by Haroon.

During the period of the Mir government, this formal division within the League leadership continued with the two groups struggling for supremacy in a conflict that symbolized the tension inherent in the theme of province-centre relations. The League ministers, with their concern for restoring amicable communal relations in Sindh represented the provincial perspective while Haroon's group, with its prosecution of All-India League policy, stood for the centre's position. In the clashes between the two groups, the ministerial party consistently emerged with the upper hand, but while they managed to consolidate their position within the League, their position in the wider context of Sindh politics gradually weakened owing to their inability to undertake constructive governmental action.

The erosion of the Leaguers' position in the government reflected the overall decline in the strength of the Mir ministry which, upon further deterioration, prompted the intervention of all-India leaders, first of the Congress and then of the Muslim League. When Jinnah chose to confront the League ministers, he was motivated by the all-India consideration that Sindh, as a Muslim majority province, demonstrate its unwavering solidarity with the All-India League, but his involvement in Sindh's affairs was, in effect, a catalyst that transformed the configuration of Sindhi Muslim politics, particularly League politics, for the remainder of the period of provincial autonomy. The response of the Sindh League leadership to Jinnah's challenge was to forge a position of solidarity under the full authority of the All-India Muslim League. This development was of vital significance, for it represented the first time since the 1938 conference that the League leadership in Sindh demonstrated simultaneously unity in their ranks and an outlook that balanced all-India and provincial considerations. But the difference between 1938 and 1941 was crucial. Following the 1938 conference, the League leadership had once again become weak and divided. But in 1941, they maintained their unity even to the extent of resigning ministerial office, at considerable personal cost, and entering the opposition.

The Sindh Leaguers, by achieving unity and a balanced outlook in terms of province-centre relations, in a sense, fulfilled the terms of their political apprenticeship and beyond that, they prepared the ground for the firm implantation of the League in Sindh. They learned to accommodate conflicting loyalties,[3] to moderate their personal political ambitions, and to reserve a place for principle in their political outlook—evidence of their newly-acquired political sophistication as well as their readiness to shoulder the full burden of responsible provincial leadership. They assumed that burden in October 1942 when the League took office and formed the first, full-fledged Muslim League ministry in Sindh. The League's ascension to power in 1942 marked the beginning of a period of strong League leadership which continued until 1947, when the League's ultimate goal was finally achieved and Sindh joined the new nation-state of Pakistan.

NOTES

1. *Asbiyyat* which means the binding link holding a polity together is a term Kazi borrows from the great Arab historian Ibn Khaldun. I.I. Kazi, Foreword to *Thoughts on the Political Problem of India,* by Sheikh Abdul Majid Sindhi (Karachi: Daily Press, 1945), pp. iii-iv.

2. Siraj-ul Haque, a prominent Sindhi editor, in his discussions with the author stressed that during the 1920's and 1930's the tribal and feudal basis of Sindhi society was breaking down, and in its place the clan emerged as the dynamic unit of political behaviour. He defined a clan as a sub-caste of blood relatives who traced their clan's origins to a forbearer several generations earlier who, by distinguishing himself, gave his name to the clan by which it was subsequently known. Interview in Karachi, 11 September 1975.

3. The Leaguers in Sindh were able to integrate their conflicting loyalties to the League on the one hand and to their region and caste or clan on the other. In a related study, R.W. Nicholas has shown the interrelations between factions and other loyalties such as caste, economic dependence and territory, particularly the tendency for factional loyalties to cut across other loyalties. See his 'Village Factions and Political Parties in Rural West Bengal,' *Journal of Commonwealth Political Studies,* 2 (November 1963), 17-32. See also Paul R. Brass, *Factional Politics in an Indian State: The Congress in Uttar Pradesh* (Berkeley: University of California Press, 1965), pp. 234ff.

GLOSSARY

Amil	A Hindu sub-caste prominent in high levels of Sindh government service.
anjuman	an association or organization usually literary but sometimes political in nature
Asbiyyat	an Arabic term meaning a polity's 'binding link' or common sentiments holding a society together.
asal Sindhi	those having a genuine claim to be old and true Sindhis (see pukkha Sindhis)
Azad	free, independent
badmashes	rowdy, disruptive characters, usually listed by the police as criminal elements
bania	Hindu moneylender of the *vaisya* caste
Baluch	name given to the group of tribes west of Sindh, some of which settled in Sindh
Bhaibund	a Hindu merchant sub-caste
Bohra	a largely urban Muslim business community
durbar	a ceremonial court or reception held in British times to honour prominent Indians
Hanuman Mandir	a temple dedicated to the Hindu monkey god, Hanuman
hari	generally landless cultivators, tenants-at-will
hijrat	a mass migration of Muslims for religious purposes
Imam	Leader; the title given to Hasan and Hussain, the sons of Ali, and the grandsons of the Prophet Muhammad
Ittihad-i-Millat	the name of a Sukkur Muslim organization which means the 'unity of the religious nation'
Jamiyyat el-ulama-i Hind	a land-grant awarded for military or meritorious service
Khoja	a Muslim trading community some of whom are the followers of the Aga Khan
lakh	a term denoting one hundred thousand, written as 100,000

Lakhiari	a prominent sub-group of Sindhi Saiyyids
Lohano	Sindhi Hindus of *vaisya* origin some of whom claim Brahman status
Manzilgah	a term meaning garden of rest, park or caravanserai
Matiari	a prominent sub-group of Sindhi Saiyyids
maulana	a Muslim scholar learned in the Quran
maulvi	a religious Muslim knowledgeable in the Quran, of lower status than a maulana
Mir	a title denoting rulership, used most often by Sindh's pre-British ruling family, the Talpurs
mofussil	the rural hinterland of the province
muhajarin	those who migrate for the purpose of Islam; religious refugees
Mukkhi	a title given to a leader of a Hindu panchayat
mullah	one who performs Muslim religious duties in the villages
Memon	A Muslim merchant community
Om Mandli	the name of a Hindu welfare society for women
panchayat	a council of five Hindu or Muslim village elders organized to adjudicate caste or clan differences
pir	a Muslim saint, invariably a Saiyyid
pukkha Sindhis	those who claim their forbearers have been Sindhis for many generations
Rais	a Baluch title denoting chieftainship (see Sardar)
Raj	Rule
rupee	a unit of currency, roughly equivalent to US $0.30 in 1947
sardar	a term used by the Baluch to denote tribal chieftainship
satyagraha	a non-violent campaign of civil disobedience
Saiyyid	one who traces his ancestry to the Prophet Muhammed
Sheikh	a title; also adopted by Hindu converts to Islam
swaraj	self-rule
taluka	a unit of land measurement for administrative and revenue purposes
Tehrik Reshmi Roomal	a conspiratorial movement in which secret communications were written on silk handkerchiefs

vaisya	the third caste in the classic Hindu four fold caste hierarchy
wadero	a Sindhi term for a landlord of extensive properties
zamindar	a landholder responsible for paying land revenue to the government

SELECTED BIBLIOGRAPHY

Primary Sources

Alavi Papers, Hatim. Correspondence of Hatim Alavi. On Micro film (11 Files). Quaid-i-Azam Papers Cell, Islamabad.

Alavi Papers, Mazhar. Correspondence and Papers of Mazhar Alavi, 1936. Mahmudabad, Karachi.

Gazdar Papers, Mohammed Hashim. Correspondence of M.H. Gazdar. On Microfilm (4 Files). Quaid-i-Azam Papers Cell, Islamabad.

Hidayatullah Papers, Daulat. Correspondence and Papers of Abdullah Haroon. Seafield House, Karachi.

Hidayatullah Papers, Ghulam Hussain. Correspondence of G.H. Hidayatullah. On Microfilm (13 Files). Quaid-i-Azam Papers Cell, Islamabad.

Jinnah Papers, Mohammed Ali. Jinnah's Correspondence with Sindh League leaders from 1939 to 1942. Unbound volumes. Muslim League Archives, Karachi.

_____. Jinnah's Correspondence with Sindh League leaders from 1936 to 1942. On Microfilm (67 Files). Quaid-i-Azam Papers Cell, Islamabad.

_____. Jinnah's Correspondence with Sindh League leaders from 1941 to 1942. 2 volumes. Syed Shamsul Hasan Collection, North Nazimabad, Karachi.

Khuhro Papers, Mohammed Ayub. Correspondence of M.A. Khuhro. On Microfilm (7 Files). Quaid-i-Azam Papers Cell, Islamabad.

Linlithgow Papers. Correspondence on the Marquis of Linlithgow as Viceroy and Governor-General of India from 1936 to 1942. Mss Eur F 125, India Office Records, London.

Sayed Papers, G.M. Correspondence and Papers of G.M. Sayed. Sann village, Dadu district, Sind.

_____. Correspondence of G.M. Sayed. On Microfilm (9 Files). Quaid-i-Azam Papers Cell, Islamabad.

Saiyid Papers, Matlubul Hasan and Rizwan Ahmed. Correspondence between Jinnah and the Sindh League leaders. Pakistan Movement Foundation, Spencer Building, Karachi.

Sindhi Papers, Sheikh Abdul Majid. Correspondence and Papers of Majid. Former Brahmo Samaj Center, Karachi.

Suleman Papers, Inayatullah. Press Clippings. Jehangir Kothari Building, Karachi.

Government Records and Documents

Great Britain. 1935-1947 India Office Records. Information Department Records. Series 1.

_____. 1935-1945 India Office Records. Public and Judicial Records. Series 9.

_____. Laws, Statutes, etc. *Government of India Act, 1935.* 26 Geo 5 ch. 2.

_____. Parliament. *Parliamentary Papers* (Commons), *1930-31,* vol. 12 (Reports, vol. 3). Cmnd. 3772, 'Report of the Sub-committee No. IX (Sind).'

_____. Parliament. *Parliamentary Papers* (Commons), *1932-33,* Vol. 5), Memorandum 53, 'Sindh's Separation from Bombay by Khan Bahadur M.A. Khuhro, M.L.C.'

_____. Parliament. *Parliamentary Papers* (Commons), *1935-36,* vol. 9 (*Reports,* vol. 3) Cmnd. 5099 'Report of the committee appointed in connection with the Delimitation of Constituencies and connected matters.'

_____. 1930 *Report of the Indian Statutory Commission* (Simon) 17 vols. London: His Majesty's Stationery Office.

Government of India. 1925 *Histories of the Non-cooperation and Khilafat Movements.* By P.C. Bamford. Delhi: Government of India Press.

_____. 1933 *India. Census of India 1931.* Compiled by J.H. Hutton. Delhi: Manager of Publications.

_____. 1943 *India. Census of India 1941.* Compiled by M.W.M. Yeats. Delhi: Manager of Publications.

_____. *Report of the Sind Conference, 1932.* By A.F.L. Brayne. Calcutta: Government of India Central Publications Branch, 1932.

_____. 1937 *Return Showing the Results of the Elections in India, 1937.* Delhi: Manager of Publications.

_____. 1931 *Sind as a Separate Province.* By Miles Irving. Simla: Government of India Press.

Government of Bombay. 1933 *A Handbook of the Government Records Lying in the Office of the Commissioner-in-Sind and in District Offices.* Karachi: Commissioner's Printing Press.

_____. 1928 *Gazetteer of Sind, Sukkur District.* Compiled by J.W. Smyth. B. Series, Vol. III. Bombay: At the Government Press.

_____. 1907 *Gazetteer of the Province of Sind.* Compiled by E.H. Aitken. Vol. A. Karachi: Printed for the Government at the Mercantile Steam Press.

_____. 1886 *History of Alienations in the Province of Sind Compiled from the Jagir and other Records in the Commissioner's Office.* 2 vols. Karachi: Printed at the Commissioner's Press.

_____. 1917 *Report of the Committee appointed to enquire into the advisability of extending the period of Settlement in Sind from 10 to 30 years.* Bombay Castle: Government of Bombay, Revenue Department.

_____. 1935 *Report of the Sind Provincial Delimitation Committee.* Bombay: At the Government Press.

_____. 1927 *Report on the Subject of Legislation to Restrict the Alienation of Land in Sind by Members of the Agricultural Classes.* Written by S.H. Covernton. Karachi: The Commissioner's Printing Press.

_____. 1855 *Selections from the Records of the Bombay Government No. XVII—New Series.* Edited by R. Hughes Thomas. Bombay: printed for the Government at the Bombay Education Society's Press.

Government of Sind. 1954 *A Short Sketch, Historical and Traditional of the Mussalman Races Found in Sind, Balochistan and Afghanistan.* Written by Sheikh Sadik Ali Ansari. Karachi: Sind Government Press.

_____. 1936-1942 Fortnightly Reports from the Sind Government and Administration on the Political Situation in Sind for the First and Second Half of the Month.

_____. 1948 *Hari Report: Minute of Dissent.* Submitted by M. Masud. Karachi: Printed at the Government Press.

_____. 1936-1937 *Proceedings of the Sind Advisory Council,* Karachi: Printed at the Government Press.

_____. 1937-1942 Proceedings of the Sind Legislative Assembly. Karachi: printed at the Government Press.

_____. 1940 *Report of the Court of Inquiry appointed under Section 3 of the Sind Public Inquiries Act to inquire into the Riots which occurred at Sukkur in 1939.* By E. Weston. Karachi: At the Government Press.

_____. 1948 *Report of the Hari Committee: The Majority Report.* Written by Sir Roger Thomas. Karachi: Printed at the Government Press.

_____. 1941 *Report of the Inquiry appointed under Section 3 of the Sind Public Inquiries Act to enquire into the nature of the Manzilgah Buildings at Sukkur.* By E. Weston. Karachi: Printed at the Government Press.

_____. 1938 *Report of the Sind Reorganization Committee.* Karachi: Printed at the Government Press.

_____. 1939 *Report of the Special Officer appointed to examine the relations between Jagirdars and Zamindars and their Tenants and Haris, 1939.* By Nur Nabi. Karachi: Printed at the Government Press.

_____. 1937 *Sind Government Gazette,* Part 1., January to February 1937. Karachi: Printed at the Government Press.

Government of West Pakistan. 1968 *West Pakistan Gazetteer: The Former Province of Sind.* Compiled by H.T. Sorley. Karachi: Government of West Pakistan Press.

All-India Muslim League Records and Documents

Muslim League Archives, Karachi:

Records
All-India Muslim League Annual Sessions. 1908, 1924-25, 1933-41. 26 Bound Volumes.

All-India Muslim League Committee of Action Meetings. 1944-47. 10 Bound Volumes.

All-India Muslim League Constitutional Development. 1919-43. 1 Bound Volume.

All-India Muslim League Council Meetings. 1920-23, 1926-37. 23 Bound Volumes.

All-India Muslim League Membership and Subscriptions. 1916-17. 1 Bound Volume.

All-India Muslim League Working Committee Meetings. 1932-47. 7 Bound Volumes.

The Sind Provincial Muslim League. 1912-38. 2 Bound volumes.

Documents

All-India Muslim League Central Board: Policy and Programme. n.p. 1936.

List of Members of the Council of the All-India Muslim League, 1937. Delhi: National Printing and Publishing House, 1937.

List of Members of the Council of the All-India Muslim League, 1938. Delhi: National Printing and Publishing House, 1938.

Resolutions of the All-India Muslim League from March 1939 to March 1940. Delhi: Published by the All-India Muslim League, n.d.

Rules and Regulations of the All-India Muslim League. Aligarh: Institute Press, 1909.

The Constitution and Rules of the All-India Muslim League. Delhi: National Printing and Publishing House. 1937.

The Constitution and Rules of the All-India Muslim League. Published by Liaquat Ali Khan, 1940.

Other Documents:

Ahmad, Jamil-ud-Din. *Historical Documents of the Muslim Freedom Movement.* Lahore: Publishers United Ltd., 1970.

Allana, G. *Pakistan Movement Historic Documents.* Karachi: Paradise Subscription Agency, 1967.

Causes of (the) Sukkur Disturbances: Important Findings of the Court of Inquiry into (the) Sukkur Riots of November, 1939, presided over by Judge Weston. Karachi: Sind Provincial Muslim League, 1940.

Pirzada, Syed Sharifuddin., ed. *Foundations of Pakistan: All-India Muslim League Documents, 1906-1946.* Karachi: National Publishing House, 1970.

Report of the Inquiry Committee appointed by the Council of the All-India Muslim League to inquire into Muslim grievances in Congress provinces. Written by Raja of Pirpur, Chairman. 1938.

Report of the Enquiry Committee appointed by the Work Committee of the Bihar Provincial Muslim League to inquire into some grievances of Muslims in Bihar. Drafted by S.M. Shareef. 1939.

198   SELECTED BIBLIOGRAPHY

Contemporary Biographies, Memoirs, Printed Papers, Pamphlets and Speeches

Abbassi, M.U., ed. 1944 *The Colourful Personalities of Sind.* Karachi: Pak Abbassi Publications.

Aga Khan, 1954 *The Memoirs of the Aga Khan: World Enough and Time.* London: Cassell & Co., Ltd.

Ahmad, Jamil-ud-Din. 1960 *Quaid-i-Azam, as seen by his contemporaries.* Lahore: Publishers United Ltd.

_____. 1960 *Speeches and Writings of Mr Jinnah* 2 vols. Lahore: Sheikh Mohammed Ashraf.

All Parties Conference, 1928. *Proceedings of the All Parties National Convention.* Allahabad: General Secretary, All-India Congress Committee.

Allah Baksh, *Presidential Address of Khan Bahadur Allah Baksh to the All-India Independent Muslim Conference, 27 April 1940.* Delhi: National Journals Press, 1940.

Bhurgri, Jan M. Khan. 1920 *The Provincial Khilafat Conference, Hyderabad (Sind) 4th January 1920: Address of Jan Mohammed Khan Bhurgri.* Hyderabad: 'Bharataasi' Press.

Gwyer, M.l. and Appadorai, A. 1957 *Speeches and Documents on the Indian Constitution, 1921-1947.* 2 vols. Bombay: Oxford University Press.

Haroon, A. 1939 Foreword to *The Muslim Problem in India together with an alternative Constitution for India,* by Syed Abdul Latif. Bombay: Times of India Press.

Hasan, Syed Shamsul., ed. 1976 *...Plain Mr Jinnah: Selections from Quaid-i-Azam's Correspondence.* Karachi: Royal Book Co.

Hassain, Azim. 1946 *Fazl-i-Hussain: A Political Biography.* Bombay: Longmans Green and Co.

India's Problem of her Future Constitution. Bombay: Published by M.H. Saiyid, n.d.

Isa, Qazi. 1946. Foreword to *It Shall Never Happen Again,* n.a. Delhi: Published by Syed Shamsul Hasan.

Jinnah, M.A. 1942. Foreword to *Pakistan and Muslim India,* n.a. Bombay: Home Study Circle.

Joyo, Mohammed Ibrahim. 1947. *Save Sind—Save the Continent.* Karachi: By the author.

Khaliquzzaman, Choudhry 1961. *Pathway to Pakistan.* Lahore: Longmans, Green and Co.

Khuhro, Mohammed Ayub 1930. *A Story of the Sufferings of Sind: A Case for the Separation of Sind from the Bombay Presidency.* Karachi: Bharat Printing Press.

————. 1933 *Evidence of Khan Bahadur Mohammed Ayub Khuhro, M.L.C. on behalf of the Sind Separation Conference taken before the Joint Parliamentary Select Committee on Indian Constitutional Reform.* Bombay: Appeal Press.

Manshardt, Clifford. 1936. *The Hindu-Muslim Problem in India.* London: George Allen and Unwin.

Mehta, Asoka and Patwardhan, Achyut 1942. *The Communal Triangle in India.* Allahabad: Kitabistan.

Moman, Mohammed 1942. *Muslim India: Rise and Growth of the All-India Muslim League.* Allahabad: Kitabistan.

Noor, Mohammed 1928. *The Backwardness of Sind Mussalmans in Education.* Poona: Scottish Mission Press.

Rahmat Ali, Choudhary 1942. *What does the Pakistan National Movement stand for?* Cambridge: Pakistan National Movement.

Saiyid, Matlubul Hasan 1945. *Mohammad Ali Jinnah: A Political Study.* Lahore: Sheikh Mohammed Ashraf.

Sayed, G.M. 1974. *Chund Adabi Mazmun-valayat ja Khat* (Selected Essays and Letters written from 1933-1960). Karachi: Naiyen Sindh Publication.

————. 1970 *Khat-i-Mazmun 1937-1958* (Correspondence of Ali Mohammed Rashidi with the author). Hyderabad: Hamid Sindhi.

————. 1967 *Janab guzamrim ginse* (Those with whom I have spent my life). Hyderabad: Sindhi Adabi Board.

————. 1968 *Jadid Siyasat ja nan Ratan* (Nine Great Politicians in Indo-Pakistan). Hyderabad: Hydiri Printing Press.

————. 1949 *(The) Struggle for (a) New Sind: An Account of the Workings of Provincial Autonomy in the Province.* Karachi: Sind Observor Press.

Shafi, Al-Haj Mian Ahmad n.d. *Haji Sir Abdoola Haroon: A Biography.* Karachi: Pakistan Herald Press.

Shah, Sayid Ghulam Mustapha 1943. *Understanding the Muslims of Sind.* Karachi: Alwahid Printing Press.

Sindhi, Sheikh Abdul Majid n.d. *Report of Sheik Abdul Majid, Secretary, Jamiat Khilafat of Sind.* Karachi: Alwahid Printing Press.

————. 1945 *Thoughts on the Political Problem of India.* Foreword by I.I. Kazi. Karachi: Daily Gazette Press.

Sherwani, L.A., ed. 1969 *Pakistan Resolution to Pakistan, 1940-1947.*
Karachi: National Publishing House, Ltd.
Some Features of Bureaucratic Administration in Sind. Hyderabad:
Sind Publishing House, 1918.
*The Khilafat Day in Sind: The Presidential Address of Seth Haji
Abdullah Haroon Sahib and a Brief Report of the Proceedings of
some of the Important Meetings.* Karachi: By Mohammed Khan,
Secretary, Sind Provincial Khilafat Committee (1918).

Newspapers, Annuals

Alwahid (Sindhi)
Civil and Military Gazette
Daily Gazette
Jang (Urdu)
Muslim Advocate
Sind Observor
Statesman
The Indian Annual Register. Edited by Nriprendra Nath Mitra.
Calcutta: The Annual Register Office, 1935-1942.
The Indian Yearbook and Who's Who, 1947. Edited by Francis Low.
Vol. XXXIII Bombay: Bennett, Coleman and Co., 1947.
Times of India
Unity

Interviews

Alavi, Hatim. Alavi Company office, Karachi. Interview, September
18 and October 7 1975.
Alavi, Mazhar. Alavi residence, Karachi. Interview, January 23, 1976.
Allana, G. Allana Watch Store, Karachi. Interview, October 1, 1975.
Baksh, Pir Illahi. Baksh residence, Karachi. Interview, January 15,
1975.
Bhurgari, Ghulam Mustapha. Bhurgari Residence, Karachi. Interview,
September 28, 1975.
Bokhari, Jamal-ud-Din. Bokhari residence, Larkana. Interview,
December 14, 1975.

Dakhan, Taj Mohammed. Dakhan village, Sukkur district. Interview, December 15, 1975.

Fazlullah, Kazi. Fazlullah residence, Larkana. Interview, January 22, 1975.

Gazdar, Shaukat. Gazdar residence, Karachi. Interview, September 23, 1975.

Hafiz, *Moulvi* Mohammed Ismail. Khadda Seminary, Karachi. Interview October 25, 1975.

Hidayatullah, Daulat. Seafield House, Karachi. Interview, February 25, 1976.

Khalid, Karim Baksh. Sind Government Information Office, Sukkur. Interview, December 22, 1975.

Khuhro, Mohammed Ayub. Larkana residence, Larkana. Interview, January 22, 1975., Karachi, residence, Karachi. Interview, January 28, 1976., Planning Commission, Islamabad. Interview, December 22, 1976.

Lambrick, H.T. Lambrick residence, Oxford, England. Interview, April 24, 1976.

Mujtiba, Kazi. Mujtiba residence, Karachi. Interview, December 12, 1975.

Ohidi, Khair Mohammed. *Sind Zamindar Press,* Sukkur. Interview, December 18, 1975.

Pathan, Agha Ghulam Nabi. Pathan residence, Karachi. Interview, February 26, 1976.

Rashidi, Pir Ali Mohammed. Rashidi residence, Islamabad. Interview, May 29-June 3, 1975.

Rashidi, Pir Hissamuddin. Rashidi residence, Karachi. Interview, September 30, 1975.

Sayed, G.M. Sann village, Dadu district. Interview, April 8 1975, February 12, 1976.

Siraj-ul-Haque. *Hilal-e-Pakistan* office, Karachi. Interview, September 11, 1975.

Soomro, Moula Bux. Soomro residence, Karachi. Interview, September 10, 1975.

Talpur, Mir Ali Ahmed. Talpur residence, Karachi. Interview, February 26, 1976.

Secondary Sources

A. Books

Abbas, Sayed Ali and Mughal M. Rafique 1963. *A Chronology of Muslim India, 1932-1947.* 2 vols. Lahore: Punjab University Press.

Abbott, John 1924. *Sind, a Re-interpretation of the Unhappy Valley.* New York: Oxford University Press.

Abdul Hamid 1967. *Muslim Separatism in India: A Brief Survey, 1958-1947.* Lahore: Oxford University Press.

Abdullah, Ahmed 1973. *The Historical Background of Pakistan and Its People.* Karachi: Tanzeem Publishers.

A History of the Freedom Movement. 1967-1970. 4 vols. Karachi: Pakistan Historical Society.

Ahmad, Aziz 1967. *Islàmic Modernism in India and Pakistan, 1958-1964.* London: Oxford University Press.

Ahmad, Aziz and Von Grunebaum, G.E., eds. 1970. *Muslim Self-statement in India and Pakistan.* Wiesbaden: Otto Harrossowitz.

Ahmad, Aziz 1964. *Studies in Islamic Culture in the Indian Environment.* Oxford: Clarendon Press.

Ahmad, Jamil-ud-din 1969. *Middle Phase of (the) Muslim Political Movement.* Lahore: Publishers United.

———. 1963. Muslim Political Movement, Early phase. Karachi: By the author.

Ali, Chaudhri Mohammed 1973. *The Emergence of Pakistan.* Lahore: Research Society of Pakistan, University of the Punjab.

Ali, Imran 1975. *Punjab Politics in the Decade before Partition.* Lahore: University of the Punjab Press.

Allana, G. 1967. *Quaid-i-Azam Jinnah: The Story of a Nation.* Lahore: Ferozsons, Ltd.

Ambedkar, B.R. 1946. *Pakistan or the Partition of India.* 3rd Edition. Bombay: Thacker and Company, Ltd.

Azad, Maulana Abul Kalam 1959. *India Wins Freedom: An Autobiographical Narrative.* Bombay: Orient Longmans, Ltd.

Aziz, K.K. 1968. *Ameer Ali: His Life and Work.* Lahore: Publishers United.

———. ed. 1972. *The All-India Muslim Conference, 1938-1935, A Documentary Record.* Karachi: National Publishers House.

———. 1970. *The Historical Background of Pakistan, 1957-1947.* Karachi: The Pakistan Institute of International Affairs.

———. 1972. *The Indian Khilafat Movement, 1915-1933: A Documentary Record.* Karachi: Pak Publishers.

———. 1967. *The Making of Pakistan: A Study in Nationalism.* London: Chatto and Windus.

Bahadur, Lal 1954. *The Muslim League: Its History, Activities and Achievements.* Agra: Agra Book Store.

Baillie, Alexander F. 1975. *Kurrachee, Past, Present and Future.* Karachi: Oxford University Press.

Banerjee, D.N. 1945. *Partition or Federation? A Study in the Indian Constitutional Problem.* Calcutta: General Printers & Publishers Ltd.

Bolitho, Hector 1954. *Jinnah, Creator of Pakistan.* London: John Murray.

Braibanti, Ralph J. and Joseph Spengler, eds. 1961. *Tradition, Values and Socio-Economic Development.* Duke University Commonwealth Studies Center Publications, Vol. 13. Durham, North Corolina: Duke University Press.

Braibanti, Ralph J., and associates 1966. *Asian Bureaucratic Systems Emergent from the British Imperial Tradition.* Duke University Commonwealth Studies Center Publications, Vol. 28. Durham, North Carolina: Duke University Press.

Braibanti, Ralph J. 1966. *Research on the Bureaucracy of Pakistan.* Duke University Commonwealth Studies Center Publications, Vol. 26. Durham, North Carolina: Duke University Press.

Brass, Paul R. 1965. *Factional Politics in an Indian State: The Congress party in Uttar Pradesh.* Berkeley: University of California Press.

Burton, Richard E. 1968. *Sindh: And the Races that Inhabit the Valley of the Indus.* Karachi: Oxford University Press.

Chablani, S.P. 1951. *Economic Conditions in Sind, 1592-1843.* Bombay: Orient Longmans, Ltd.

Chandra, Kailash 1943. *Tragedy of Jinnah.* 2nd Revised Edition. Lahore: Varma Publishing Co.

Coupland, R. 1944. *The Indian Problem: Report of the Constitutional Problem in India.* New York: Oxford University Press.

Desai, A.R. 1948. *Social Background of Indian Nationalism.* Bombay: Oxford University Press.

Dwarkadas, Kanji 1966. *India's Fight for Freedom 1913-1937: An Eyewitness Story.* Bombay: Popular Prakashan.

Feldman, Herbert 1970. *Karachi Through a Hundred Years: The Centenary History of the Karachi Chamber of Commerce and Industry, 1960-1960.* Karachi: Oxford University Press.

Gallagher, John, Johnson, Gordon and Seal, Anil., eds. 1973. *Locality, Province and Nation.* Cambridge: Cambridge University Press.

Gidumal, Dayaram 1932. *Hiranand-The Soul of Sindh.* Karachi: Kevalram Dayaram.

———. 1882. *Something about Sindh.* Hyderabad: Blavatsky Press.

Haider, Azimusshan 1974. *History of Karachi with Special Reference to the Educational, Demographical and Commercial Developments, 1839-1900.* Karachi: By the author.

Hardy, Peter 1971. Partners *in Freedom and True Muslims: The Political Thought of Some Muslim Scholars in British India* 1912-1947. Lund: Student Literature.

———. 1972. *The Muslims of British India.* Cambridge: At the University Press.

Hughes, A.W. 1973. *A Gazetteer of the Province of Sindh.* London: George Bell & Sons.

Hussain, S. Abid 1965. *Destiny of Indian Muslims.* London: Asia Publishing House.

Huttenback, Robert A. 1962. *British Relations with Sind, 1799-1843; An Anatomy of Imperialism.* Berkeley: University of California Press.

Ikram, S.m. 1965. *Modern Muslim India and the Birth of Pakistan.* Lahore: Sheikh Muhammad Ashraf.

Isphani, M.A.H. 1967. *Quaid-i-Azam as a I Knew Him.* Karachi: Forward Publication Trust.

Kabir, Humayun 1969. *Muslim Politics, 1906-1947 and Other Essays.* Calcutta: Firma K.L. Mukhopadhyay.

Karaka, D.F. n.d. *This India.* Bombay: Thacker and Co.

Khera, P.N. 1963. *British Policy towards Sindh, up to its Annexation, 1943.* Delhi: Ranjit Printers and Publishers, 1963.

Lambrick, H.T. 1964. *Sind: A General Introduction.* Hyderabad: Sindhi Adabi Board.

———. 1973. *Sind: Before the Muslim Conquest.* Hyderabad: Sindhi Abadi Board.

———. 1952. *Sir Charles Napier and Sind.* Oxford: Clarendon Press.

———. 1972. *The Terrorist.* London: E. Benn Ltd.

Madani, Hussain Ahmed 1960. *Tahrik Reshmi Roomal.* Lahore: Classic. (Urdu).

Majumdar, R.C. 1962-63. *History of the Freedom Movement in India.* Vols. Calcutta: Firma K.L. Mukhopadhyay.

Majumdar, S.K. 1966. *Jinnah and Gandhi: Their Role in India's Quest for Freedom.* Calcutta: Firma K.L. Mukhopadhyay.

Malik, Hafeez 1963. *Moslem Nationalism in India and Pakistan.* Washington, D.C.: Public Affairs Press.

Masoom, Mohammed 1955. *A History of Sind, Embracing the Period from 710 to 1590.* Bombay: Government of Bombay Education Society Press.

Mayne, Pater 1956. *Saints of Sind.* London: John Murray.

McDonough, Sheila, ed. 1970. *Mohammed Ali Jinnah: Maker of Modern Pakistan.* Lexington, Mass.: D.C. Heath and Co.

Menon, V.P. 1957. *The Transfer of Power in India.* Princeton, N.J.: Princeton University Press.

Majeeb, M. 1967. *The Indian Muslims.* London: George Allen and Unwin.

Nagarhar, V.V. 1975. *Genesis of Pakistan.* Delhi: Allied Publishers.

Napier, W.F.P. 1851. *History of General Sir Charles Napier's Administration of Sind.* London: Chapman & Hall.

———. 1845 *The Conquest of Sinde.* London: Boine.

Outram, J. 1946. *The Conquest of Scinde - A Commentary.* Edinburgh: C.W. Blackwood and Sons.

Pandey, B.N. 1969. *The Break-up of British India.* New York: St. Martin's Press.

Parsram, Jethmal 1924. *Sind and its Sufis.* Madras: Theosophical Society.

Pasha, Mohammed Akbar 1947. *Pakistan Achieved.* Madras: Madras Presidency Muslim League.

Phillips, C.H. and Wainwright, Mary D., eds 1970. *The Partition of India, Policies and Perspectives 1935-1947.* London: George Allen and Unwin, Ltd.

Pirzada, Syed Shariffuddin 1963. *Evolution of Pakistan.* Lahore: All-Pakistan Legal Decisions.

Pithawalla, Maneck B. 1951. *An Introduction to Sind: Its Wealth and Welfare.* Karachi: Sind Observor Press.

———. 1959. *A Physical and Economic Geography of Sind.* Karachi: Sindhi Abadi Board.

Prasad, Rajendra 1947. *India Divided.* 3rd Edition. Bombay: Hind Kitabs Ltd.

Qureshi, I.H., gen. ed. 1967 *A Short History of Pakistan.* 4 Vols. Karachi: University of Karachi Press.

———. 1962. *The Muslim Community of the Indo-Pakistan Subcontinent.* The Hague: Mouton & Co.

———. 1969. *The Struggle for Pakistan.* Karachi: University of Karachi Press.

Qureshi, Saleem M.M. 1969. *Jinnah and the Making of a Nation.* Karachi: Council for Pakistan Studies.

Rahman, Matiur 1970. *From Consultation to Confrontation, Study of the Muslim League in British Indian Politics 1906-1912.* London: Luzac & Co.

Rajput, A.B. 1947. *Muslim League: Yesterday and Today.* Lahore: Sheikh Mohammed Ashraf.

Ram Gopal 1964. *Indian Muslims, A Political History, 1958-1947.* Bombay: Asia Publishing House.

Robinson, Francis 1974. *Separatism among Indian Muslims: The Politics of the United Provinces' Muslims, 1860-1923.* Cambridge: Cambridge University Press.

Sayeed, Khalid bin 1960. *Pakistan: The Formative Phase.* Karachi: Pakistan Publishing House.

Seal, Anil 1968. *The Emergence of Indian Nationalism.* Cambridge: At the University Press.

Sen, Sachin 1955. *The Birth of Pakistan.* Calcutta: General Printers and Publishers Ltd., 1955.

Siddiki, N.M. A. 1936. *Co-operation as it Stands today in Sind, 1936.* Published by D.N. Abichandani.

Sitaramayya, Pattabhi 1947. *The History of the Indian National Congress.* 2 Vols. Bombay: Padma Publications.

Smith, C.W. 1957. *Islam in Modern History.* New York: Mentor.

———. 1947. Modern Islam in India: A Social Analysis. Lahore: Minerva Book Shop.

Suleri, Zia-ud-Din Ahmad 1945. *My Leader.* Lahore: Lion Press.

Symonds, Richard 1950. *The Making of Pakistan.* London: John Murray.

Thakur, U.T. 1960. *Sindhi Culture.* University Of Bombay Sociology Series. No. 9. Bombay: University of Bombay.

1960 *The Sind Madressah-Tul-Islam Platinum Jubilee Book.* Karachi. Ehsan Buduwi.

Weiner, Myron 1957. *Party Politics in India: The Development of a Multi-Party System.* Princeton: Princeton University Press.

Articles

Bhutto, M.H. 'Role of Sind in The Awakening of Indian Muslims, 1943-1947.' *Sind University Research Journal: Art Series, Humanities and Social Sciences* 3 (1963), 44-61.

Khuhro, Hamida, 'The Separation of Sind and the Working of an Autonomous Province: An Analysis of Muslim Political Organization in Sind, 1843-1938.' Paper presented at Sind Through The Centuries Seminar, Karachi, March 25, 1975.

Mohammed, Khawaja Ali, 'A History of Sind Madressah-tal-Islam,' *The Sind Madressah-tal-Islam Platinum Jubilee Book.* Karachi: Ehsan Buduwi, 1960.

Nicholas, R.W., 'Village Factions and Political Parties in Rural West Bengal.' *Journal of Commonwealth Political Studies,* 2 (November 1963), 17-32.

Rustomji, Behram Sohrab H.J., 'A Short Historical Survey of the Beginnings of the Corporation of Karachi.' *Proceedings of the All Pakistan History Conference.* Karachi: Times Press, 1951.

'Sheikh Abdul Majid.' *Sindhi Publications,* 4 (1975), 1-42. (Sindhi).

Dissertations and Typed Manuscripts

Becker, Mary Louise 1957. 'The All-India Muslim League, 1906-1947.' Ph.D. dissertation, Harvard University.

Flynn, B.W. 1974. 'The Communalization of Politics: National Political Activity, 1926-1930.' Ph.D. dissertation, Duke University.

Khuhro, Hamida 1965. 'British Administration in Sind, 1943-1865.' Ph.D. dissertation, University of London.

Sipe, Keith 1976. 'Karachi's Refugee Crisis: The Political, Economic and Social Consequences of Partition-Related Migration.' Ph.D. dissertation, Duke University.

Ghulamally, Ziaullah G. 1970. 'Some Historical Personalities of Sind,' Hyderabad. (typed manuscript.)

Nasar, Hasan. 'History of the Hari Movement in Sind.' Communist Party of India document, n.d. (typed manuscript.)

INDEX